Series Editors:
Dario Castiglione (University of Exeter) and
Vincent Hoffmann-Martinot (Sciences Po Bordeaux)

european integration and its limits

intergovernmental conflicts and their domestic origins

Daniel Finke

© Daniel Finke 2010

First published by the ECPR Press in 2010

The ECPR Press is the publishing imprint of the European Consortium for Political Research (ECPR), a scholarly association, which supports and encourages the training, research and cross-national cooperation of political scientists in institutions throughout Europe and beyond. The ECPR's Central Services are located at the University of Essex, Wivenhoe Park, Colchester, CO4 3SQ, UK

All rights reserved. No part of this book may be reprinted or reproduced or utilised in any form or by any electronic, mechanical, or other means, now known or hereafter invented, including photocopying and recording, or in any information storage or retrieval system, without permission in writing from the publishers.

Typeset by the ECPR Press
Printed and bound by Lightning Source

British Library Cataloguing in Publication Data
A catalogue record for this book is available from the British Library

Paperback ISBN: 978-0-9558203-7-3

www.ecprnet.eu/ecprpress

acknowledgements

This book has benefited from the input of numerous colleagues whom I would like to thank cordially. Most importantly, the book has gained from the fruitful discussions with members of the research project "Domestic Structures and European Integration" (DOSEI). This project has been coordinated by Thomas König to whom I am very grateful for giving me the opportunity to become a member of the project, for setting me back on track when I was running the risk of losing it and for the innumerable insightful comments he provided along the course of the last years. Other members of the DOSEI project include Simon Hug, Kenneth Benoit, George Tsebelis, Madeleine Hosli, Christophe Crombez, Christine Arnold, Simon Hix and Han Dorussen. The discussion among this group gave me confirmation that explaining the domestic origins of governmental preferences is indeed a very valuable contribution to our understanding of European treaty reforms.

Moreover, I am very thankful for the inspiring and helpful comments from a group of colleagues at the University of Mannheim including Berthold Rittberger, who read the entire first draft of the manuscript, Thomas Bräuninger, Brooke Luetgert, Tanja Dannwolf, Dirk Junge, Lars Mäder, Janina Thiem and Stephanie Daimer. Over the years individual chapters of the book have benefited from the discussion at numerous conferences and workshops. To avoid the risk of forgetting someone I would like to express my full hearted thanks to all colleagues who commented on my work over the last years, especially in their capacity as discussants or reviewers. My participation in the EITM summer program at the Washington University in St. Louis provided me with the methodological know-how for measuring actors' policy positions. During the editing stage Henrik Wedekind provided valuable assistance with the figures and tables. Finally, I would like to thank Mark Kench and Rebecca Knappett at ECPR Press for producing the book and the patience which they had to exercise with me on occasions. Needless to say: all remaining errors are my own.

The researching and writing of this book has been a time consuming effort. Fortunately, I have friends and family who not only support me without reservation, but are even sympathetic to my research. My parents promoted my studies and research whenever necessary and possible. Ellen and Charlotte are giving me their love, encouragement and confidence every day anew. Without them this book would not have been possible.

Daniel Finke
Heidelberg, Germany 2010

contents

List of Figures and Tables	vii
Chapter One: Perspectives on European Integration	5
The Question	5
The Arguments	11
Agenda and Conflicts	12
Actors and Process	13
Positions	17
The Method	18
Chapter Two: The Conceptual Framework	23
The Calculus of European Treaty Reforms	23
Europe's Constitutional Quandary	23
Why Efficiency is Difficult to Attain	29
Legitimacy and Political Integration	42
A Cross-sectional Perspective	44
Patterns of Intergovernmental Conflict	47
Preferences	47
How Preferences Transform into Positions	50
The Origins of Governmental Reform Positions	55
The Process and Set of Relevant Actors	63
Relevant Actors	63
Procedural Constraints	67
Summary	70
Chapter Three: Patterns of Intergovernmental Conflict	73
Empirical Methodology	73
Spatial Models	73
Data	75
Model	78
Results	80
Governmental Positions	81
Substantial Interpretation	84
Summary	96
Chapter Four: A Short History of EU Treaty Negotiations	97
Amsterdam	97
Nice	106
Rome II	115
The Convention	126
Summary	131

Chapter Five: What Explains Governments' Positions on European
        Integration? 133
    The Unitary Actor Assumption 134
    The Economy 138
    The Voters 143
    Parties and Parliament 149
    Discussion of Results 160

Chapter Six: The Effect of Nonseparable Preferences in EU Treaty
        Negotiations 167
    Theoretical Relevance 167
    Estimating the Nonseparability of Governmental Preferences 171
    Simulation of Endogenous Change 183
    Discussion of the Results 201

Chapter Seven: Solving Europe's Constitutional Quandary 205
    Steering the Fleet Through Heavy Waters 205
    European Integration and its Limits 213

References 219

Appendix 231

Index 233

list of figures and tables

Figures

Figure 1.1:	Europe's post-Maastricht constitutional quandary	7
Figure 1.2:	Schematic Illustration of the Spatial approach: positions in the intergovernmental conflict space representing heterogeneous domestic actors and change across time	22
Figure 2.1:	Development of heterogeneity cost and economics of scale subject to the level of vertical integration	25
Figure 2.2:	Development of heterogeneity cost and economics of scale subject to a change in decision rules from higher to lower voting thresholds	26
Figure 2.3:	Effect of different decision rules in case of separable preferences	28
Figure 2.4:	Effect of different decision rules in case of non-separable preferences	28
Figure 2.5:	An illustration of the set of alternatives, the governmental position, the outcome and the status quo for three issues contained in the Rome II data	48
Figure 2.6:	An illustration of how the subtraction and addition of actors and dimensions as well as the shift of positions may reshape the unanimity core and the win-set of the status quo	67
Figure 3.1:	Governmental positions on European integration at Amsterdam, Nice and Rome II	83
Figure 3.2:	Governmental positions on reforming the decision rule at Amsterdam, Nice and Rome II	85
Figure 4.1:	Governments' positions at Amsterdam in two-dimensional conflict space	105
Figure 4.2:	Governments' positions at Nice in two-dimensional conflict space	114
Figure 4.3:	Governments' ideal positions at Rome II in two-dimensional conflict space	124
Figure 4.4:	Positions of the 25 governmental delegations to the European Convention located in the intergovernmental conflict space	129
Figure 5.1:	The changing reform position of European governments: From Amsterdam over Nice to the Constitutional IGC	136
Figure 5.2:	Governmental positions plotted against the balance of intra-EU trade as percentage of GDP	141

Figure 5.3: Governmental positions plotted against the net payer position measured as the log ratio of received EU transfer to EU contribution in the year preceding each IG   142

Figure 5.4: Governmental positions plotted against the median voters' position on European integration   146

Figure 5.5: Governmental positions plotted against the short-term trend in public opinion on European integration   147

Figure 5.6: Governmental positions plotted against the short-term trend in the public opinion on European Integration by ratification instrument   148

Figure 6.1: Governmental positions conditional upon the minimal compromise reached in June 2003   190

Figure 6.2: Governmental positions conditional upon the Convention Draft   190

Figure 6.3: Governmental positions conditional upon the compromise reached by the Italian presidency in December 2003   196

Figure 6.4: Governmental positions conditional upon the compromise reached shortly ahead of the final summit in June 2004   197

Figure 6.5: Governmental positions conditional upon the Constitutional Treaty   199

Tables

Table 1.1: Most important reform issues of the post-Maastricht agenda assigned to two prevalent intergovernmental conflict dimensions   14

Table 2.1: A comparison of the most important reform issues on the agenda of the Amsterdam, Nice and Constitutional IGC   31

Table 3.1: Model comparison: predictive power of the one- and two-dimensional model as compared to chance   81

Table 3.2: Item discrimination and difficulty parameters, labels, theoretical assignment to either of the two conflict dimensions and short descriptions for 138 issues   87

Table 3.3: Means and standard deviation of the estimated item and person parameters   96

Table 5.1: Analysis of variance of governmental positions at Nice and Rome II (EU15)   138

Table 5.2: Partisan Affiliation and position of the heads of government and foreign ministers during the three IGCs   150

Table 5.3: OLS Regressions to explain governmental positions on vertical
    integration (without lagged dependent variable)   161
Table 5.4: OLS Regressions to explain governmental positions on vertical
    integration (including lagged dependent variable)   164
Table 6.1: Estimated effect of governments' nonseparable preferences
    in 95% confidence interval   174
Table 6.2: Analysis of the variance of the estimated nonseparability in
    governments' preferences   175
Table 6.3: OLS regression on the estimated nonseparability in governments'
    preferences   176
Table 6.4: Item-level effect of the nonseparability in governments'
    preferences   177
Table 6.5: Analysis of the observed variance in governmental positions
    including an endogenous predictor for change   185
Table 6.6: Sequence of intergovernmental decisions   187

introduction | plan of the book

Chapter 1 explores the history of European integration since 1992 and the underlying agenda for this process of integration, which has become a constitutional quandary for many member states. It introduces the research question: How did the European Union cope with this constitutional quandary? The chapter commences with identifying and explaining the interests of member states in order to understand the collective reform agreements concluded after Maastricht. The nature of this reform agenda, the intergovernmental conflicts, the set of relevant actors and their reform positions are explored further, whilst the latter part of the chapter details the methodologies utilised throughout the book.

In Chapter 2, the basic two-parameter model of constitutional choice is introduced, specifically, focusing on a discussion of the government's cost-benefit calculation for alternative constitutional designs as a function of the level of vertical integration and the decision rule in place. The post-Maastricht reform agenda is analysed using these two parameters and the empirical literature on the EU's political economy. Subsequently, the origins of intergovernmental conflict are discussed with particular reference to the argument that domestic politics involving voters, parties and parliaments are responsible for changes of position in the medium term. The focus on national governments is justified through the conceptualisation of the history of post-Maastricht treaty revisions as a sequence of equilibrium and disequilibrium. Next, the importance of procedural constraints for the post-Maastricht treaty revisions is discussed, in particular, the procedures which may be of importance for Rome II because it had been prepared by a novel method, i.e., the Convention on the Future of Europe.

Chapter 3 is devoted to the operationalisation of my dependent variable – governmental position on European treaty reforms. The data set, and its genesis, is introduced, followed by a brief discussion of its validity. Next, how the spatial model of politics translates into a statistical model of ideal point estimation is shown. The results of the statistical estimation are discussed, firstly the substantive interpretation of the two-dimensional conflict space, after which the governmental positions at each of the three IGCs are presented.

In Chapter 4, each of the three IGCs are discussed in chronological order. First, the most important issues on the agenda are discussed, in particular how member states (or groups of states) positioned themselves on these issues. For this purpose, a comparison of the information in official documents and public statements with my statistical results is presented. This comparison is followed by additional information on the negotiation process and the actors, such as the duration of the process, dates of most important summits, and identification of the Council Presidents and the partisan composition of the national governments. The impact of the European Convention as a new method for preparing for IGCs is also discussed.

Chapter 5 identifies and explains the domestic origins of governmental positions on EU treaty reforms. The empirical analysis reveals that the positions on the design of the decission rule are relatively stable, whereas the positions on the vertical dimension reveal significant changes across time. The subsequent sections of Chapter 5 analyse the importance of economic and political factors for understanding these changes. In particular, the role of the parliament and voters in the domestic preference formation process is analysed.

In Chapter 6, the relation between a government's position on vertical integration and its preference for the decision rule is discussed, specifically the argument that a government's position on the decision rule cannot be considered independent of its de facto or expected level of political integration. The theoretical relevance of this interdependence is elaborated and a hypothesis formulated about how its importance may vary across member states and reform issues. It is argued that the above-mentioned interdependence presents an alternative, endogenous explanation for the observed changes in governmental positions.

Chapter 7 offers a summary and discussion of my findings, specifically by discussing the relevance of the empirical results for the analyses of international treaty negotiations and the implications for the future of European integration.

List of Abbreviations

AFSJ	Area of Freedom Security and Justice
CAP	Common Agricultural Policy
CFSP	Common Foreign and Security Polity
COSAC	Conference of Community and European Affairs Committees of Parliaments of the European Union
DG	Directorate General
EADS	European Aeronautic, Defence and Space Company
ECA	European Court of Auditors
ECJ	European Court of Justice
EMU	European Monetary Union
EP	European Parliament
EPIN	European Policy Institutes Networks
ESC	Economic and Social Committee
EU	European Union
IGC	Intergovernmental Conference
JHA	Justice and Home Affairs
LT	Lisbon Treaty
MEP	Member of the European Parliament
NATO	North Atlantic Treaty Organisation
QMV	Qualified Majority Voting
SEM	Single European Market
SGCI	Secrétariat Général du Comité Interministériel pour les questions de cooperation économique européenne
ToA	Treaties of Amsterdam
ToM	Treaty of Maastricht
ToN	Treaty of Nice
WEU	West European Union

chapter one | perspectives on european integration

THE QUESTION

On February 7th, 1992, the foreign and finance ministers from twelve member states of the European Communities signed a treaty that, according to the British press,[1] aimed 'to turn the European Community into an economic union and a global political power, before the end of the decade'. However, commentators and political leaders were fully aware that the European Union had to face a stiff breeze from the moment of birth. The ambitious agenda of the political integration process listed the enhancement of social and economic cohesion, which was intended to guarantee the effectiveness of the Single European Market (SEM) and the European Monetary Union (EMU). Concrete measures discussed to achieve this goal ranged from minimum standards in social protection and employment law over loose coordination mechanisms to a more fully-fledged European social policy including the nucleus for a redistributive policy scheme. The restructuring of foreign and security policy ranked even higher on the political to-do list. Only two years after the fall of the Berlin Wall, Europe faced an intense discussion over its future security architecture. Of particular importance in this discussion was the potential dissolution or reorganisation of the West European Union and the enlargement of the North Atlantic Treaty Organisation. The same was true for future cooperation in the areas of justice and home affairs. This stronghold of the sovereign nation-state had been increasingly challenged by integrationist politicians who argued that common European decisions would be an inevitable step guaranteeing a successful economic integration. Other projects contained conflicts at the interface between the common market and environmental as well as social standards. Finally, closer cooperation in fiscal policy affairs emerged as one of the most hotly-debated issues on the agenda.

It goes without saying that this agenda for political integration has been and still is heavily disputed among politicians, academics and the interested general public. This is an ongoing debate between the so-called 'Europeanists' and the 'Euro-sceptics'. Contemporary witnesses of the final steps to what would become the Treaty of Maastricht had to face three developments that turned the contentious issue of substantial integration into a quandary that provoked lasting discussion of the Union's legitimacy, its efficiency and its ultimate purpose. According to Schofield (2004: 16), a 'constitutional quandary' is characterised by political trade-offs accompanied by a high degree of uncertainty among the political ac-

---

1. Palmer, J. 'Second Treaty of Maastricht brings full Union closer', *The Guardian*, February 7th 1992.

tors and, in particular, among their electorate. Such a situation requires a group of constitutional architects who agree on a path to the resolution of the quandary. The purpose of this book is to identify and explain the interests of these architects and to understand the collective reform agreements concluded after Maastricht. In particular, the Intergovernmental Conferences (IGCs) of Amsterdam (1996/7), Nice (2000) and Rome II (2003/4) will be analysed in more detail.

What were the three challenges at the time of Maastricht that turned the issue of European integration into a constitutional quandary? First, political leaders found themselves under pressure from a growing queue of would-be member states. To accommodate them, the existing twelve member states had to agree on how to move toward a political union well before the 1996 review date specified in the Treaty of Maastricht. At the time of Maastricht, many thought that even including Austria, Finland and Sweden would stretch the existing decision-making mechanisms beyond any tolerable limits of efficiency. However, the true challenge at the time was that central European countries would sooner or later become full or associate members of the Union. Given the weak economic conditions of the former communist countries, as well as their historic and geographic differences from the existing member states, it was obvious that enlargement threatened the ambitious goals of political integration. Even worse, Eastern enlargement appeared to be somewhat incompatible with the SEM (e.g. freedom of movement) and with the Common Agricultural Policy (CAP), one of the cornerstones of the integration project.

Second, as a consequence of the Single European Act (1986), legal activities at the European level had drastically increased in number and complexity (König *et al.* 2006). Although the amount of EU legislation had reached its temporary peak around 1990, the political system had been pushed to the limits of its capacity. Although an increase in staff assigned to the European institutions could have solved this problem, another phenomenon appeared even more troublesome. The quantity of EU legislation slowly decreased after 1990, but the average length of decision-making increased (König *et al.* 2006), largely because of the changing character of European legislation. After the first wave of single market directives had been approved, member states were left with the more contentious issues, which were harder to solve. The origins of political conflict in the EU are found among the divergent interests of its member states. Following this logic, Eastern enlargement implied a further decrease in decision-making efficiency, unless member states could agree to reform the decision-making procedures significantly. However, any reform plans might well threaten the principles of equality and consensus, especially the extension of majority voting, lower voting thresholds and the empowerment of supranational actors.

Finally, as the legal activities of the European Communities increased and political decisions became more and more contentious, Europe's political leaders had to face increasing debate about the democratic legitimacy of the European integration project (e.g. Kohler-Koch and Rittberger 2007). In particular, scholars and Euro-sceptics began to question the extent to which voters were democratically represented by a primarily intergovernmental decision-making body and a nontransparent supranational bureaucracy, such as the European Commission. This criticism increased with the extension of qualified majority voting (QMV) in the Council of Ministers, which could allow a member state to be outvoted on matters of vital national interest. The lack of transparency and accountability were, and still are, the keywords of this debate. As a consequence, it was no longer safe to assume that voters were either favourably disposed or indifferent to the integration project. The end of this 'permissive consensus' (Inglehart 1971) was most evident when Danish voters rejected the Treaty of Maastricht in 1992, which eventually led to the Danes opting out of the last stage of the EMU as well as from cooperation in defence and home affairs (Edinburgh Agreement). Only two months after the Danish 'no' vote, the French referendum on the Treaty of Maastricht passed with a razor-thin majority (50.5 per cent).

On January 1st, 1993, the Treaty of Maastricht took effect and the European Union was born. Even at this early stage, its political leaders found themselves in a multidimensional constitutional quandary, represented by the pyramid in Figure 1.1. Against the backdrop of approaching Eastern enlargement, they had to strike a balance between three partly conflicting goals: efficiency, legitimacy and political integration. Any reform of one of these goals would have come at the expense of another. Obviously, not all goals had equal weight in the political debate, and even more importantly, not all relevant political actors attached the same level of salience to the goals. In retrospect, it is known that member states moved in a stepwise fashion to resolve this quandary.

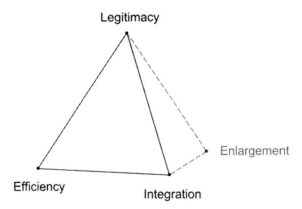

Figure 1.1: Europe's post-Maastricht constitutional quandary

The present book explains Europe's approaches to solving its constitutional quandary. For this endeavour, the history of European integration is perceived as a sequence of major reforms that usually occurred via treaty revisions agreed upon by European governments. The classic IGC has three stages: first, a taskforce (or wise-men group) elaborates the reform agenda. Second, the Council President settles the less contentious issues in bilateral shuttle diplomacy. Third, hotly- contested issues are negotiated in a concluding summit. However, the IGC in 2003/4 (henceforth: Rome II) was prepared by the European Convention, which involved delegates of national parliaments and governments representing a broader spectrum of domestic interests.

As mentioned earlier, the IGCs before Maastricht (1992) had a clear focus on deepening economic coordination and integration. This development culminated in the completion of the SEM, agreed to in the Single European Act (1986), and the establishment of the EMU, agreed to in the Treaty of Maastricht (ToM). Compared with previous IGCs, those after Maastricht dealt 'primarily with questions of constitutional design and institutional balance', not least to prepare for the approaching Eastern enlargement (Laffan 1997: 289). Therefore, the analysis here focuses on the negotiations at Amsterdam (1996/7), Nice (2000), the European Convention (2002/3) and Rome II (2003/4), which would eventually be modified by the Lisbon Treaty (2007). The adoption of the Lisbon Treaty by Irish voters in October 2009 marks the preliminary end of this reform process that began almost two decades earlier. Although integration during the pre-Maastricht era resulted in an unexpectedly high level of economic coordination, member states in the post-Maastricht era have been continuously struggling to reform the Union's constitutional design, to prepare for enlargement and to adapt to external challenges such as globalisation, structural economic changes, global warming and energy shortages (Majone 2006).[2]

Compared with some of the radical reform proposals that have been discussed by national governments during the past fifteen years, the actual treaty modifications may appear modest. However, even if only the most prominent reforms are considered, there is little doubt that the Treaties of Amsterdam (ToA) and Nice (ToN), as well as the Lisbon Treaty (LT), significantly altered the distribution of political powers in the EU.

- Step-by-step, the EU's policy competences have been extended, especially in the areas of employment, environmental protection and the second and third pillars. Besides, governments strengthened the so-called Enhanced Cooperation provision, an instrument that allows a group of member states to foster integration within the institutional framework of the Union. The ToA extends Enhanced Cooperation to the areas of justice and foreign policy (Schouthetee 2001: 164).[3] The ToN lowered the minimum number of participating states to eight, and with few exceptions, abolished the veto right of individual states (Janning 2001: 146). Finally, the LT provides for closer cooperation in European Security and Defence Policy ('Permanent Structured Cooperation'),

---

2. That said, the subsequent analysis touches upon explanations for the date and terms of enlargement only marginally and only where necessary for understanding the intergovernmental negotiations. As a consequence, Figure 1 is reduced to a triangle of legitimacy, efficiency and political integration.

3. Although the official voting rule for closer cooperation in the first and third pillar was qualified majority voting, each member state could nonetheless veto closer cooperation for vital domestic reasons, as under the Luxembourg compromise (de Schouthetee 2001: 162).

though initiation would still require the consensus of all member states.

- Regarding the Council of Ministers, the ToN introduced voting weights and the triple majority threshold.[4] The LT would completely abandon voting weights and set the threshold at 55 per cent of the member states, representing at least 65 per cent of the EU's population. To block a proposal, at least four member states must be against it. However, the real impact of the QMV rules depends on their applicability. Each of the three treaty reforms provides for a case-wise extension of QMV (Moravcsik and Nicolaidis 1999: 77; Baldwin *et al.* 2001: 10; Piris 2006: 94).

- Regarding the European Parliament (EP), the ToA simplified the codecision procedure and extended it to certain aspects of policies against social exclusion and fraud, and for public health. Its applicability has been further extended under the ToN to antidiscrimination action, as well as to additional aspects of asylum, social, structural, and industrial policies and justice and home affairs (JHA). The LT adds provisions concerning agricultural policy and further aspects of JHA, now calling codecision the 'ordinary legislative procedure'. In addition, it would strengthen the EP's say in the annual and multiannual budgeting process, including agricultural budgets. Furthermore, the ToN and the LT marginally changed the distribution of seats in the EP toward a system increasingly proportional to population size.

- Regarding the European Commission, the ToN introduced a ceiling for the number of Commissioners, which was to be applied in 2005, with the status quo[5] retained until then. Thereafter, the large member states would have lost their second Commissioner. However, according to the revised version of the LT every member state maintains one Commissioner.

- The personalisation of EU politics has been enhanced by introducing the office of the High Commissioner, Europe's 'Minister of Foreign Affairs'. The ToA demanded that the Commission President, chosen by common accord of all member states, must be approved by the EP. In addition, the LT proposed that a team of three member states should preside over the European Council for eighteen months[6] to foster the continuity of EU politics.

- Regarding the representation of domestic interests, the ToA strengthened the autonomy and competences of the Committee of Regions and the Economic

---

4. The Nice threshold demands between 71 per cent and 74 per cent necessary weighted 'yes' votes (depending on enlargement), a majority of member states, and if a member requests it, 62 per cent of the total EU population.

5. From 2005, the large member states would lose one Commissioner, while all member states will have one Commissioner until the number of member states exceeds twenty-seven. In that case, rotation on an equal basis will take place (Yataganas 2001:37).

6. However, considering the close cooperation that current and past presidents have established with their predecessors and successors, this reform more or less reinforces the current practice.

and Social Committee (ESC).[7] Under the same treaty, national parliaments were granted a minimum time to consult documents during the drafting stage. The LT leaps ahead, introducing a 'subsidiary early warning system', which makes the national parliaments responsible for monitoring the division of competences in the EU. The ToA fostered transparency by ensuring the accessibility of official documents, and the ToN opened the formerly secret Council meetings to the public. Finally, the LT introduces a popular initiative.

In sum, these reforms were intended to guarantee efficient decision-making in an enlarged Union, to foster integration when the benefits outweighed the drawbacks, and to boost legitimacy. Overall, they mirror a significant redistribution of powers among member states, as well as between domestic and European levels of government. In this book, the treaty changes that the first fifteen (then twenty-seven) member states agreed to during the post-Maastricht era are explained and the reform positions of national governments explored in greater depth. It is important to understand that these positions are crucial for our understanding of reform outcomes. It is also critical to identify the political and economic factors that explain the observed variation in governmental reform positions across member states and across time. A few examples may illustrate the underlying research puzzle.

Why did European governments agree to extend Enhanced Cooperation to Common Foreign and Security Politics at the Nice IGC when the British and other governments had vetoed it at Amsterdam in 1997? Is it because Britain had recently elected a Labour government? Or did the changing context of world politics put additional pressure on the 'masters of the treaties'? Why did the Greek government suddenly prefer the extension of Enhanced Cooperation? Did the unexpected prospect of joining the EMU from the start contribute to a complete reevaluation of a reform that would promote a multispeed Europe? Why did the French government successfully veto the hotly debated reform to modify the voting rule in the Council of Ministers during the Nice IGC, while a few years later, the same government turned around to support a much more drastic reform of the Council's voting rule at the Brussels IGC? Did its foreign counterparts coerce the French government? Or did France come to realise some hidden benefits of this reform for domestic politics?

In particular, the findings presented in this book address four research questions:

1. What are the major intergovernmental conflicts underlying European treaty negotiations since Maastricht?
2. How do these conflicts contribute to our understanding of treaty negotiations and reform?
3. Are there domestic-level political and economic factors that can help us explain the observed governmental reform positions? To what extent are changes in these positions caused by domestic political dynamics?

---

7. However, as a reaction to the successive enlargements, the number of representatives in the Committee of Regions and ESC has been steadily increased.

4. To what extent do governmental positions on integration depend on their (expected) reform of the Union's institutions and decision rules?

THE ARGUMENTS

More than ten years after Maastricht, in October 2004, the heads of state and government signed the Treaty Establishing a Constitution for Europe. The treaty was the result of a lengthy negotiation process that had been prepared by the Convention on the Future of Europe. Its purpose was to solve Europe's constitutional quandary, at least in the medium term. Hence, it was designed to increase decision-making efficiency, transparency and the democratic legitimacy of the enlarged EU. Only six months later, failed referenda in France (May 29th, 2005) and the Netherlands (June 1st, 2005) buried hopes for successful ratification. It took more than two years of collective reflection before the political leaders of all twenty-seven member states signed a pared-down version of the Constitutional Treaty in Lisbon. However, this time, the first, negative Irish referendum (June 2008) delayed the ratification and it took another sixteen months before Irish voters adopted the treaty on the second attempt.

These events polarised the debate about the future of European integration. Against the background of modest integration progress at Nice and the failures to ratify the Constitutional Treaty, a first camp of scholars concluded that 'the failure of Constitutional reform is, paradoxically, evidence of the success and stability of the existing European constitutional settlement' (Moravcsik 2006: 219; Franklin 2006; Rabkin 2006). The primary argument here is that the reforms agreed in the ToA and (though almost irrelevant) the ToN have successfully solved Europe's constitutional quandary. In other words, the common market project and limited cooperation in selected policy areas represent an optimal split of competences between national and European levels of government, existing decision-making procedures and institutions are sufficiently efficient, and finally, the democratic deficit does not exist (Moravcsik 2006; Majone 2002).

This perspective is strongly contested by other scholars. Again, the normative criticism follows the conflicting goals described in Figure 1.1. First, the EU suffers from a democratic deficit that could be reduced by particular institutional reforms (for a recent discussion, see Follesdal and Hix 2006; Hix 2008). Specifically, proponents of the democratic deficit thesis criticise the fact that European institutions cannot be held accountable for their politics (Crombez 2003). Second, economists argue that the current division of competences violates the principle of fiscal equivalence, meaning that it creates policy externalities that should be internalised (e.g., Alesina *et al.* 2001, 2002; Alesina and Wacziarg 1999; Collignon 2002). These scholars argue that agricultural, regional and structural policies (among others) should be renationalised, whereas certain aspects of environmental, fiscal and tax policies should be Europeanised. Third, Eastern enlargement led to increasing heterogeneity of preferences among member states and more contentious conflicts, which in turn increase the danger of grid-lock and standstill (Sapir *et al.* 2003; Zimmer *et al.* 2004; König and Bräuninger 2004).

The empirical analysis presented in this book reminds us not to confuse the normative dimension of Europe's constitutional quandary with positive explanations for observed successes and failures in revising the European treaty framework. There might be good reason to reject the idea that Europe faces a constitutional quandary. But as a matter of fact, Europe's political leaders invested a lot of resources in the post-Maastricht reform agenda and, eventually, agreed on a list of quite important reforms. In the remainder of this section, the nature of this reform agenda, the intergovernmental conflicts, the set of relevant actors and their reform positions are explored further.

AGENDA AND CONFLICTS

Economic coordination dominated pre-Maastricht treaty negotiations, generating economic benefits for all member states (Majone 2006, 1998). Those negotiations can be characterised by one primary conflict: some member states expected higher gains from intensified economic coordination than others did. These same member states were eager to ensure the credible commitment of all others to the realization of the European treaties. Hence, they preferred more delegation and pooling of sovereignty (Moravcsik 1998: 76).

The post-Maastricht IGCs faced a different agenda, one that turned the previous positive-sum game of economic coordination into a mixed-motive game. The historic setting described above would lead to an expectation that the conflicts among Europe's constitutional architects would resemble the conflicting goals of the constitutional quandary; i.e. legitimacy, efficiency and integration. The empirical analysis shows that intergovernmental disputes centred on political integration and those institutional reforms that would have altered the distribution of powers among member states, a reform debate primarily driven by efficiency considerations. This is not to say that democratic legitimacy has been irrelevant to our understanding of post-Maastricht treaty revisions. The debates at and decisions of the European Convention as well as the ratification processes (with their unparalleled number of announced referenda) proves that the opposite is true, legitimacy considerations are less important for understanding the conflicts among national governments because, at the level of concrete reform issues, they coincide with either of the two other dimensions. If, for example, a government prefers an elected President of the Commission or the empowerment of the European Parliament, these reforms imply both a transfer of sovereignty from the national to the European level and an increase in transparency (or at least visibility) and accountability.

The intergovernmental reform agenda, which was surprisingly stable throughout the period of observation, was dominated by 1) institutional reforms, many of which imply a redistribution of political power; and 2) the empowerment of the EU in so-called 'new policy areas', some of which imply a redistribution of the benefits of EU membership. As a consequence, the post-Maastricht IGCs revealed two conflicts that reflect standard constitutional theories (e.g. Lijphart 1999; Buchanan and Tullock 1962). The first conflict deals with the horizontal distribution of power among member states at the EU level. This conflict contrasts those who espouse consensus and equality as a means of horizontal power distribution with those who prefer majoritarianism and proportionality. The second conflict illustrates the standard 'integration-independence' dimension, where conflict centres on the vertical distribution of competences between European and domestic levels of government. In short, this dimension contrasts the supporters of a fully-fledged political federation with those favouring a loose confederation of sovereign states.

Table 1.1 assigns each of the most prominent reform issues of the post-Maastricht agenda to one of these two conflict dimensions. Here, the concept of vertical integration contains three subgroups of issues. The first group of issues defines the political mandate of the EU and includes the transfer of legislative and judicial competences. Judicial competences concern strengthening the legal status of the individual, especially with respect to fundamental human rights. Finally, the EU's prospective mandate is defined by its objectives, such as full employment, social markets and competitiveness.

The second group of vertical integration issues concerns the democratic legitimacy of the EU, especially with respect to the participation of domestic actors at the EU level. These actors include individual voters, national parliaments, regions and social partners. Issues in this group comprise the empowerment of the EP in legislation, nomination and budgeting; the empowerment of national parliaments, the ECJ, and the ECA; and a stronger and independent role for the ESC and the Committee of Regions. These issues also concern stronger political rights for individual voters, such as access to courts, suffrage and direct democratic elements. Finally, the third group of issues relates to how vertical integration is affected by the accessibility of information and the increasing political accountability of EU-level actors. The former point concerns access to official documents and Council meetings, and the latter refers to further personalisation of internal and external political representation.

The horizontal dimension in Table 1.1 refers to the impact that national governments have on EU decisions. Most prominently, it addresses voting, agenda setting, informational and budgetary powers (Bailer 2006). Accordingly, it concerns such issues as the reform and extension of QMV, the compositions of the Commission, the ECJ, the ECA, the ESC and the Committee of Regions, the allocation of seats in the EP, and the organisation of the European Council presidency.

Table 1.1 offers a heuristic for understanding the intergovernmental conflicts underlying Europe's constitutional quandary. It is by no means self-evident, so the next logical step is to discuss the relevant actors and the origins of their reform positions.

ACTORS AND PROCESS

In his groundbreaking analysis, Moravcsik (1998) explains European integration prior to Maastricht by focusing on the three *largest member states*. If necessary, these large countries would offer either 'financial side payments or symbolic concessions' to the smaller ones to achieve their grand economic bargains (1998: 65f.). As a consequence, intergovernmental bargaining resulted in treaty reforms that benefited the three larger member states (Pareto superior), whose governments were able to strike the optimal bargain (Pareto efficient).

Table 1.1: *Most important reform issues of the post-Maastricht agenda assigned to two prevalent intergovernmental conflict dimensions*

Vertical Integration		Horizontal Integration	
Issues	Effect	Issues	Effect
Transfer of legislative competencies	Definition of EU's political mandate	Extension of QMV	Redistribution of voting, informational, agenda setting and budgetary power; Decision Making Efficiency
Strengthening individual legal rights (e.g fundamental and human rights)		QMV threshold	
Introduction of objectives and principles (e.g. high level of employment)		Council of Ministers: allocation of votes & internal reform	
Empowerment of EP in legislation, budgeting & nomination	Empowerment of domestic actors at the EU level	Commission: composition & allocation of budgets	
Empowerment of national parliaments in legislation		Enhanced Cooperation	
Empowerment ECJ and ECA		European Council: Presidency	
Empowerment of Committee of Regions		ECJ & ECA: size, composition and internal reform	
Direct Democracy (popular initiative)		EP, Ctte. of Regions & ESC: size, composition and internal reform	
Empowerment of Social and Economic Council			
Strengthening individual political rights (e.g. suffrage, access to courts)			
Transparency of the decision-making process & legal simplification	Reduction of information asymmetries; democratic accountability		
Personalisation (President of European Council, Minister of Foreign Affairs, Commission president)			

However, Moravcsik's original work deals with a maximum of twelve member states since 1986, and with even fewer states before the first Northern (1973) and subsequent Southern (1981, 1986) enlargements. When the Treaty of Maastricht was negotiated (1991), the total GDP of Germany, France and the UK outweighed that of the remaining nine member states by a factor of 1.8. In terms of population size, this factor was 1.3. Hence, the three largest member states held an economic power almost twice as strong as all the other countries combined. In contrast, the Northern (1995) and Eastern (2004/7) enlargements added another fifteen small to medium-sized countries to the Union, the majority of which had relatively weak economies at the time they entered. Today, the total economic power of the UK, Germany and France is roughly equal to that of the remaining twenty-four countries, though these three states account for only 201 of the 485 million EU inhabitants. Given this shift in the balance of economic power, making financial side payments to smaller countries appears to be a less feasible strategy. In addition, the focus of the IGCs since Maastricht shifted away from economic integration and coordination toward institutional reforms and political integration. In other words, it is highly doubtful that any member state could have offered economic bargains large enough for financial side payments to be a profitable strategy.

Against this background, it comes as little surprise that recent researchers writing in the tradition of LI argue that large and small member states are equally important for our understanding of EU treaty reforms (e.g. König and Hug 2006). In his empirical analysis of the Amsterdam IGC, Slapin (2006) found that large member states did not have any more power than the average member state at the bargaining table.

In the spatial analysis of politics, a bargaining outcome is *Pareto superior* if it is located in the win set of the status quo, and it is *Pareto efficient* if it is located in the core (Tsebelis 2002: 39). Accordingly, one would expect to find the outcome of intergovernmental negotiations since Maastricht to be located in the win set of all member states. This presumes that the status quo ante must be situated outside the core of all member states. Presuming that the reform agenda remained relatively stable throughout the post-Maastricht period, it follows that the positions of national governments must have changed between one IGC and the next. In other words, the history of European treaty reforms is conceived of as a sequence of equilibrium and disequilibrium (Caporaso 2007). The empirical results support this argument for Amsterdam and Nice. However, Rome II adhered to a slightly different logic. Here, the data suggest that the Treaty of Nice was more or less in equilibrium as defined by member states' positions in spring 2004. Nevertheless, the heads of state and government signed a progressive reform; namely, the Treaty Establishing a Constitution for Europe. Why did some member states sign the Constitution, even though they preferred the Treaty of Nice?

One possible answer highlights the importance of procedural constraints. The classic liberal intergovernmentalist perspective argues that treaty reforms are a result of pure and unconstrained intergovernmental bargaining. In a Union of six, nine or even twelve governments, such an unconstrained bargaining game might produce efficient outcomes, especially if the table is dominated by the three senior partners of France, Germany and the UK. However, the efficiency of such an unstructured bargaining game decreases with the number of participants. Moreover, many of the institutional reforms on the post-Maastricht agenda imply a redistribution of political power among member states, most prominently discussed in connection with issues such as the design of voting rules and the composition of the European Commission. As a consequence, the nature of intergovernmental conflict shifts from being a coordination problem toward being a complex and strongly redistributive issue, which is substantially more difficult to solve.

These arguments are well grounded in the theoretical literature. First, and most obviously, the number of participating actors raises the transaction costs of international negotiations (e.g. Cross 1969). Second, without any procedural constraints on the agenda, neither multidimensional spatial voting models (McKelvey 1976) nor multilateral strategic bargaining models identify a unique subgame-perfect equilibrium (Muthoo 2002: 300). In other words, both the social choice and the bargaining literatures would expect a unique and stable equilibrium in multilateral negotiations only if process matters.

The traditional IGC restricts bargaining by the powers granted to the Council Presidency who perform the crucial tasks of preparing political agreements and organising the IGC itself. Therefore, it has been argued that the President holds a certain degree of agenda-setting power (Elgström 2003). Usually, the President prepares the IGCs via bilateral shuttle diplomacy to settle the less important issues on the agenda (which are identified a priori by an expert committee). The more important and contentious issues are saved for the decisive summit, where it is the President's responsibility to set the agenda and propose a political compromise.

However, the Constitutional Treaty was prepared by a novel method; namely, the Convention on the Future of Europe. The President of the Convention (Giscard D'Estaing) held considerable agenda-setting powers (Tsebelis 2008; Tsebelis and Proksch 2007). He could pick and choose among amendments suggested by the working group, alter the rules of the game during the procedure, and iterate the agenda *ad libitum* – and he did not intend to have an explicit vote on the complete draft. In December 2004, the IGC adopted the Convention draft almost without modification. This raises the question of why the Convention enjoyed such a high degree of de facto agenda-setting power.

In Chapter 2, there is an in-depth analysis of the three possible answers to this question. First, in the course of the unexpectedly strong Convention, member states began to see a dilemma. Either they had to disempower the Convention via intergovernmental overrule (which would tarnish both international and domestic reputations) or they could play along with the Convention and its President by upgrading the ranks and status of their delegations.[8] Ultimately, their deci-

---

8. Note that the second option (upgrade) dominates the first (disempower) in the sense that a disempowerment of the Convention would have required collective action, which was unlikely as some member states, most notably France and Germany, realised that the president was largely promoting their goals. Accordingly, member states with different preferences were forced to counterbalance their power in the Convention at the expense of upgrading the committee's power.

sion to exchange their delegates for high-profile politicians raised the reputation costs of disrespecting the Convention draft. Second, the Laeken declaration prescribed a clear timeline for the entire process, which would end with elections to the European Parliament in June 2004. This fixed deadline provided additional pressure to keep the box closed and renegotiate only the most controversial issues. Finally, procedural innovations left governments with incomplete and imperfect information. At the time the Laeken declaration was issued, nobody expected the Convention to deliver a fully-fledged draft of a Constitution for Europe. Under these circumstances, bargaining theory ascribes an even higher importance to process. In addition, theory does not necessarily expect bargaining outcomes to be Pareto efficient and superior.

POSITIONS

So far, it has been argued that 1) the history of European treaty reforms can be considered as a sequence of equilibrium and disequilibrium; 2) the post-Maastricht agenda remained relatively stable; and 3) national governments are the relevant actors, and they did not change during the period of observation. Therefore, it follows logically that governmental positions must have changed. From a long-term perspective, it is hard to imagine the history of European integration without changing positions anyway. From such a perspective, it is also clear that Charles De Gaulle would not have welcomed a European Minister of Foreign Affairs, nor would Margaret Thatcher have signed a treaty rendering the EP an almost coequal legislator.

In this book, how domestic interests and institutions shape member states' reform positions is analysed in the short and medium terms. From my theoretical perspective, the official governmental position is a result of competing domestic interests. Hence, the main focus is on the preferences of voters, political parties and their representatives in national parliaments. An additional argument explored in this book is that member states' economic characteristics define a corridor for governmental positions. However, the final position that governments take at any particular IGC is determined by domestic politics.

With regard to the preferred level of vertical integration, the results provide ample support for the relevance of the domestic arena. Whereas economic variables can explain international variation, positional changes reflect both public opinion and party politics. These findings deal a severe blow to all those who criticise the process of European integration for its elitist and undemocratic nature. In particular, when formulating the national position, a government's discretion is limited by short-term trends in public opinion. In addition, formal parliamentary scrutiny (where present) and government partisanship are important determinants of the governmental position on integration.

As for conflicts over the decision rules, member states at first appear to be truly unitary. Domestic actors always prefer more powers for their own government relative to foreign governments. The variation across member states is best explained by varying degrees of unilateral policy discretion. Large and economically affluent member states prefer reforms toward majoritarianism. Furthermore, member states' positions on the decision rule reflect governments' fear of being outvoted in the Council of Ministers, and the Ministers' de facto discretion in the implementation of community law.

Finally, the fact that governments' positions on reforming the decision rule depends on the set of competences delegated to the EU is explored further. In technical terms, governments' preferences for vertical and horizontal integration are nonseparable. The crucial idea here is that nonseparability might go both ways. For example, France might prefer deeper cooperation in justice and security politics only if decision-making in this area becomes more efficient by extending majority voting and lowering the voting thresholds. Ireland, on the other hand, might prefer deeper cooperation in the same area only if it retains its veto right. One important consequence of this bidirectional conditionality is that it reduces the size of the win set for potential reforms. Another, more general consequence of nonseparable preferences is that the sequences in which member states adopt positions on integration and decision rules matter. Hence, nonseparability provides an endogenous explanation for changing policy positions (Lacy 2001).

Elaborating on constitutional theories, it could be said that wealthier member states (net payers) prefer a more majoritarian and efficient decision rule when they are confronted with more vertical integration than they wanted. This is because they possess alternative means of power and, accordingly, would gain in relative strength once veto power loses its overall importance in EU decision-making. In other words, rich member states are able to avoid the rising heterogeneity costs implied by a higher level of integration.

In sum, the following arguments can be made: First, Europe's constitutional quandary, which emerged at the time of Maastricht, can be divided into two intergovernmental conflicts. The first conflict centres on governments' disputes over vertical political integration, and the second on issues of horizontal distribution of powers. Second, all member states are relevant to our understanding of post-Maastricht treaty revisions. However, because of an increased number of member states, our understanding of intergovernmental bargaining must consider procedural constraint. This is particularly evident with regard to the Convention method. Third, governmental positions are located within a corridor defined by socio-economic factors. However, their position on any particular IGC must be conceived of as a product of domestic politics. Finally, governments condition their preferences for political integration on the reforms of the decision-making rules, and vice versa.

THE METHOD

How solid is the empirical foundation for these claims? Methodologically, the dependent variable used in this book is based on governmental leaders' preferences on all relevant reform issues in the agendas at Amsterdam, Nice and Rome II. Their preferences on these issues have been systematically measured for each IGC, as well as for the European Convention (Hug and König 2002; König and Luetgert 2003; Thurner and Pappi 2006; König und Hug 2006). These datasets were generated through a mixture of face-to-face interviews with experts, Internet questionnaires filled out by experts, and document analysis. They contain information on the governmental positions of all member states on more than 150 issues. Overall, the validity of this information has been cross-checked in various ways and is considered very high (Hix and Crombez 2005; Dorussen *et al.* 2005; König *et al.* 2005; König 2005; Slapin 2006). The issues comprise matters of both institutional reform and the further transfer of policy competences.

The period of observation minimises possible external impacts on the agendas. When the ToM was ratified (1993), the two major economic projects of the Union had been completed – the SEM as agreed in the Single European Act (1986), and the EMU. The reflection group presented its first suggestion of issues to be discussed at Amsterdam in December 1995. Up until then, the SEM had been implemented by a tremendous amount of law making by European institutions during the late 1980s and early 1990s (König *et al.* 2007). In addition, the date of the EMU's third and final phase had been fixed. Ever since then, the European integration project has been characterised by the constitutional quandaries described in the previous sections. The report of the reflection group presented at the European Council held in Madrid (December 1995) set the stage and placed new issues on the agenda.[9] This agenda remained more or less stable throughout the period of observation.

In January 1995, Austria, Finland and Sweden completed the Union of fifteen. However, at that time, every government knew that Eastern enlargement was just a matter of time (Schimmelfennig 2001). Hence, it is plausible to assume that member states anticipated the possible consequences of enlargement in 1996. Therefore, observed changes in member states' national positions between 1996 and 2004 can hardly be attributed to Eastern enlargement. Figure 1.2 illustrates that Eastern enlargement led to a slight increase of the unanimity core.[10] Nevertheless, it is advisable to determine empirically the extent to which the participation of ten new member states influenced the old member states' preferences and the resulting intergovernmental conflict patterns. In sum, the period beginning with the negotiations of Amsterdam (1996) and ending with the Constitutional Treaty in June 2004 controls for two important variables: it defines a stable agenda and a stable set of relevant actors. Therefore, observed changes in member states' positions must be rooted in concrete social, political and economic developments during the period of observation.

To evaluate the extent to which member states' positions changed during the

---

9. The headings of the report are: 1.1. Citizenship and Fundamental Rights; 1.2 Third Pillar; 1.3 Employment; 1.4 Overseas Territories; 1.5 Environment; 1.6 Subsidiary; 1.7 Transparency and Simplification; 2.1 The European Parliament; 2.2 National Parliaments; 2.3 The Council; 2.4 The Commission; 2.5 The Court of Auditors; 2.6 The European Court of Justice; 2.7 Fight against Fraud; 2.8 Differentiated Integration and Flexibility; 2.9 The Committee of Regions; 2.10 Hierarchy of Legal Acts and Budgetary Matters; 2.11 New Policy Areas; 2.12 The Economic and Monetary Union; 3.1 The Common Foreign and Defence Policy; 3.2 The Defence Policy and the WEU.

10. The unanimity core defines the set of alternatives that cannot be altered without leaving at least one actor worse off.

period of observation, two different methodological approaches could be utilised. First, every member state's position on each and every issue discussed at Amsterdam, Nice and Rome II could be analysed. In Chapter 4, my analysis benefits from this qualitative approach. However, with respect to systematic hypothesis testing, this issue-by-issue approach has certain limitations.

- First, only a minority of the 140 issues in the data set are directly comparable. Not only does the wording of questions differ across questionnaires but also the answer and reference categories change. The following example illustrates the problem. The Dutch government preferred more EU competences in employment at Amsterdam but was satisfied with the EU's employment competences at Nice. There are two possible explanations for this discrepancy. First, the different answers might be due to the reforms agreed to under the Treaty of Amsterdam. Second, the substantial position of the Dutch government might have changed. However, because of differences in how the pertinent questions and answer categories were worded, we cannot know which of these two explanations is true. Fortunately, this ambiguity does not characterise all questions. For a sufficient number of questions, a direct comparison between different data sets was possible. These questions build bridges across the different points in time. By contrast, qualitative analysis of the remaining issues must go back to the original governmental documents, which are very incomplete. In addition, any *ex post facto* interpretation of individual documents entails danger of subjectivity and arbitrariness.
- Second, subjectivity and arbitrariness are two potential sources of coding error when doing issue-by-issue comparisons and interpretations. Further sources of error are induced by cross-country comparisons: member states publish different documents of varying quality regarding their positions. Any *ex post facto* attempt to compare these documents is difficult, not least because many of them are joint statements from two or more governments, often issued during the negotiation process.
- Finally, my theoretical approach is founded in the spatial analysis of politics, which specifies the distances between actors and policies in political conflict spaces. By contrast, the qualitative issue-by-issue analysis provides for a very low level of abstraction. Although one might start with different policy areas and institutional facets and then aggregate these individual issues by means of deductive categorisation, this aggregation process remains rather arbitrary and irreproducible in comparisons across time.

Against this background, a statistical approach has been chosen to be supplemented by qualitative illustration where necessary. To identify and anchor the latent conflict spaces of the different IGCs, statistical models that can be grouped under the label 'ideal point estimation' are used (e.g. Martin and Quinn 2002; Clinton, Jackman and Rivers 2004; Bailey 2007). Most of these methods are developments of the Item Response model and allow for the estimation of multilevel effects (De Boeck 2004). Most of the applications refer to Bayesian estimators, which allow for large quantities of missing data.

For the identification of domestic interests, the attitudes of the voters, political parties, and their representatives in national parliaments should be considered. In particular, the Eurobarometer surveys contain valuable information on public opinion in all member states. Party preferences have been measured by means of Manifesto analysis and expert interviews (Benoit and Laver 2006; Hooghe et al. 2006; Klingemann et al. 2006).

In addition, how institutions shape the domestic preference formation process is examined in more detail. Fortunately, previous researchers have already gathered information on very specific provisions such as the involvement of the national parliament, the hurdles of the ratification process, and the intragovernmental coordination process (see Stoiber 2003; König and Hug 2006). Standard macro and socio-economic indicators are used to account for the relevant socio-economic and political information across member states.

Figure 1.2 illustrates the three methodological cornerstones of this book; namely, the 'reformability' of a treaty, the collective nature of governmental preferences, and changes in governmental positions over time. This illustration foreshadows some of the findings of the empirical analysis.[11] It displays only those six countries that demarcate the boundaries of the unanimity core at Rome II (Denmark, Slovakia, Ireland, Greece, France and Italy), even though the estimation takes into account the governmental positions of all member states. If a treaty is located within the unanimity core, it will be impossible to find a reform alternative that improves all member states; i.e. the status will remain in equilibrium.

The horizontal and vertical bars indicate the 95 per cent confidence intervals of the estimates for each governmental preference. These errors would be very small if a governmental leader consistently presented issue-specific positions on either of the two dimensions. For example, if Greece preferred more European integration on all of those issues than a prointegrationist country typically does, the standard errors would be very small. It can be seen that the size of these errors differs across countries. Denmark, for example, seems to fit very well into the model on both dimensions, whereas Italy reveals a considerably larger error on the horizontal dimension.

Figure 1.2 also indicates that the preference of the French government changed across three IGCs. Compared with Rome II, the French cohabitation government proposed a significantly stronger degree of European integration and about the same degree of institutional reforms at Nice. At Amsterdam, the French position on substantial integration is located between its positions at Nice and Rome II, but it proposed more drastic reforms of the decision rules. Similar changes in other countries can be found too. Such changes may alter the win set and the unanimity core. Only such a longitudinal analysis can provide insights into the push and pull factors of European treaty reforms.

---

11. Horizontal and vertical bars indicate 95 per cent confidence intervals. FR^{t-2} and FR^{t-1} depict the French position at the Amsterdam and Nice IGCs, respectively.

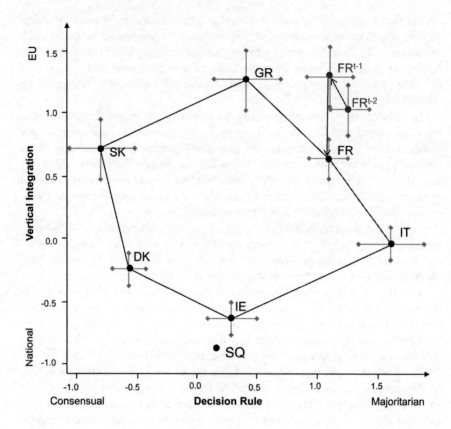

Figure 1.2: Schematic illustration of the Spatial approach: Positions in the intergovernmental conflict space representing heterogeneous domestic actors and change across time

chapter two | the conceptual framework

THE CALCULUS OF EUROPEAN TREATY REFORMS

This section briefly summarises why (and under which conditions) national governments may be willing to surrender national sovereignty to the EU. It lays the groundwork for all subsequent discussions. Buchanan and Tullock (1962), argue that constitutional rules can be evaluated with a simple cost-benefit calculation under uncertainty. On one hand, the transfer of competences produces benefits according to the economics of scale and scope (D). On the other hand, an additional transfer of competences may cause heterogeneity costs (C). Hence, actors' most preferred level of integration maximises the simple additive utility function D-C. Next, this section discusses how particular reforms may impact this cost-benefit calculation. It emphasises the difference between the choice of rules and the choice within rules. Understanding the latter is a precondition for any explanation of the former. Finally, it discusses the origins of, and the individual issues on, the post-Maastricht reform agenda.

EUROPE'S CONSTITUTIONAL QUANDARY

What are the essential functions of constitutions? What are the consequences of different institutional designs with respect to an actor's power in the policy-making process? In their classic analysis of *The Calculus of Consent,* Buchanan and Tullock (1962) identify two questions that any constitutional design has to answer.[1] First, 'when will it prove desirable to shift one or more sectors of human activity from the realm of private to that of social choice, or vice versa?' (1962: 7). Second, which 'decision-making rule' shall apply to each of the collectivised sectors of human activity? (1962: 48) Accordingly, constitutions assign decision-making competences to different levels of government and define the corresponding decision rules. With regard to the EU, the first question refers to the substantial division of competences between actors located at subnational, national and European levels. In contrast, the second question refers to the political system of the EU, and in particular, the distribution of power among the member states. Buchanan and Tullock (1962: 50) differentiate between three modi for dividing competences: private, collective and public. Private refers to the case in which the constitution assigns competences to the individual lower-level actor. In the EU, this would be

---

1. In connection with the Treaty Establishing a Constitution for Europe, several alternative definitions of the term 'constitution' have been mentioned. However, most definitions are normative. Many require that a constitution should realise at least three core principles: rights, the separation of powers and representative democracy (e.g. Wiener 2005; Day and Shaw 2003).

to individual member states. Collective decisions are based on ad hoc collaborations of different subsets of individual actors, as is the case for most multilateral agreements among nation-states. Public decisions are binding for all lower-level actors. Accordingly, public decisions imply the delegation of sovereignty from the member states to the supranational level, a step henceforth referred to as integration. It goes without saying that, compared with other international organisations, the EU has reached a unique level of public decision-making.

From the perspective of individual actors, each constitutional design implies different costs and benefits. In other words, an actor's constitutional preferences depend upon this cost-benefit calculation (Buchanan and Tullock 1962). On the one hand, the transfer of competences to the European level of government produces benefits according to the economics of scale and scope (D): integration causes the average unit costs of public goods to fall. The foundation of the European Armament Agency constitutes one example. Founded in 2004, its mission is to support and coordinate member states' research in, and buying of, arms. Another example would be the envisaged European consular corps. Its creation would avoid duplication, optimising the use of member states' consular services. Furthermore, the benefits of integration cover the internalisation of external costs created by individual action. The most prominent examples are negative external effects caused by environmental pollution, as discussed in Ostrom's (1990) classic *Governing the Commons*. An example from the field of foreign and security politics is the thwarting of individual (single-state) diplomatic missions. Such missions would likely fare better if the decisions over their direction and aim were taken jointly at the European level. Note that the economics of scale and scope, D, increases monotonically in the degree of vertical integration, but the marginal benefits of integration diminish because policy areas with higher benefits are integrated first, i.e. $D'(e) \geq 0$ and $D''(e) < 0$.

On the other hand, an additional transfer of competences may raise heterogeneity or decision-making costs (C). Heterogeneity costs are induced by conflicting policy interests and realised whenever actors are forced to make concessions because they were outvoted and must implement unfavourable legislation. These political costs of collective decision-making originate in member states' conflicting political interests, and they increase continuously with the degree of vertical integration. For example, unfavourable product standards may cause high adaptation costs for the affected branch of the national economy. Or even worse, a reform of the common agricultural policy may hurt the national agricultural sector. However, the marginal costs increase because actors prefer areas with low heterogeneity costs to be integrated first. Besides heterogeneity costs, C covers the transaction costs of collective decision-making. Hence, *ceteris paribus*, the decision-making costs C increase monotonically in the degree of integration with increasing marginal costs (Ostrom, 1990: 70), i.e. $C'(e) \geq 0$ and $C''(e) > 0$.

As a result, actor i's most preferred level of integration E_i^* maximises the simple additive utility function $D_i(e) - C_i(e)$ (see Figure 2.1). In other words, Figure 2.1 allows us to derive an actor i's optimal level of integration given a particular design of the decision rules k at the EU level. For the subsequent theoretical discussion, two standard assumptions are made.

the conceptual framework | 25

Assumption 1: For any decision rule k, an actor's utility function $U_i[D_i(e), C_i(e)]$ is single peaked. This important characteristic follows from the presumption that low-cost, high-benefit sectors are collectivised first.

Assumption 2: For any decision rule k, an actor's utility function $U_i[D_i(e), C_i(e)]$ is symmetric around the optimal level of integration E_i^*.[2]

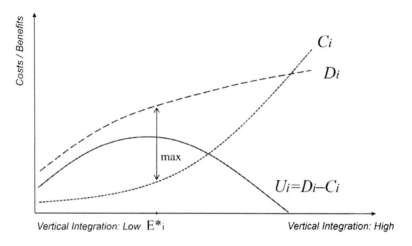

Figure 2.1: Development of heterogeneity cost (C_i) and economics of scale (D_i) subject to the level of vertical integration. The most preferred level of Integration E_i^* maximises the utility $U_i = C_i + D_i$

In the next step, let us assume that the level of integration is exogenously given and that the exclusive subject of constitutional choice is the decision rule k. For now, the only matter of relevance is the absolute power that actor i would exert under different decision rules, assuming that a given decision rule grants equal relative power to all actors. The horizontal axis in Figure 2.2 spans the range between two extremes; namely, actor i holds veto power or actor i's power is reduced to a minimum. With an exclusive focus on voting rules, the horizontal axis in Figure 2.2 spans the range between unanimity and simple majority. If all actors hold veto power, heterogeneity costs (C_i) are low, but so are the benefits of integration (D_i) because decision-making is inefficient and the danger of grid-lock is high.

When the overall voting thresholds are lowered, the characteristics of the cost-benefit function depend on actor i's evaluation of the present level of integration. In Figure 2.2, the concave slope of D_i outperforms the convex slope of C_i for decision rules close to unanimity. In this case, actor i places a higher value on increasing

---

2. On closer inspection of Figure 2.1, U_i will in many cases deviate from assumption 2. However, I argue that the minor deviations from this assumption are outweighed by the analytical advantage of a symmetric utility function.

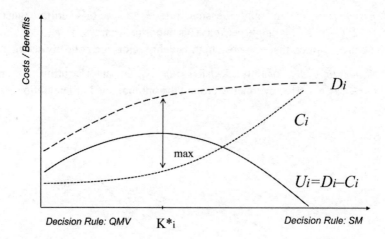

Figure 2.2: Development of heterogeneity cost (C_i) and economics of scale (D_i) subject to a change in decision rules from higher to lower voting thresholds. The most preferred level of Integration K_i^* maximises the utility $U_i = C_i + D_i$

decision-making efficiency than on the potential heterogeneity costs implied by unfavourable decisions. However, as we move along the horizontal axis toward simple majority decision-making, at some point, the slope of C_i equals the slope D_i, and the additive utility function reaches its maximum. This point K_i^* denotes the optimal choice of the decision rule that, in Figure 2.2, corresponds to a qualified majority voting rule located halfway between unanimity and simple majority voting. With respect to the post-Maastricht treaty revision, Figure 2.2 corresponds to the perspective of the German, French or Italian governments who, as will be shown in the empirical section, argued that voting thresholds should be lowered and that the realm of majority voting should be extended.

For other member states, such as Denmark or Ireland, the optimal decision rule K_i^* has been located further to the left. In other words, these member states preferred higher voting thresholds. In the most extreme case, the slope of D_i never outperforms the slope of C_i. In that case, the optimal decision rule K_i^* is unanimity, as any lower voting thresholds would touch upon vital national interests. However, with the conclusion of Maastricht, the EU treaty framework already provided for qualified majority voting for more than eighty articles.[3] The empirical analysis shows that member states rarely reclaimed their veto power in these areas.

Thus, Figure 2.2 allows us to derive an actor's optimal decision rule K_i^* given a particular level of integration (e). As for the choice regarding the division of competences, two standard assumptions are made.

---

3. "The Extension of Qualified Majority Voting from the Treaty of Rome to the European Constitution." House of Commons Research Paper 54(4), July 2004 . Online: www.parliament.uk/commons/lib/research/rp2004/rp04-054.pdf, (accessed 15 January 2009).

Assumption 3: For any level of integration e, an actor's utility function over the choice of decision rules $U_i[D_i(k), C_i(k)]$ is single peaked.

Assumption 4: For any level of integration e, an actor's utility function $U_i[D_i(k), C_i(k)]$ is symmetric around the optimal decision rule K_i^*.[4]

From assumptions 1 and 3, it follows that an actor's two-dimensional utility function $U_i[D_i(e,k), C_i(e,k)]$ is single peaked too. In other words, actor i's unique ideal position in the two-parameter space is given by $\{K_i^*; Ei^*\}$.

The next crucial question concerns the extent to which actors' preferences for the design of decision rules and the level of integration are separable. The separability assumption implies that actors' preferences for the level of integration are independent of the de facto design of decision rules at the EU level (Enelow and Hinich 1984); or, vice versa, their preferences for the design of EU decision rules are independent of the competences delegated to the EU. However, with regard to constitutional politics in the EU, this assumption of separable or unconditional preferences appears to be unrealistic. For example, France might prefer deeper cooperation in justice and security politics *only if* decision making in this area would become more efficient by extending majority voting and lowering the voting thresholds. Ireland, on the other hand, might prefer deeper cooperation in the same area *only if* it retained its veto right. One important consequence of this bidirectional conditionality is that it may alter the size of the win set for potential reforms. Another, more general consequence of nonseparable preferences is that the sequence of decisions matters (Enelow and Hinich 1984; Lacy 2001). In Chapter 6, how governments adjusted their preferences on one issue dimension in response to the outcome on another dimension is illustrated. As a consequence, conditional preferences grant additional powers to the agenda setter.

Generally speaking, actors' preferences for integration are nonseparable if the slope of either $D_i(e)$ or $C_i(e)$ is a function of the effective decision rule K. Overall, potential integration gains are realised faster and more completely if the decision rules are efficient; i.e. voting hurdles are generally lower. At the same time, lower voting thresholds might increase actors' expected heterogeneity costs. Hence, every constitution has to solve the trade-off between maximising decision-making efficiency and minimising the potential heterogeneity costs for individual actors (Buchanan and Tullock 1962: 97). Figure 2.3 illustrates the effect of lowering the decision hurdles from QMV to SM on $U_i(e)$. For now, it is assumed that actors hold *separable preferences* across both dimensions of constitutional reform. In this case, the decision rule does not alter the slope of either $D_i(e)$ or $C_i(e)$. Instead, the effect of the change in decision rule is restricted to the intercept. In the current example lower decision hurdles facilitate the realisation of integration benefits, D_i, and raise the potential decision making costs, C_i. However, in Figure 2.3 this reform does not alter an actor's ideal position on the level of integration

---

4. On closer inspection of Figure 2.2, U_1 will in many cases deviate from Assumption 4. However, I argue that the minor deviations from this assumption are outweighed by the analytical advantage of a symmetric utility function.

($E_i^* \mid qmv = E_i^* \mid sm$). In the same way, an actor's most preferred decision rule (under the assumption of separable preferences) does not depend on shifts in the level integration.

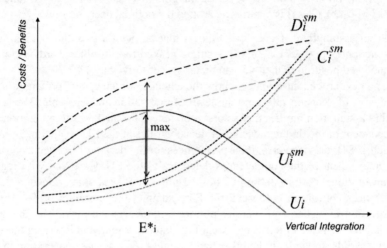

Figure 2.3: Effect of different decision rules in case of <u>separable preferences</u>. The upward move of C_i^{sm} and D_i^{sm} indicates a shift to a lower decision threshold (e.g. simple majority) as compared to Figure 2.1. The ideal level of Integration E_i^* does not dependent on the decision rule and vice versa ($E_i^* \mid qmv = E_i^* \mid sm$)

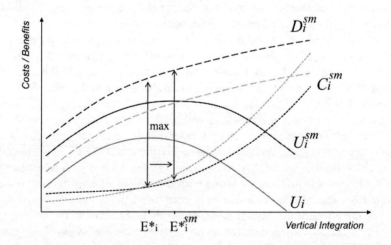

Figure 2.4: Effect of different decision rules in case of <u>non-separable preferences</u>. The upward move of C_i^{sm} and D_i^{sm} indicates a shift to a lower decision threshold (e.g. simple majority) as compared to Figure 2.1. The ideal level of Integration E_i^* depends on the decision rule and vice versa ($E_i^* \mid qmv \neq E_i^* \mid sm$)

By contrast, Figure 2.4 illustrates the effect of the decision rule under the assumption of *nonseparable preferences*. In this case, lowering the decision rule from QMV to SM alters the slope of the utility curve $U_i(e)$ and its intercept. As a consequence, a reform of the decision rule would alter actor i's preferred level of integration ($E_i^* \mid qmv = E_i^* \mid sm$). This (by no means unrealistic) assumption could have consequences for the collective reform. For example, the UK might be willing to delegate competences for regulating the armament industry only if it retained veto power on these matters. On the other hand, France might be unwilling to collectivise this sector of its industry unless regulations were decided under a flexible and efficient rule. Without other bargaining chips, this example leaves little room for reform.

The above model of constitutional preferences is rather simple. However, it is a very helpful starting point for an analytical inquiry into the puzzle of European treaty revisions since Maastricht. The next sections will put flesh on this analytical skeleton by discussing how the issues on the post-Maastricht reform agenda affect governments' evaluation of the heterogeneity costs C and their expected benefits D, beginning with a review of the institutional reform issues. The integration of specific policy areas following the insights provided by economic theories of federalism is then discussed. Later in the chapter there is an exploration of the extent to which an aggregation across individual issues and policy areas is admissible, followed by a discussion of the domestic origins of governmental positions. Finally, potential explanations for collective reform agreements, especially with respect to the set of relevant actors and the relevance of procedural constraints is sought.

WHY EFFICIENCY IS DIFFICULT TO ATTAIN

To understand the effect of different institutional rules on actors' perceived costs and benefits, it is important to realise the difference between the choice within rules and the choice of rules. A successful explanation of constitutional choice must consider its effects on the process and outcomes of EU policy making as expected by the actors (Diermeier and Krehbiel 2003). Given the theoretical model discussed above, we are interested in those characteristics of institutions that impact either the efficiency of EU decision-making procedures or heterogeneity costs. The latter refers to those institutions that alter an individual member state's ability to impact European policies. Fortunately, political scientists have come a long way in understanding the institutions that characterise the EU's political system (for an overview, see Hix 2005). Decision-making institutions determine actors' powers in the political process and, accordingly, their impact on political decisions. The most prominent means of impact are informational, budgetary, voting and agenda-setting power (Bailer 2006: 43). More generally speaking, constitutions allocate a) decision, and b) control rights. The former refers to the power that an actor holds to impact political decisions directly. These rules affect the horizontal distribution of power. The latter refers to the means that principals have to control their agent's decisions; for example, member states' ability to control the Commission. Subsequently, a brief overview, pertaining to the most important institutional issues on the post-Maastricht reform agenda, will be given. The discussion will begin with institutions that determine the allocation of decision rights across member states, many of which relate to the goal of efficiency, and will continue with institutions of relevance for vertical integration; i.e. the allocation of control rights and its common ground with democratic legitimacy.

Table 2.1 summarises the key issues of the agenda. It is primarily based on the questionnaires of the survey data used for the empirical analysis (see Chapter 3) and the official documents issued by governmental delegations (see Chapter 4). Table 2.1 is arranged according to the three goals that guided the post-Maastricht reform agenda: political integration, efficiency and legitimacy. However, as the subsequent discussion will clarify, those issues intended to boost legitimacy and those associated with political integration overlap significantly.

The most prominently discussed institutional reforms refer to the design of the voting rules, the extension of majority voting into additional policy areas, and a reform of the Council of Ministers' internal structures and procedures. In particular, the last set of issues refers to the number of separate Councils and a clearer separation of their legislative and executive functions. Table 2.1 finds all of the issues on the Amsterdam, Nice and Rome II agendas, with the exception of internal reforms, which were temporarily omitted from the Nice agenda. As for the extension of QMV, the wish list of potential policy areas has significantly increased since Amsterdam.

Why do member states pool their sovereignty by subjecting political decisions to majority voting in the Council of Ministers? According to Moravcsik (1998: 73), member states chose to delegate powers to supranational actors and introduced majority voting in the Council to overcome a credible commitment problem. Member states might agree to delegate certain policy areas to the EU. The problem is that, for many policy areas, there would be limited hope that they would ever translate international treaties into secondary legislation. Instead, many decisions might violate the vital interests of one or another preference outlier, who might then veto European law proposals. To counteract this enforcement problem, member states pool their sovereignty over secondary legislation by means of majority voting.

This rule raises the decision probability in the Council of Ministers and solves the credible commitment problem between the 'founding fathers' and ministerial interests. This problem matches exactly the trade-off between heterogeneity costs (C) and the benefits of integration (D) discussed by Buchanan and Tullock (1962). Using a similar logic, several researchers have explained the introduction and expansion of qualified majority voting by citing the implied reduction in transaction costs (Schulz and König 2000; Golub 1999; 2008; König 2008). This effect should worsen with enlargement, which increases the likelihood that a single country will stall the decision-making process unless its vital interests are accommodated.

There are few empirical approaches that explicitly model the relationship between conflicting policy preferences and the expected policy outcomes implied by different decision-making rules. So far, the project 'Decision Making in the European Union' (DEU) constitutes the most comprehensive study to distinguish the effects of preferences on the one hand from the effects of decision-making rules on the other (Thomson *et al.* 2006). The DEU data set includes detailed information on sixty-six legislative proposals by the Commission. To be considered for inclusion, a legislative project needed to raise at least a minimum level of

Table 2.1: A comparison of the most important reform issues on the agenda of the Amsterdam, Nice and Constitutional IGC

	Reform Agenda: Democratic Legitimacy		
	Amsterdam	Nice	Constitutional IGC
EP (power in legislation)	Ext. of co-decision: 1.) to all areas under QMV; 2.) to specific areas: AFSJ; environment, anti-corruption); ext. of assent procedure to international treaties & treaty revision; intro. right of initiative for EP; EP's role in comitology; EP's right to summon and inquire the Commission (hearing).	Right of initiative; co-decision as 1.) general rule; 2.) co-decision if QMV; 3.) case wise: environment; health; immigration; employment; agriculture; CFSP; asylum; anti-drug; anti-corruption; workers' rights; basic rules for media & press; research; education; regional; currency; taxation; currency; development aid.	Right of initiative; co-decision as 1.) general rule; 2.) if QMV; 3.) case wise: agriculture; region; ASFJ; internal market; taxation; currency; economy; employment; social; social security; CFSP; EP approval for enhanced cooperation.
EP (power in budgeting)	Ext. of assent procedure to own resources; ext. of co-decision procedure to budgeting.		Rights in annual budget and multi-annual framework.
EP (power to nominate & control)	Stronger role in ECJ nominations; nomination of Commissioners.	Nomination and control of Commissioners; vote of confidence for Commission president.	Election of the president of the European Council; election of Commission president; nomination and control of Commissioners; appointment of EU Foreign Minister.
EP (transparency)	Uniform election procedure; simplification of co-decision; control administrative implementation of EU legislation.	Rules for the organisation of supranational parties.	Uniform election procedure (all over Europe).

	Reform Agenda: Democratic Legitimacy		
	Amsterdam	Nice	Constitutional IGC
Direct Democracy			Direct election of the president of the European Council; popular initiative; election of Commission president; right of initiative.
National Parliaments (information)	Ext. of COSAC to AFSJ; control of subsidiarity via COSAC; restrict 'general authorisation' of the Council; automatically gets all consultation documents; minimum number of days Nat. Parl. can deal with draft legislation; right to summon and inquire the Commission.		Early warning system (watchdog).
National Parliaments (intervention)	2nd EP chamber for national MPs.		Right to veto Commission proposal if violation of subsidiarity; right of initiative; election of the president of the European Council; election of Commission president; 2nd EP chamber (involvement if EP not involved).
Council (transparency)	Access & publication of documents; public meetings.	Public meetings.	Public meetings.
Commission (election of president)	Council and/ or EP.	Council and/ or EP.	Council / EP / national parliament / citizens.
Commission (nomination of commissioner)	Council and/or EP and/or Commission president.	Council and/or EP and/or Commission president.	Council and/or EP and/or Commission president.
European Council (presidency)	Elected president(cy).		Elected president(cy).

	Reform Agenda: Democratic Legitimacy		
	Amsterdam	Nice	Constitutional IGC
ECJ (empowerment)	Intro. of 2nd chamber; term of office; ext. powers with respect to ASFJ, CFSP and Schengen; relationship to Council (responsibility of MS, control by Council); intro. of internal appeals.	Internal reform: number of judges.	Scope of jurisdiction (see Amsterdam plus fundamental rights).
ECA (empowerment)	Number of members; ext. powers with regard to anti-corruption, CFSP and ASFJ; national administration shall be obliged to collaborate.	Internal reform: number of members.	
Committee of Regions (empowerment)	Financial and administrative independence; ext. powers for policy areas in his "sphere"; access to ECJ.	Internal reform: number of members.	
Social & Economic Council (empowerment)	Extension of obligatory consultation; access to ECJ.	Internal reform: number of members.	
Citizenship (individual legal rights)	Charter of Fundamental Rights & additional chapter of Fundamental and Human Rights in TEU; ext. of social & economic rights; status of EU citizenship in addition to national.	Charter of Fundamental Rights.	Charter of Fundamental Rights.
Citizenship (individual political rights)	Direct access to ECJ; possible sanctions against MS violating fundamental rights; access to all official documents from Council, EP & Commission; active & passive suffrage at regional level.	Worker's rights *vis-a-vis* their employers.	Worker's rights *vis-a-vis* their employers.

	Reform Agenda: Democratic Legitimacy		
	Amsterdam	Nice	Constitutional IGC
Objectives & Principles	High level of employment; protection of the environment; transparency; subsidiarity.	Transparency; limit to geographical ext.	References to religion and/ or philosophical tradition in preamble; free single market vs. social market; high level or full employment; competitiveness; subsidiarity.
Legal Simplifications	Reorganisation of treaty structure; catalogue of competences; fusion of exiting legal texts.	Reorganisation of treaty structure; catalogue of competences; fusion of exiting legal texts.	Reorganisation of treaty structure; catalogue of competences; fusion of existing legal texts.

	Reform Agenda: Political Integration		
	Amsterdam	Nice	Constitutional IGC
CFSP	Voluntary peace corps; fight against terrorism; intro. right of initiative for Commission; trade policy; international legal personality of EU; embassies & diplomatic service outside the EU; passage on mutual solidarity; High Representative; incorporation of WEU.	Extended cooperation in defence, development aid; embassies & diplomatic service outside the EU; coordination of foreign policy.	Foreign Minister (accountable to Council and/ or Commission); extended coordination of foreign policy; extended coordination of defence policy (progressive framing; common armament; mutual commitments; European army).
AFSJ	Cooperation on different issues (see Läufer 1998: 11ff.); ext. of Passarelle; fight against drugs, corruption; ext. of Europol; incorporating Schengen.	European Public Prosecutor; basic rules for media & press; fight against drugs.	European Public Prosecutor; general extension of competences; data protection electronic; judicial cooperation (civil and criminal law).
Visa, Asylum and Immigration	Cooperation in all three areas; cooperation in external border control.	Extended cooperation in all three areas.	Management system for external borders (integrated system, common guard-corps); cooperation and harmonisation in all three areas.

Reform Agenda: Political Integration

	Amsterdam	Nice	Constitutional IGC
Employment	Intro. of the social protocol & new title on employment into TEU; resolution of Cannes, Essen & Madrid; employment committee; Commission shall elaborate package of measures.	Extended cooperation.	General extension of competences.
Environment	Maintenance of superior national standards; limited ext. (importance of sustainability, animal rights, environmental impact assessment).	Extension similar to Amsterdam.	General extension of competences.
EMU	Introducing enhanced fiscal coordination.	Introducing enhanced fiscal coordination.	More flexible stability and growth pact; intro. of debt/ GDP ratio as criterion into the pact.
Enhanced Cooperation (areas/ general approach)	Possibility to opt out; cooperation outside the EU's institutional framework; enhanced cooperation (within EU's institutional framework) for: pillars 1 and/or 2 and/or 3.	Scope (incl. CFSP/ defence).	Scope (incl. CFSP/ defence).
Enhanced Cooperation (realisation)	Realisation via Commission initiative; consent or QMV; role of Council and EP in budgeting; right to vote for participating MS only.	Intro. of specific enabling clauses to unease enhanced cooperation; no. of MS necessary to start procedure; no veto right (except for CFSP).	No. of MS necessary to start procedure; approval by EP.
Regional policy		Reform of criteria (adaptation to enlargement).	Reform.
Agriculture and Fishing		Reform (adaptation to enlargement).	Reform.
Additional areas	Energy, tourism, taxation, consumer protection.	Health; social welfare; education & research; taxation; culture.	Taxation; social welfare; health; education; research.

Reform Agenda: Rules of Decision Making

	Amsterdam	Nice	Constitutional IGC
Council (internal organisation)	Reorganisation to initiate legislation regarding AFSJ.		Simplification of internal procedures (number of Councils, separation of executive & legislative functions).
Council (ext. of QMV)	Employment; ASFJ; environment; CFSP to all legislation under co-decision; reservation of unanimity in sensitive areas.	QMV as general rule or case wise application: environment; currency; develop. aid; health; immigration; employment; agriculture; CFSP; anti-drug; anti-corruption; workers' rights; rules for media & press; research; education; regional; currency; taxation; asylum.	QMV as general rule of case wise: agriculture; region; ASFJ; internal market; taxation; currency; economy; employment; social; social security; CFSP.
Council (criteria for QMV)	Threshold; double majority; voting weights.	Threshold; double majority; voting weights.	Threshold; double majority; voting weights.
EP	Limitation to three procedures; max. of 700 seats; simplification of co-decision procedure; deadline in consultation procedure.	Maximum number of seats.	Maximum number of seats.
European Council (presidency)	Rotation or election; duration of presidency.		Rotation or election; duration of presidency.
Commission	Number of Commissioners; role of Commission president in selection of Commissioners; right of initiative in CFSP.	Number of Commissioners; internal organisation (hierarchy & budget).	Number of Commissioners; internal organisation (hierarchy & budget).
Budgetary procedures	Simplification		Extended rights for EP.
ECA (organisation)	Internal reform: number of members.	Internal reform: number of members.	Internal reform: larger governing committee, but small executive board.

Reform Agenda: Rules of Decision Making

	Amsterdam	Nice	Constitutional IGC
ECJ (organisation)	Internal reform: number of judges.	Internal reform in light of enlargement.	
EP	Allocation of seats.	Allocation of seats.	Allocation of seats.
Council	Relative voting power under QMV (weights, threshold, criteria); maintenance of veto.	Relative voting power under QMV (weights, threshold, criteria); maintenance of veto.	Relative voting power under QMV (weights, threshold, criteria); maintenance of veto.
Commission	Composition and allocation of budgets; possible system of rotation.	Composition and allocation of budgets; possible system of rotation.	Composition and allocation of budgets; possible system of rotation.
ECJ	Allocation of judges.	Allocation of judges.	Allocation of judges.
Economic and Social Council / Committee of Regions		Representation in ESC & Ctte.Reg.	
European Council	Organisation of council presidency (system of rotation).	Organisation of council presidency (system of rotation).	Organisation of council presidency (system of rotation).

Sources: Amsterdam: Hug and König (2002) prepared the 'Report of the EP Task Force'. The original report is downloadable at: www.europarl.eu.int; Doc. No. JF/bo/ 290/97, last accessed 27 May1997; Thurner *et al.* (2002); Laursen (2002); Weidenfeld (1998) (provides archive with official documents); Kölliker and Milner (2000); Mahncke (1997); Moravcsik and Nicolaidis (1999); Monar and Wessels (2001).

Nice: König and Luetgert (2003); Weidenfeld (2001) (provides archive with official documents); Bond and Feus (2001); Heinemann (2003); Yataganas (2001).

Constitutional IGC: König and Hug (2006) (incl. DOSEI data and on line archive with official documents); 'Analysis of EP Task Force (AFCO)', downloadable: www.europarl.eu.int; DV\512456EN.doc, last accessed 6 November 2003.

controversy, effectively eliminating very technical issues that were of only minor political importance. The selected legislative proposals were subject to either the consultation or the codecision procedure. Both procedures can require unanimity or qualified majority as voting threshold in the Council of Ministers. Among the many results of this ambitious project, three stand out. First, procedures matter. Those models that took into account the involvement of the EP and the voting rule had a higher explanatory power. Second, at the level of individual proposals, member states rarely use their veto power, even if the new law would leave them worse off. However, veto power becomes important and visible when considering member states' negotiation success over a set of legal proposals within a single policy area (König and Junge 2008). Finally, alternative means of bargaining power, such as information, bargaining skills or the power of the purse, matter (Bailer 2005; Schneider *et al.* 2009). Overall, the results of the DEU project justify a careful design of decision rules, though at the same time, they remind us that other factors determine EU policy making too.

König and Bräuninger (2000, 2004) took a different approach when comparing decision rules defined in the ToN with those proposed by the European Convention. Using sector-specific economic data,[5] they located the member states in an issue-specific policy space for employment and agricultural policies. Their results illustrate how the shape of the QMV core[6] after enlargement has depended upon the applicable voting rules. Dobbins *et al.* (2004) used a similar approach and applied it to a larger number of policy fields. Their data were based on expert surveys, but their findings were broadly identical.

Other scholars argue that governments hold limited foresight with regard to the future distribution of preferences in the Council of Ministers. In other words, they face the veil of constitutional ignorance. Therefore, it is sufficient to analyse member states' voting power. According to Shapley and Shubik (1954), voting power is defined by the percentage of minimal winning coalitions in which a player is pivotal; i.e. he can turn a losing into a winning coalition. A second concept identifies the so-called passage probability of a decision rule. This is the number of winning coalitions in relation to the total number of possible coalitions (Coleman 1971). In short, these studies illustrate how a shift from unanimity to different types of QMV enhances the passage probability and redistributes member states' relative veto power (e.g. König and Bräuninger 2000). The opposite effect emerges from enlargement (e.g. Steunenberg 2001; Widgren and Baldwin 2003).

The *European Parliament* (EP) is the only directly elected decision-making body of the EU. Therefore, it comes as little surprise that its overall strength relative to the Council or the Commission is related to political integration. However, some aspects of reforming the EP and its role in the EU's decision-making proce-

---

5. For agricultural policy, they refer to the agricultural sector's percentage of total gross value-added product and the general gross domestic product per capita. For employment policy, they replace the first indicator with the unemployment rate (König and Bräuninger 2001: 52)

6. The QMV core defines the set of alternatives that cannot be changed by a winning coalition without leaving at least one member of the coalition worse off.

dures affect the goal of decision-making efficiency and the horizontal distribution of power. The underlying reason is that Members of the EP (MEPs) are considered to be agents of two principals (Hix 2002). On the one hand, they are responsible toward their domestic electorate, especially if they intend to stand for reelection. In this respect, they will frequently defend regional or, depending on the electoral system, national interests. On the other hand, they are organised in European party groups that manage legislative behaviour via the standard tools of party discipline (e.g. roll call votes, whips, administrative and financial incentives). The seven European party groups can be separated along two predominant conflict dimensions, the 'left-right' and 'integration-independence' dimensions (Hix *et al.* 2007). For this reason the EP must be considered a potential veto player in its own right.

Table 2.1 reveals that all three IGCs debated the distribution and maximum number of seats in the EP. Furthermore, governments discussed several procedural reforms intended to reduce transaction costs, which had been increased by extending the EP's powers to a broad number of additional policy areas at Maastricht. In particular, this concerns the reform of the newly introduced codecision procedure at Amsterdam[7] as well as an overall streamlining of the legislative process by means of mandatory deadlines.

A growing number of scholars are convinced that the empowerment of the EP resulted in substantially different policies, a finding which explains the conflict over any reallocation of seat shares among member states (König 2008; Bräuninger *et al.* 2001; Crombez 1996; Moser 1996; Scully 1997). With regard to transaction costs, the empowerment of the EP prolonged EU decision-making, especially with the introduction of the EP as coequal legislators under the codecision procedure (Schulz and König 2000; Golub 1999, 2008). For the same reasons, its involvement in the EU's budgeting process was under scrutiny at Amsterdam and Rome II. Furthermore, the plurality of decision-making procedures led to confusion and a lack of transparency among the general public and politicians alike. In its 2001 white paper on 'European Governance',[8] the Commission itself highlights this problem, demanding the simplification of intra- and inter-institutional decision-making procedures.

The second supranational player is the *European Commission*. As with the EP, many discussions during the post-Maastricht period regarding reform of the Commission pertain to issues of vertical integration. Nevertheless, Table 2.1 reveals that some of the more concrete reform issues related to the Commission have direct implications for decision-making efficiency and the horizontal distribution of power. There has been general agreement among scholars and practitioners that a college of twenty-seven equal Commissioners is not the most efficient, let alone the most transparent, organisation. However, any potential limitation to the number of Commissioners raised the question of whether large member states,

---

7. At Amsterdam, governments abolished the third reading of the codecision procedure (Crombez 2000).
8. Available online: http://eur-lex.europa.eu/LexUriServ/site/en/com/2001/com2001_0428en01.pdf, (accessed 7 June 2006).

which each had two Commissioners, should be granted compensatory privileges. Hence, the issue of size was, almost automatically, accompanied by a distributive issue. One possible suggestion was a rotation system, with or without privileged access for large member states. An alternative proposal created so-called junior Commissioners to avoid the temporary absence of nationalities from the powerful college. These proposals, of course, caused heated debates among the Directorate Generals (DGs) about the internal hierarchy and the allocation of the budget. Furthermore, a question emerged regarding how the Commission President should be elected, and whether or not he/she should exercise his/her powers in selecting individual Commissioners.

In integration theory, the Commission fulfills three functions that, again, are comparable to those found in the theory of constitutional choice discussed earlier (Pollack 2003: 21). It sets the political agenda, thereby solving the credible commitment problems among member states, and it fills in incomplete contracts by drawing on expert information. The Commission monitors the principals' compliance to agreements. This holds for primary as well as for secondary European law. With respect to primary law, the delegation of national sovereignty to supranational institutions has a similar effect as the pooling of sovereignty by means of majority voting (Moravcsik 1998). Both actions are intended to overcome credible commitment problems among member states. In other words, the Commission ensures that the necessary European laws are crafted and the benefits of integration are realised (Franchino 2005). However, even though laws encouraging commitment are written, they still need to be enforced (Börzel 2001). The enforcement problem is typical of international organisations, which rarely build up their own executive administrations (Koremenos *et al.* 2001: 763). With respect to secondary legislation, the Commission monitors member states' compliance to EU law; i.e. its translation into national legal instruments. If the Commission faces repeated noncompliance, it can ultimately transfer the case to the ECJ (Luetgert and Dannwolf 2009).

Furthermore, in most policy areas, the Commission holds the sole right of initiative. Therefore, the Commission enjoys tremendous agenda-setting power whenever member states want to change the status quo but are in dispute over the concrete shape and direction of reform.[9] These theoretical arguments are broadly consistent with the empirical analysis of decision-making in the EU (e.g. Thomson *et al.* 2006; Garrett and Tsebelis 1996; Pollack 2003).

Given its role in the legislation and implementation stages, it comes as little surprise that the distribution of power within the Commission is hotly contested among national governments. Accelerated by enlargement, the issues of total size, allocation and internal organisation emerged in all of the European suprana-

---

9. Within the spatial analysis of politics, the power of an agenda setter increases with the size of the win-set relative to the status quo, the latter being defined as the set of possible outcomes that would improve at least a minimum winning coalition of member states. However, with respect to the codecision procedure, the question of whether the EP or the Commission enjoys agenda-setting powers has been hotly debated (e.g. Crombez 1996, Moser 1996, Scully 1997).

tional bodies, such as the EP, the Commission, the ECJ, the ECA, the ESC and the Committee of Regions. As Table 2.1 shows, this was true of the three IGCs under study, with only minor differences (of note among these minor differences was the failure to discuss the rearrangement of representation in the ESC and the Committee of Regions at Amsterdam and the Constitutional IGC). Among these decision-making bodies, the ECJ stands out as the sole representative of the EU's judiciary. However, although the origins and scope of its powers remain the object of intense scholarly debate (e.g. Garrett *et al.* 1998; Alter 1998; Carruba *et al.* 2008), it has been subject to the same issues of horizontal power distribution; namely, the allocation of judges and the internal hierarchy.

Finally, the reform of the *Council presidency* has been another, very prominently discussed issue. For example, Tony Blair has been an outspoken critic of the principle of rotating the presidency in the council:

> The six-monthly rotating presidency was devised for a common market of six: It is neither efficient nor representative for a Union of 25 or more. How can the Council with constantly shifting leadership be a good partner for the European Commission and Parliament? How can Europe be taken seriously at international summits if the Chair of the Council is here today and gone tomorrow? The old system has reached its limits. It creates for Europe a weakness of continuity in leadership. (Devuyst 2002: 4)

It is obvious that publicly-stated arguments like this must be taken with a grain of salt. However, empirical research proves that the Council President enjoys significant discretion in steering the legislative activities of the Union (Warntjen 2007). Hence, it constitutes a perfect example of the tensions between efficiency concerns and power politics.

In sum, the empirical literature on the EU's political system allows us to evaluate reform proposals with regard to their potential effects on decision-making efficiency and the distribution of powers among member states with obvious implications for their expected heterogeneity costs. This makes it possible to assign individual issues to the two dimensions of the theoretical model described earlier. From a normative perspective, the decision-making procedures of the EU have been criticised as inefficient. Unfortunately, many reforms that increase decision-making efficiency raise issues of redistributing powers. Accordingly, a positive-sum reform goal such as efficiency is transformed into a zero-sum conflict over power. Even worse, there is little normative guidance to resolve this issue. In other words, there is no unique answer to the quest for a just distribution of power across member states. Should the power distribution reflect the population size or even economic power? Or should each member state be treated alike; i.e. one state, one vote?[10]

---

10. For example, the current system of weighted votes combined with a threefold threshold constitutes a somewhat arbitrary compromise between the two extremes. A mathematically more transparent voting scheme has been suggested. Known as the Penrose method, it would allocate seats or votes in legislatures based on the square root of the population size.

LEGITIMACY AND POLITICAL INTEGRATION

In this section, all institutional reform issues of relevance to the discussion surrounding Europe's putative democratic deficit will be examined. Normative political theory demands 'no integration without representation' (Rittberger 2006: 1211). The reproaches against the existing system are twofold (for an overview, see Follesdal and Hix 2006). First, it has been said that the EU suffers from insufficient democratic representation meaning that European institutions cannot be held accountable for their politics (e.g. Lodge 1994; Crombez 2003), and European and national parliamentarian control cannot outweigh the increasing shift of legislative powers toward the executive (Raunio 1999).

The second point of criticism refers to deficient process legitimacy. The lack of accountability leads to unresponsiveness among European voters. At the same time, a strict politicisation of the European public is assumed to be a necessary precondition of a functioning democracy. No truly European elections exist because elections for the EP are dominated by national issues (Hix 1999; Franklin and van der Eijk 1995). The root of this procedural illegitimacy has been identified as a lack of transparency in the Commission's politics and secret decisions in the Council (Magnette 2001; Wallace and Smith 1995).

However, not all scholars agree with these accusations. Moravcsik (2002, 2004) argues that the Council of Ministers is controlled via national elections, and the EP could be controlled via European elections. Furthermore, Majone (2002) argues that the EU primarily deals with regulatory and Pareto-improving policies, which do not require the same democratic representation and accountability as redistributive policies.

Assuming that these criticisms are nevertheless warranted, which reform issues should have been placed on the agenda? All those issues that enhance voters' control of, and participation in, EU decision-making (Follesdal and Hix 2006: 551). This contains elements of both direct and representative democracy. Being concrete, the latter would suggest the empowerment of the EP (with respect to legislation, budgeting and nomination), a stronger role for national parliaments (with respect to information and intervention powers in the legislative process), more transparency in the EU decision-making procedures, and a reform of the Commission to make it a democratically elected and accountable executive. Furthermore, the enormously complex system of European treaties should be simplified, and citizens should be aware of the Union's political objectives. In addition, strong and independent courts, such as the ECJ and the ECA, should be empowered to protect the rights of the voters and other domestic actors. Moreover, the Committee of Regions and the ESC should be empowered as the direct representatives of domestic interests at the EU level. Finally, it has been argued that the EU's post-Maastricht constitution should strengthen individual legal and political rights, which are considered an indispensable building block of democratic constitutions (e.g. Wiener 2007; Day and Shaw 2003), and thus a personalisation of EU politics might help to strengthen the accountability and transparency of the Union.

Table 2.1 reveals that many of these reform issues were indeed on the agenda of all three post-Maastricht IGCs. Exceptions are the elements of direct democracy (e.g. popular initiative, a directly elected President of the Council or the European Commission), which were not on the agenda before Rome II. Furthermore, the Nice agenda lacked the issues on the empowerment of national parliaments, the empowerment of the EP in the budgeting procedure and the possible introduction of an elected President of the European Council. Rome II also excluded reforms of the ECA, the ESC and the Committee of Regions. With respect to personalisation, governments discussed having a stronger Council President who would be elected by the EP and serve a longer term. Other proposals along these lines included an upgrade of the Commission President and the introduction of a European Minister of Foreign Affairs.

Given that all of these issues are considered suitable means to enhance the Union's democratic legitimacy, questions arise regarding how they are related to the constitutional theory described earlier. It can be argued that these issues do nothing more than complement the vertical division of competences. Accordingly, they can be assigned to the integration dimension. To illustrate this, the general logic of principal agent theory is applied.

Following Buchanan and Tullock (1962), actors weigh the benefits of integration (determined by economics of scope and scale) against the potential costs (implied by either transactions or unfavourable policies) when expressing preferences for a constitution.[11] However, to maximise possible gains, the constitutional design must ensure efficient decision-making and effective enforcement. In contrast to the voluntary commitments presumed by collective decisions, public decisions must provide institutions to overcome the credible commitment problem (1962: 51). Otherwise, the choice for Europe may be reduced to mere lip service, because international treaties in general, and European treaties in particular, are rarely self-enforcing. In the realm of international relations, this problem is sometimes solved by a transfer of sovereignty from the nation-state to a supranational institution, the 'guardian of the treaties'. However, such institutions, which are designed to ensure commitment among participants, must be controlled as well. Otherwise, they exploit their position to line their own pockets (Epstein and O'Halloran 1999). As a consequence, the benefits of integration remain unrealised, and the likelihood for unfavourable decisions increases.

One approach that takes the conflict inherent in delegation seriously can be found in the principal-agent literature. The primary reason for delegation is to realise efficiency gains by reducing transaction costs, ensuring the credible commitment[12] of third parties and increasing expertise available for policy making.

---

11. In their general analysis of the delegation problem, Epstein and O'Halloran (1999) highlight the trade-off between transaction costs implied by the central provision of public goods versus the control costs implied by delegation. Hence, the delegation problem is about 'choosing the lesser of two evils' (1999: 28).

12. This refers to the collective action problem in the provision of public goods, also termed the pooled resource allocation problem (Dixit 1996: 65). To overcome this problem and ensure compliance with collective agreements, 'political sovereigns are willing to delegate important power to independent experts in order to increase the credibility of their policy commitments' (Majone 1997: 139–40).

However, diverging interests between agent and principal creates the danger of agency loss (e.g. Fiorina 1977; Kiewit and McCubbins 1991; Cox and McCubbins 1993; McNollgast 1987; Epstein and O'Halloran 1999).[13] In the case of suboptimal outcomes, agents will mix two strategies: 1) obscure the outcome and 2) shift the blame to other actors. Against this background, the principal's response necessarily depends on beliefs rather than perfect information.[14] Obviously, both strategies lower accountability and transparency, two critical aspects of democratic legitimacy.

Matters get worse with respect to international agencies that must be considered delegates of a second or even third order.[15] The following factors are frequently held responsible for the severe information asymmetry between domestic principals and international organisations such as the EU: a) higher transaction costs (e.g. language, distance); b) reduced ability to compare the 'performance of different political agents (yardstick competition)' and c) negotiations behind closed doors, which make it impossible for the principals to hold individual agents accountable for the policy outcome (Vaubel 2006: 128).

The current decision-making modus in the EU is predominantly intergovernmental. Hence, governments are able to exploit their informational advantages over domestic actors. Even worse, governments themselves must control the supranational institutions they installed to overcome their credible commitment problem. Consequently, the issue of democratic legitimacy collapses to a large extent to the issues discussed in the principal-agent literature. Relevant aforementioned institutional reforms deal with the vertical allocation of decision and control rights; i.e. vertical integration. However, a second screw exists to decrease democratic deficit: the limitation of EU policy competences (Majone 2006: 618). An evaluation of this approach must analyse the benefits of European integration for different policy sectors.

A CROSS-SECTIONAL PERSPECTIVE

This section is devoted to the split of decision-making competences between national and European levels. Economic theories of federalism seek the optimal division of policy competences between different levels of government (Mundell 1961; Kenan 1969; Oates 1972). They highlight the general trade-off between efficiency gains via 'economics of scale and the internalization of externalities' on

---

13. Formal works on delegation have a predominantly US focus (Epstein and O'Halloran, 1994, 1999; Krehbiel 1991), so they disregard specific incentive structures of a multilevel political system such as the EU.

14. The information asymmetry between principals and agent has been frequently highlighted as the most important aspect determining the principals' ability to detect and sanction defection. McCubbins and Page (1987) even reduce the delegation model to two factors, the level of uncertainty (asymmetric information between agent and principal) and the level of conflict (potential agency loss).

15. The voters elect their members of parliament, who in turn elect the government, and the government is involved in revision of international and European treaties; i.e. it delegates competences to international agencies.

the one hand, and 'the costs of heterogeneity of preferences' on the other (Alesina *et al.* 2002). Obviously, these are the same aspects discussed by Buchanan and Tullock (1962). However, whereas the latter authors focus on the individual actors' expected utility, the former evaluate the collective outcome.[16]

Policy competences should only be centralised when efficiency gains exceed heterogeneity costs, which are induced by preference asymmetry among the states. A formalisation of this trade-off has been suggested by Alesina *et al.* (2001) and Alesina and Wacziarg (1999). Building upon the economic theory of federalism, Collignon (2002) distinguishes between type-I and type-II inefficiencies, focusing on democratic representation. Type-I inefficiency occurs whenever a constituency's policy preferences for a public good are not represented at the jurisdictional level, and the principle of *perfect correspondence*[17] is violated (Oates 1972). Type-II inefficiency occurs whenever policy externalities are not internalised, and thus the principle of *fiscal equivalence*[18] is violated (Olson 1969).

Several economic studies have evaluated the current split of policy competences in the EU (Alesina *et al.* 2002; Friderich 2002). However, Collignon (2002:125) concludes that it is rather 'difficult to distinguish among policy domains'. It turns out that nearly every policy domain in the European dimension has both inclusive and exclusive public goods[19] with different strategic implications. This makes a coherent assignment to a small number of policy sectors almost impossible. The work of the 'Convention on Europe's Future has also come to this realisation. Talk of a catalogue of competences has ceased' (2002:125). Nevertheless, any discussion of the trade-off between heterogeneity costs and efficiency gains among policy areas quickly reveals that the current split of competences in the EU is far from optimal. With the notable exception of regulations intended to ensure the smooth functioning of the common market, the EU is too powerful in many areas.

---

16. Although this refers to the normative economic theories of federalism, other economists analyse individual actors' utility and action (e.g. Hirshman 1971; Stehn 2002). Stehn (2002) concludes that we should expect an inverse monotonic relationship between the degree of homogeneity of preferences within the jurisdiction and the size of the jurisdiction: 'If the latter [central government, D.F.] centralizes too many competences, several countries may not join because they are too distant from the 'median' union member, given that the chosen policy is close to the median preference. On the other hand, if the union centralizes too little, it does not fully benefit from economy of scales and from externalities, which motivate the creation of a Union in the first place' (Stehn 2002: 12).

17. Following Oates (1972), the principle of perfect correspondence demands 'a public sector with both centralized and decentralized levels of decision-making in which choices are made at each level concerning the provision of public services and are determined largely by the demands for the services of the residents of (and perhaps others who carry on activities in) the respective jurisdiction' (Collignon 2002: 69).

18. According to Olson (1969), the principle of 'fiscal equivalence' demands that the geographical incidence of the benefits of a public programme should coincide with the jurisdiction of the government operating and financing the programme.

19. Following Olson (1969), ex*clusive public goods* do not include all people affected by a good's spillovers, while *inclusive public goods* do include all people affected by this public good (no spillovers).

As a result, the EU does not respond to the heterogeneity of voters' preferences. Typical examples include most aspects of the common agricultural policy as well as regional and structural policies. On the other hand, some policy areas still under the realm of the nation-state can affect actors living outside the state's borders. Here, the nation-state is too small and not capable of internalising such externalities. Examples comprise the area of environmental protection, certain aspects of fiscal policy and taxation, nonsectoral business relations, foreign relations, the fight against cross-border crime, defence, research and technology. Still other areas should remain primarily under the realm of the nation-state, especially education and culture (e.g. Oates 1999; Alesina *et al.* 2002).

The post-Maastricht reform agenda depicted in Table 2.1 largely mirrors this discussion. However, reform of the two holy cows, structural cohesion and agricultural policy, does not appear on the agenda before Nice. Furthermore, education and culture appear on the agenda as candidates for additional EU competences, although economists suggest that they should not. As expected, closer fiscal coordination pops up in connection with EMU. Finally, a central aspect of the post-Maastricht agenda is defined by the areas of the second and third pillars (e.g. foreign relations, defence, energy, external borders, visas and asylum, fighting cross-border crime, European public prosecutor). Within the theoretical framework introduced earlier, the division of competences lies at the heart of the intergovernmental conflict over vertical integration.

The theoretical and empirical analysis of the EU's political system is rapidly progressing. However, these results have been rarely related to member states' preferences over European treaty reforms. For the post-Maastricht era, such a combined analysis can only be found for single IGCs (e.g. Bräuninger *et al.* 2001; Moravcsik and Nicolaidis 1999; Laursen 2002, 2006) and for specific institutions (e.g. Rittberger 2005; König-Archibugi 2004). Moravcsik's (1998) original analysis of European integration from Messina to Maastricht has demonstrated that only a long-term perspective enables us to uncover the fundamental dynamics of European integration.

In this section, a model of constitutional choice is derived around two parameters – the level of integration and the decision rule. This model is followed by a discussion of the most prominent reform issues on the post-Maastricht agenda. In particular, it is proved that the post-Maastricht reform agenda allows for such a longitudinal analysis because it has been relatively stable. To do this, the existing literature is examined to explore the consequences of reforming the Union's decision rules for the distribution of power and decision-making efficiency. Then the level of vertical integration is shown to comprise two aspects, the allocation of decisions and control rights. The former refers to the division of competences and the delegation of sovereignty, and the latter refers to the responsiveness of domestic actors' representatives in the Union's decision-making bodies. Hence, legitimacy and integration are two sides of the same coin. In addition, concrete reform issues are assigned to the two-parameter model of constitutional choice, integration and the decision rule. The next section explains how and why actors' preferences for a bundle of individual reform issues can be assigned a position in an intergovernmental conflict space.

PATTERNS OF INTERGOVERNMENTAL CONFLICT

In the previous section, it was seen that the reform agenda matches Europe's constitutional quandary: it comprises reform proposals intended to strengthen the EU's democratic legitimacy, improve the allocation of competences, and reduce decision-making inefficiencies. Now, the concept of revealed preferences will be introduced which will be empirically examined for the multitude of individual reforms described in the previous section. The extent to which governments' conflicts over the multitude of individual issues can, for the sake of analysis, be reduced to a lower-dimensional conflict space will then be discussed. The first step will be to define preferences for individual reform issues as an analytical concept, followed by an explanation of the patterns of intergovernmental conflict and a discussion concerning governments' positions within this conflict space, given their preferences for individual reform issues. Finally, explanations for the observed variation among governmental positions across countries and time will follow.

PREFERENCES

The present analysis focuses on official governmental preferences (e.g. Moravcsik 1998), based on the standard assumptions that preferences are *sincere, realistic, intransitive, comparable* and *stable*.[20]

> *Assumptions 5-9:* Revealed governmental reform preferences are sincere, realistic, intransitive, comparable and stable.

For the purposes of this study, an agenda topic is considered an issue whenever different actors hold conflicting interests with regard to its reform. A *sincere preference* is defined as a choice from a set of *realistic* alternatives for a single issue that can be resolved in a single decision. In contrast, strategic preferences define choices from a set of realistic alternatives for a group of issues that might be resolved in either a single decision or a sequence of decisions. Accordingly, strategic preferences differ from sincere preferences in presuming interdependencies across issues and actors, such as package deals, compromises, threats and promises. Strategic preferences are stated with the intention to impact other actors' decisions with regard to the same or other issues. Hence, they are formulated in anticipation of others' reactions.

Figure 2.5 illustrates the preferences of a national government 'X' on three issues; namely, the reform of the qualified majority voting rule, the applicability of Enhanced Cooperation, and the introduction of a popular initiative. For the same issues, the figure shows a status quo alternative, as defined by the ToN, and an alternative equal to the bargaining outcome of Rome II, the Constitutional Treaty. Issues 1 and 2 are polytomous, providing five and four possible alternatives, re

---

20. For an introduction to spatial preferences and the standard assumptions, see McCarty and Meirowitz (2007: 6).

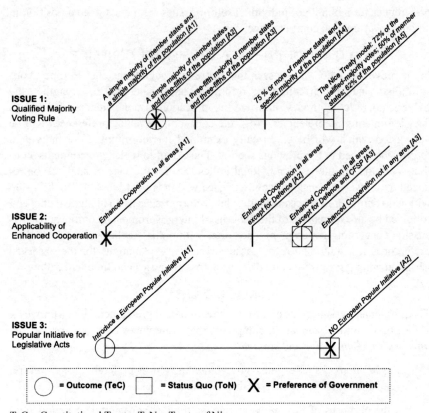

Figure 2.5: An illustration of the set of alternatives (A), the governmental position (x), the outcome and the status quo for three issues contained in the Rome II data

spectively, whereas issue 3 is dichotomous. All issues are rank ordered and *intransitive*, which means that an actor who prefers alternative 1 (A1) over A2, and A2 over A3, will always prefer A1 over A3. Though other, intermediate alternatives are possible (e.g. a popular initiative for a very limited set of policy areas with a very high threshold), the available information is restricted to the set of most prominently discussed alternatives.

Comparability implies that different actors choose from the same set of alternatives. With respect to the examples in Figure 2.5, this means that different national governments share a common understanding of the available alternatives and their order. Comparability does not imply that actors attach similar importance to the same issues.

Figure 2.5 is restricted to the set of *realistic* alternatives. For example, Germany would most likely prefer a solution for Issue 1 that skips the prescribed number of supporting member states and merely requires a simple majority of the EU population. Obviously, this is an unrealistic alternative.

It can be argued that, in the short run, governmental preferences are *relatively stable* because they are a result of a process of forming structured domestic preferences (Moravcsik 1998: 24). Stoiber's (2003) analysis of interministerial coordination in the run-up to the Amsterdam IGC, as well as the volume edited by König and Hug (2006) on processes of forming domestic preferences before Rome II, illustrates that national positions emerge from a process of highly- structured negotiation and coordination. As a result, Moravcsik and Nicolaidis (1999) found that at the Amsterdam IGC, short-term changes occurred in only 5 per cent of all issues. From a long-term perspective, they found that most changes were connected to 'salient, predictable, structural changes in domestic politics' (1999: 24), especially changes in the partisan compositions of either government or parliament. For example, the new Labour government in Britain formulated a clearly more prointegrationist position than its conservative predecessor. By contrast, the end of the Kohl era in Germany is widely associated with a change in the opposite direction.

Nevertheless, the stability assumption is hotly contested, not only between constructivists and rationalists but also among rationalists. For example, König and Finke (2007b) find that governmental delegates revealed strategic preferences during the endgame of Rome II.[21] Thurner *et al.* argue that a proper analysis might consider 'learning and developing preferences only in interaction with evolving constraints' (2003: 166). During the course of negotiations, governmental delegates may improve their information about domestic and international constraints and adapt their revealed preferences accordingly. As a consequence, short-term preference changes might be observed, which Thurner *et al.* (2003: 169) call the 'negotiation dance'.

To constructivists, policy preferences are conditioned not merely by self-interest calculations but rather by ideational considerations such as legitimacy and norms (Kratochwil and Ruggie 1986).[22] They stress the importance of ideas and ideals for the process of European integration (e.g. Sandtholz 1996; Jupille *et al.* 2003). As a consequence, constructivists regard preferences as endogenous to the negotiation process (Jorgensen 1997). Therefore, the outcome of the negotiations is unpredictable (Jupille *et al.* 2003).[23] Unfortunately, this perspective often com-

---

21. Their findings suggest that delegates from status quo-prone governments may gain the necessary credibility for a strategic maneuver if they are backed by status quo-prone ratification actors (König and Finke 2007c).
22. Krasner (1999) refers to these perspectives as the 'logic of consequence' and the 'logic of appropriateness'.
23. Cohen *et al.* (1972) describe negotiations as a 'garbage can' process: ideas, beliefs and actors go in and start to interact in various modes, such as problem solving, social learning and mutual justification.

plicates the statement of falsifiable hypotheses (Moravcsik 1999).[24] Another consequence of this analytical perspective is a methodological self-restriction to thick empirical descriptions of the emerging compromise and the substantial political results (e.g. Weidenfeld 1998, 2001, 2005; Monar and Wessels 2001; Pijper and Edwards 1997; Eriksen *et al*. 2004; Dinan 2004; Magnette 2004).

HOW PREFERENCES TRANSFORM INTO POSITIONS

Every explanatory approach to European treaty revision must make simplifying assumptions. In other words, they reduce the complex real world into a model. This section will examine the extent to which preferences for concrete reform issues can be reduced to a position in an abstract, lower-dimension conflict space. As one of the primary interests of this book is the origins and solutions of intergovernmental conflicts over European treaty revisions, the analysis is therefore restricted to those topics on the reform agenda (see Table 2.1) on which governments held conflicting interests. However, for each IGC, the agenda comprises between forty and sixty-five highly contested issues, multiplied by fifteen to twenty-five member states. Hence, we are dealing with roughly 2900 bits of information on revealed preferences.[25] Obviously, a detailed discussion would significantly extend the scope of this book. Even worse, such a low level of abstraction fits neither its analytical purpose nor its research question. Accordingly, the preference data will be summarised by identifying governments' positions on the most prevalent patterns of intergovernmental conflict.

One approach to such a summary is to identify typical conflict constellations, coalitions or alignments. For example, going back to Figure 2.1, it might be the case that the German, French and Italian governments prefer the most progressive alternative on each of the three reform issues; i.e.,the introduction of a popular initiative, the extension of Enhanced Cooperation to all policy areas and a simple majority voting rule. On the other hand, the British, Czech and Danish governments may prefer the least progressive alternative; i.e. no popular initiative, the abolition of Enhanced Cooperation and the maintenance of the voting rules established at Nice. In this case, we could reduce the three issues to a one-dimensional conflict space spanning the gap between a coalition of three progressive governments at one extreme and a coalition of three regressive governments on the other.

Unfortunately, it is much more difficult to summarise fifteen or even twenty-five governments across the multitude of real-world issues. Thus, there

---

24. Exceptions are Rittberger's (2005) analysis of the empowerment of the EP and Schimmelfennig's (2001) study of Eastern enlargement. They explicitly state theoretical expectations and argue that political actors can entrap others via rhetorical action whenever they have the normative system of beliefs on their side. As a result, actors' preferences converge, and the political outcome will reflect prevalent social norms, such as democratic representation (Rittberger and Schimmelfennig 2006).

25. Chapter 3 describes the data set that contains thirty-nine reform issues for Nice, forty-six for Amsterdam and sixty-five for Rome II (39 * 15 + 46 * 15 + 65 * 25 = 2900). However, the preferences of all actors were not observed for all issues, and therefore the actual number of revealed preferences is slightly lower.

is a trade-off between complexity and analytical clarity (with its potential loss of information). However, a detailed analysis of hundreds of issues does not fit my theoretical approach, which focuses on only two dimensions – vertical integration and the decision rule. The question is, 'Can we explain intergovernmental conflict patterns using these two dimensions?' The theoretical answer to this question is explored below.

The reduction of complexity to underlying latent conflicts, such as 'left versus right', 'pro versus con integration' or 'liberal versus conservative', is part of the standard toolbox in political science. With respect to European political space, most applications concentrate on either two or three dimensions (for an overview, see Zimmer *et al.* 2004: 3; Selck 2004: 213). For example, research suggests that the predominant conflicts in the EP can be captured by a two-dimensional space defined by left-right and independence-integration dimensions (Hix *et al.* 2002; Hix *et al.* 2006; Hix 2004). These studies are based on roll-call votes (Hix *et. al.* 2002, 2006), manifesto data (Gabel and Hix 2002; Pennings 2002; Benoit and Laver 2006) and expert surveys (Hooghe *et al.* 2002).[26] Empirical studies of the Council of Ministers identify a North vs. South dimension (Mattila and Lane 2001; Thomson *et al.* 2004; Hayes-Renshaw *et al.* 2006; König and Junge 2008).

For the IGCs, the number and heterogeneity of issues render the identification of systematic actor alignments operationally difficult (Beach 2003: 12). In his classic book, Moravcsik (1998) assumes that those member states that favour more economic coordination will likewise prefer more delegation of powers and pooling of sovereignty. In other words, those states with the biggest stake in economic integration have the greatest incentive to solve the credible commitment problem among member states. Accordingly, preferences for institutional reforms are subordinated to those for the division of competences. Marks and Steenbergen (2002: 883) call this the 'International Relations Model' of European integration. In this model, all member states can be classified along a single 'integration-independence' dimension. It has been criticised for its assumption that the intergovernmental conflict space can be considered detached from ideological friction on the domestic level (2002: 883). Nevertheless, the International Relations Model is frequently used to analyse EU decision-making processes (e.g. Tsebelis and Garrett 1998; Tsebelis 2002, 2005; Crombez 2002).

Compared with my theory of constitutional choice (as outlined earlier), the International Relations Model implies a folding of the two-parameter space. By contrast, there is an assumption that governments' positions on the decision rule are uncorrelated with their positions on the level of integration. Hence, the two-

---

26. The theoretical foundation of these results is the Hix/Lord Model (Hix and Lord 1997), which argues that this configuration is based on changing coalitions between territorial and functional interests. Other authors regard the independence-integration dimension with more scepticism and argue that conflict among national parties on EU issues follows a one-dimensional, ideological left-right division (Gabel and Hix 2002; Pennings 2002).

parameter space cannot be collapsed.[27] In contrast to the International Relations Model the expectation is to find governments which reject any reform of the decision rule, but demand a far reach level of integration. Likewise, the expectation is to find governments, which reject any additional integration, but prefer drastically lower voting thresholds and the extension of majority voting. Note that this does not imply that governmental positions on one dimension are independent of the real or expected outcomes on the other dimension. Such cross-issue conditionality between positions and outcomes will be discussed in detail in Chapter 6, under the heading of nonseparable preferences.

Assumption 10: Governmental positions on the level of integration are uncorrelated with their position on the decision rule.

Prior empirical work supports Assumption 10. Hix and Crombez (2005) found that the intergovernmental conflict patterns observed at Rome II resemble Lijphart's (1999) classification of political systems along 'unitary-federalist' and 'majority-consensus' dimensions. However, Hix and Crombez (2005) needed to preselect reform issues carefully to construct this space empirically.[28] For the Amsterdam IGC, Bräuninger et al. (2001) followed a similar line of argument, but their operationalisation was completely different.[29] Likewise, for the Amsterdam IGC, Stoiber (2003: 135) found a 'more-or-less-integration dimension' and a 'small-vs-large member states' dimension. Unfortunately, he did not present further substantial interpretations of his findings. Examining the Maastricht IGC, Hug and König (2002) either assessed their data question by question or implicitly assumed a single underlying dimension. Regarding the revealed preferences at Rome II, König and Hug (2006), Hug and Schulz (2007) and König and Finke (2007a) identified a two-dimensional intergovernmental conflict space.

From an empirical perspective, these findings raise the question of whether two-dimensionality can be supported for all three post-Maastricht IGCs (see Chapter 3). From a theoretical perspective, the question might be asked why the conflict space differs from the elegant depiction of states along a single 'integration-independence' dimension that was observed prior to Maastricht. The following explanation has three parts.

First, a reform of the decision rule has two effects on an actor's utility. On the one hand, a lower decision threshold implies higher heterogeneity costs (C). On the other hand, a lower decision threshold implies higher decision-making efficiency, which ensures the realisation of benefits from integration (D). Lowering

---

27. The intermediate case, in which an actor's utility over e is systematically affected but there is no complete linear function of his utility over k, is discussed under the heading of nonseparability in Chapter 4.
28. The authors refer to this as the mixed deductive/inductive method of analysing policy space (Hix and Crombez 2005). However, as has been argued in Chapter 1, it appears somewhat arbitrary to select a subset of reform issues out of the entire universe of issues discussed at an IGC.
29. The authors operationalise the actors' policy preferences via their institutional preferences in each policy area (Bräuninger et al. 2001: 55).

the voting threshold causes a pooling of national sovereignty, an important means of overcoming the credible commitment problem inherent in international treaties.

Second, from a historical perspective, the member states began by integrating those sectors that promised large benefits; i.e. either market access for competitive industries (e.g. Germany and the Netherlands) or compensation payments plus market access for the rest (e.g. France, Belgium, Italy, Luxembourg). According to Moravcsik (1998), the smaller and poorer countries can be ignored, because at the time, they were easily bought off by financial side payments. Finally, the UK entered the EU in 1973 as a country that, at the time, did not expect exceptionally high benefits from either market access or the CAP coffers. As a consequence, its government appeared reluctant with respect to future integration and unwilling to delegate or pool national sovereignty. Back then, heterogeneity costs caused by secondary law were less relevant than today. The legislative activity of the EU was still marginal and the important decisions about member states' benefits were made at IGCs (Majone 2006). Nevertheless, the beneficiaries from integration were eager to solve the credible commitment problem by delegation and pooling national sovereignty. The obverse of this logic became apparent with the Empty Chair Crises (1966), when the French government made it very clear that it was unwilling to pool sovereignty unless benefits from the CAP materialised. On the contrary, the credible commitment problem has been a loophole for integration-sceptic governments.

Third, the Treaty of Maastricht completed the process of economic coordination. As a result, EU policies became increasingly redistributive in nature (Hix 2008). Although direct redistributive effects are restricted to regional and agricultural policies, many of the so-called regulatory policies produce winners and losers (Hix and Follesdal 2006: 10). Furthermore, enlargement meant that a reform of the EU budget was inevitable. As a consequence, member states' evaluation of alternative decision rules now depended on both effects; namely, increased decision-making efficiency and potential heterogeneity costs. Therefore, the expectation is to find governments who reject further integration but promote a pooling of sovereignty. Likewise, there is an expectation of finding governments who strongly prefer further integration but reject any pooling of sovereignty; i.e. any reforms toward majoritarianism.

> *Hypothesis 1:* The post-Maastricht IGCs are characterised by a two-dimensional conflict space, with the first dimension reflecting conflict over the level of integration and the second dimension reflecting conflict over the decision rule.

Most obviously, the question must be asked: are two dimensions sufficient to capture the observed multitude of governmental preferences? Ultimately, the answer to this question must and will be empirical. However, the careful reader has two reasons to suspect that a two-dimensional solution may be an oversimplification. Let me briefly discuss both potential objections.

First, in Chapter 1, Europe's constitutional quandary was characterised as being rooted in three conflicting goals; namely, efficiency, integration and legitimacy. Why not expect a third dimension of intergovernmental conflict that centres on legitimacy? An easy, though certainly provocative, answer is that legitimacy is not at the centre of intergovernmental conflict. This is not to say that governments do not care about legitimacy. However, whenever legitimacy becomes the focus of intergovernmental conflict, it collapses into issues of vertical integration. The empowerment of supranational institutions and national parliaments, the strengthening of individual political and civil rights, the personalisation of EU politics and, last but not least, the division of competences are at the heart of the discussion over Europe's democratic legitimacy. Ultimately, this debate is so prominent because advocates of both models claim legitimacy. The 'federalists' suggest enhancing democracy by granting voters and parliaments additional powers and rights in the EU's political system. By contrast, the 'confederalists' suggest that the only solution to the putative democratic deficit is a reduction of EU competences (Majone 2006: 618). In other words, whenever legitimacy is part of the intergovernmental reform debate, it is subsumed by issues of vertical integration.

Second, a very quick look at Table 2.1 shows that the post-Maastricht agenda contains a very diverse set of policy fields, ranging from foreign and security policy through justice and home affairs, environmental, employment, social and fiscal policy to the reform of the common regional and agricultural policies. How is it that the constitutional theory should result in a single two-dimensional conflict space for all these different policy areas? Should we not at least distinguish an external from an internal dimension of European integration? On second thought, these are two different questions. To begin with, it is not being suggested that governmental integration preferences should be simply summed up across policy areas, though this has been done elsewhere (e.g. Aspinwall 2007), and the logic is easily comprehensible. Nevertheless, it is more interesting to focus on those issues that are crucial to and typical patterns of intergovernmental conflict. Issues where almost all member states are in agreement appear less interesting. Instead, the aggregation mechanisms used emphasise those policy areas that reveal distinguishable and opposing coalitions. Still, it may happen that, on the external dimension, Germany and France are pitched against Sweden and Ireland, whereas, on social and employment policy, Sweden and Germany face a coalition of France and Ireland. However, the subsequent discussion of the domestic origins of reform positions will reveal why such random coalitions are unlikely. Finally, many institutional issues crosscut policy areas, including the organisation of the Commission and the Council presidency, the voting rule, budgetary procedures, the allocation of seats in supranational institutions, the internal organisation of the Council, and the intervention and information rights of national parliaments.

In this subsection, the different preferences for individual reform issues and positions in a lower-dimensional conflict space will be explained, underlined by the argument that the patterns of intergovernmental conflicts can be sufficiently captured by two dimensions that match the two-parameter model of constitutional choice; namely, the level of integration and the design of the decision rule. The discussion will then move onto the domestic origins of governmental reform positions.

THE ORIGINS OF GOVERNMENTAL REFORM POSITIONS

The very concept of an intergovernmental conflict space presumes that governments hold systematically different preferences over the issues on the reform agenda. This section asks how these differences can be explained across member states and across time. European treaty revisions are best characterised as a multistage, two-level process. Specifically, there are four recurring stages (König 2007). First, an international taskforce or working group mandated by the Council defines the need for reform, a crucial step in defining the agenda. Second, national preferences are formed, negotiated and coordinated among domestic actors. Whereas the precise set of relevant actors may differ, all member states consult the different branches of their governments. Third, governmental delegations negotiate treaty reforms at the European level. Usually, this stage begins with intensive bilateral shuttle diplomacy organised by the Council President. The heads of state then negotiate the most hotly-contested issues at a summit. This third step is the IGC in a narrow sense of the word. Fourth, to be legally binding, the modified treaty must be ratified by parliament or via referendum. As for the post-Maastricht period, the Amsterdam and Nice IGCs followed this sequence. However, after widespread disappointment over the Nice Treaty, governments agreed at the European Council in Laeken (December 2001) to alter the standard procedure. Specifically, they installed the Convention on the Future of Europe, which included delegates of governments and national parliaments. The Convention constitutes a novelty in the process of European integration. The delegates from the national parliaments intermingled aspects of the domestic coordination and the intergovernmental negotiation phases. In doing so, they might have accelerated the level of public awareness (Lenz *et al*. 2007; König and Finke 2007a). In Chapter 4, a more detailed presentation of each IGC is given. For now, it is important to note that at all three IGCs, governmental positions had been coordinated among domestic actors before entering the intergovernmental negotiation stage.

Most existing research explains the 'national interest' in European integration by politico-economic factors. The majority of these studies focus on structural differences in national economies. In particular, they consider reform positions to be a function of producer interests. Countries that stand to benefit from the enhanced trade and competition in the Single European Market are thought to favour a high level of integration (Aspinwall 2007; Moravcsik 1998). According to Aspinwall (2007), the same holds true for member states that receive high net transfer payments out of the EU budget. In contrast, König and Bräuninger (2004) highlight the limited interest that EU net payers have in further expanding the EU budget. Therefore, the authors argue, any additional public good provided by the EU implies a reallocation of the EU's scarce financial resources. Accordingly, those who receive a lot of benefits in the status quo should oppose the extended production of public goods by the EU; i.e. further integration.

Most of these economic explanations also refer to the potential heterogeneity costs of further integration. In particular, unfavourable European policies cause adaptation costs. Domestic reforms required by further integration and harmonisation of European law may lead to temporary competitive disadvantages in the SEM (Treib 2005). Koenig-Archibugi (2004) adopts this line of argument and shows that if a member state's existing policy does not conform to other member states' policies, it rejects further cooperation in the area of foreign and security policy. The importance of different economic interests in intergovernmental negotiations depends on their power in the domestic arena and on the specific issues of European integration at hand. According to Moravcsik, the pre-Maastricht era was characterised by increasing economic coordination, and the national interest was determined by highly organised producer groups. Governmental positions were 'biased in favour of those actors with concentrated intense and clearly preexisting interests and against those with more diffuse, uncertain, or unrepresented interests. In the latter category belong consumers, taxpayers and third-country producers' (1998: 39).

However, since Maastricht, public awareness of European politics has been steadily increasing (Zürn 2006: 224). Even though European matters cover roughly 4 per cent of national party manifestos, since the mid 1990s, they have been included in manifestos across member states and political groups (Volkens 2005: 274). Furthermore, the percentage of articles in the quality press with reference to European politics has risen, now covering between 25 per cent (*Politiken*) and 45 per cent (*Le Monde*) (Peters et al. 2005: 142). Given the fact that the overall EU budget covers less than 1.5 per cent of the EU's Gross National Income, this increase cannot be explained by redistributive policies.[30] Instead, the increasing awareness and coverage of the EU has been due to the enactment of (primarily regulatory) legislation, such as common market directives, and consumer and environmental protection laws (König et al. 2007). Such policies not only have indirect redistributive effects (Follesdal and Hix 2006) but also 'may mobilize not just producers, but organised public interest groups and parties that favour particular environmental, consumer, or health and safety regulations. Such matters can generate a powerful electoral response' (Moravcsik 1998: 40).

Nevertheless, few researchers have explicitly considered the public's opinions about, or attitudes toward European integration. Aspinwall (2007) found that governments' positions at Amsterdam were positively correlated to their average voter's support for European integration. Koenig-Archibugi (2004) examined a Eurobarometer question that asks respondents to rate their European identity. The results indicated that governments were less supportive of common foreign and security policies if their average voter's European identity was low. This is consistent with the public opinion literature, which indicates that support for integration is strongly correlated to European identity (Hooghe and Marks 2005).

Other explanations suggest that a member state's position on European treaty

---

30. According to the European Commission's budget report in 2004, the CAP accounts for roughly 43 per cent of the EU's total budget, including the special programmes for rural development. In addition, the structural and cohesion policies account for another 36 per cent of the budget. (Source: http://europa.eu.int/eur-lex/budget/data/D2005_VOL1/EN/, (accessed 11 January 2007)).

reforms reflects the left-right ideology of the party in office. According to the classic version of this argument, rightist (especially traditionalist, nationalist and conservative) parties are less integrationist than centrist and leftist parties (Aspinwall 2007). However, empirical studies find an inverted u-shaped relationship, according to which both rightist and leftist parties oppose further integration. Accordingly, centrist parties are the most integrationist (Aspinwall 2007; Marks and Steenbergen 2004; Wüst and Schmitt 2007).

Finally, detailed qualitative studies are plentiful, but most of them are limited to particular aspects of the reform treaty, such as advancements in particular policy areas, for example common foreign and security politics (e.g. Koenig-Archibugi 2004; Mahncke 1997), social and employment politics (e.g. Padoan 1997), or justice and home affairs (e.g. Monar 2008; 2006). Still others analyse the negotiations over institutional reforms, especially the design of council voting rules (e.g.Bräuninger et al. 2001; Moravcsik and Nicolaïdis 1999; Laursen 2005, 2002) and the empowerment of the European Parliament (e.g. Rittberger 2005; König 2008).

The majority of the existing studies do not discuss the institutional constraints to the domestic preference formation process. Notable exceptions are Stoiber (2003) and Thurner and Pappi (2006), who analysed the interministerial coordination processes in the run-up to, and during, the Amsterdam IGC. An edited volume by König and Hug (2006) brings together twenty-five country studies in a single analytical framework that combines information on the conflict constellations and processes of domestic position formation. In the empirical chapters of this book, this information will be used to test explicitly for the effects of two types of institutional rules: the involvement of national parliaments during position formation and the expected ratification instrument.

From a normative perspective, it is important how domestic preferences for European politics are aggregated, especially the extent to which governments and parliaments respond to the preferences of their voters. During the past decade, empirical researchers began to unravel the explanatory factors underlying public opinion on European integration and the link between voters and parties.[31] However, less empirical work has been done to examine the contribution of domestic politics to the formation of governments' positions on integration. Researchers have only very recently begun to locate voters' and governments' positions on the same scale to test whether or not the Schelling conjecture applies to European treaty negotiations (Hug and Schulz 2007; König and Finke 2007a). The inspection of domestic political institutions reveals that European integration politics is subject to the same mechanisms of preference aggregation that is known from other policy fields. First, the empirical literature suggests that voters' preferences in European politics depend on how much information they have, as well as other mediating factors such as ideology (Gabel 1998; Brinegar and Jolly 2005; Hooghe and Marks 2005). Second, a party's responsiveness to the electorate is limited (Schmitt and Thomassen 2000; Ray 2003; Mattila and Raunio 2006). Third, the literature

---

31. For a recent overview, see Steenbergen et al. 2007 and de Vries 2007.

appears to be divided over whether partisan preferences follow public opinion or whether partisan elites cue the public (Steenbergen *et al.* 2007). Fourth, as with other policy areas, a government's integration policy is subject to institutional rules and the domestic power distribution among political parties (König and Hug 2006; Stoiber 2003).

Although recent studies have found an increasing importance of the European issue for national elections (de Vries 2007), it is generally believed to be of subsidiary relevance for explaining electoral choice at the domestic level (Franklin *et al.* 1996; Crum 2007). Most voters are unable to specify the costs and benefits to them of future integration, although their ability to evaluate alternative levels of integration may vary across policy areas. 'Economic theories work best when economic consequences are perceived with some accuracy, are large enough to matter, and when the choice a person makes actually affects the outcome' (Hooghe and Marks 2004: 2; Luetgert 2007). In other areas, voters will follow group identities, use ideologies as heuristics, or follow opinion leaders they perceive to be competent advisers for a particular question. Overall, the veil of constitutional ignorance is more opaque for some voters than for others, and a good deal more inscrutable for most voters than for the political elite. This problem intensifies if individuals face a considerable amount of uncertainty with respect to their own economic future. As a consequence, 'the individual, unable to predict his future position', will desire 'the imposition of some additional and renewed restraints on the exercise of legislative power' (Buchanan and Tullock 1962: 82). This argument is supported by the fact that, on average, voters are less integration friendly than the parties they voted for (Schmitt and Thomasson 2000).

The correlation between the national averages in public opinion and the revealed preferences of governments most certainly includes confounding underlying variables, such as the national economic structure and development, the net payer position, intra-EU trade, satisfaction with the national democracy, and ideological factors that may have historic origins. To solve this problem in the present study, a longitudinal research design is used. If voters' preferences and the preference formation process matter beyond confounding structural variables, governmental positions not only should correspond to the position of the electorate but also should change in response to the electorate's changes in position.

Hypothesis 2.1: Governmental positions correspond to the position of their median voter and respond to changes in the position of their median voter.

Referenda constitute a second, more direct link between governmental positions and public opinion. Here, governments are forced to consider the ultimate judgment of the treaty by the median voter. In all, fifteen member states announced ratification via popular referendum[32] at the three IGCs under examination. The

---

32. At Amsterdam, the governments of Denmark, Ireland and Portugal announced a referendum. The Irish Constitution prescribes a mandatory referendum and the Irish government was the only one to announce a referendum on the Treaty of Nice. Finally, an unprecedentedly high number of eleven governments, namely Belgium, the Czech Republic, Denmark, France, Ireland, Luxembourg, the Netherlands, Poland, Portugal, and Great Britain, announced referenda on the TeC.

conjectured link between governmental positions and public opinion presumes that governments were planning to hold a referendum before they had to reveal their official position at the final stage of the IGC. However, until they are publicly announced, ratification strategies are discussed in small circles behind closed doors. Nevertheless, eleven of the fifteen referenda were announced before the final stage of their respective IGCs. The British, Polish and Belgian announcements occurred before the end of Rome II, and only the French referendum was announced after the closing summit on July 7th, 2004 (Hug and Schulz 2007: 167).

Hypothesis 2.2: The impact of the median voter upon the governmental position will be stronger in countries where the government announced ratification via referendum.

As far as European politics is concerned, the parties in office appear to be systematically more integrationist than their voters (Schmitt and Thomassen 2000; Ray 2003; Mattila and Raunio 2006). This proves that governments enjoy a considerable degree of discretion with regard to European integration politics. When exercising their discretion, governments have expectations about the likelihood of future electoral punishment. However, as governments are incapable of knowing their voters' exact future positions, they can only extrapolate from current trends. In other words, politicians assess their latitude to take various integration positions based on short-term trends in their potential voters' opinions rather than on long-term averages.

Hypothesis 2.3: Governments respond to short-term trends in the opinions of their electoral support base.

At the international level, a country's position on reform is revealed by the national government, which may be a single-party government, or, as in most EU member states, a coalition government. Hence, the expectation is that the governmental position is determined by the parties in office. Accordingly, a given government's position changes in response to changes in the partisan composition of government. However, coalition partners may hold conflicting positions on European integration, and this raises the question of how compromises are reached regarding European politics. Although a political compromise on European integration may come from a bargaining process that involves several other policy areas, a reasonable approximation is the mean position across all coalition partners weighted by their relative power; i.e. the size of their faction in the national parliament (Martin and Vanberg 2004: 15).[33]

A more interesting discussion concerns the enforcement of such a political compromise. One perspective suggests that the minister in charge of the relevant department is in a position to present the policy proposal to the cabinet, giving them a privileged position in the policy area in question. In the most radical view, this minister is free to make an autonomous decision (Laver and Shepsle 1996). A

---

33. Indeed, this weighted mean approximates the outcome of an unrestricted and asymmetric Nash Bargaining Solution (Achen 2006: 111).

less radical perspective suggests that he/she enjoys significant discretion to drift away from the coalition compromise (Gallagher *et al.* 2001; Müller and Strom 2000). However, country studies by König and Hug (2006) and by Stoiber (2003) suggest that interministerial coordination on matters of EU treaty reforms is very inclusive. The underlying reason for this high degree of inclusiveness is the fact that the post-Maastricht reform agenda touches upon a wide array of policy fields. Accordingly, national governments are not represented by the head of any particular department but by either the head of the government or the foreign minister.

> *Hypothesis 2.4:* Governmental positions correspond to the partisan composition of the government and respond to changes in the partisan composition of the government.

So far, the focus has been on the government. Viewed from this angle, it appears that parliaments play only a marginal role in the policy-making process – they are dominated by the cabinet (Martin and Vanberg 2005). However, most EU member states are parliamentary democracies. Exceptions are the semipresidential system of France and the weak semipresidentialism of Finland.[34] Therefore, the expectation is the national position to be a result of the partisan composition of the national parliament. Accordingly, the national position changes in response to changes in the partisan composition of parliaments. Parliamentary control of the government works best whenever parties compete for a common electorate. In particular, the opposition might be tempted to discredit the government over the European issue. This strategy is especially promising shortly before national elections or in referendum countries (Steenbergen *et al.* 2007). For this reason, even the most prointegrationist British Labour government must be aware of the Euro-scepticism present in public opinion (Benedetto 2006).

> *Hypothesis 2.5:* Governmental positions correspond to the partisan composition of parliament and respond to changes in the partisan composition of parliament.

The mechanisms of parliamentary control vary across member states. Empirical studies suggest that legislative institutions, such as a strong committee system with proportional assignment of seats, can have a significant impact on policy formulation (Müller and Strom 2000). Most of these studies highlight the argument that strong committees, in combination with formal parliamentary scrutiny, strengthen the opposition parties.[35] Viewed from this angle, the representatives from all major parties can successfully amend the proposal of the minister in charge ex ante the international negotiations. Prior research suggests that, in eight of the fifteen old member states, parliamentary committees were formally involved in the formation

---

34. Finish EU politics are characterised by intensive parliamentary scrutiny, and in the case of treaty reform, parliament even enjoys an explicit veto right during the preparatory stage (Finke and König 2006: 139).
35. By contrast, Martin and Vanberg (2005) suggest that formal parliamentary scrutiny reduces ministerial drift and, accordingly, is to the benefit of the governmental coalition as a whole.

of the national position (these were: Austria, Denmark, Finland, Germany, Ireland, Spain, Sweden and the UK.[36] Furthermore, parliamentary scrutiny occurred during the domestic position formation processes in Lithuania, Hungary and Estonia (Stoiber 2003: 277; König and Hug 2006).

Hypothesis 2.6: The impact of the parliament on the national position is stronger in political systems that provide formal parliamentary scrutiny.

In brief, it can be argued that a government's position on vertical integration can be explained by the short- and medium-term dynamics of the domestic position formation process. With regard to the theory of constitutional choice introduced earlier, governments evaluate a shift in vertical integration with their voters in mind. In particular, the expectation is that changes in governmental positions from one IGC to the next are caused by changes in the partisan composition of the government and parliament, changes in party preferences, and short- and medium-term trends in public opinion. Finally, the impact of domestic actors on the governmental position is mediated by the involvement of the parliament and the choice of the ratification instrument.

At first sight, the explanation of governmental positions on the choice of the decision rule appears straightforward. Above all, it depends on how governments evaluate the heterogeneity costs implied by potentially unfavourable European policies. Hence, governments that represent outlier preferences will prefer decision rules that grant them high voting power. In the 1990s, this most certainly has been the perspective of many central European governments with relatively low wages, a large agricultural sector, and relatively low social as well as environmental standards.

Hypothesis 3.1: Governments from Central European states reject any reform of the decision rule that threatens to reduce their veto power; i.e. reforms toward majoritarianism.

All realistic reforms of the decision rule discussed at Amsterdam, Nice or Rome II tried to strengthen proportional representation. In particular, the redistribution of voting weights finally agreed to at Nice, and the double majority rule[37] repeatedly discussed at all three IGCs, implied a redistribution of relative voting power to the benefit of larger member states (Baldwin *et al.* 2001). Unfortunately, with the exception of Poland, all of the new Central European states are small, which complicates any empirical disentanglement of Hypotheses 3.1 and 3.2.

Hypothesis 3.2: Larger member states favour decision rules that lower the voting threshold; i.e. reforms toward a majoritarian system.

---

36. For Rome II, see individual country chapters in König and Hug 2006. Parliamentary scrutiny exists when parliament holds a veto right during the preference formation process.

37. The voting threshold agreed to at Nice required a majority of member states, more than 62 per cent of the EU's population and about 74 per cent of the weighted votes. The voting weights ranged from 29 (Germany, France, UK and Italy) to 3 (Malta). Under a double majority scheme, the voting weights would be skipped. Accordingly, the remaining criteria for the voting threshold are a qualified majority of member states and a qualified majority of the population.

Domestic actors should reveal less heterogeneity with regard to the reform of the decision rule. After all, voters cannot control, elect or otherwise impact foreign governments. As a consequence, they will expect the position of their own government to be the best representation of their interest in the Council of Ministers. In other words, domestic actors will prefer high relative voting power for their government throughout.

The potential conditionality between vertical integration and the reform of the decision rule has already been discussed. Actors' positions on both dimensions might be conditional, in technical terms 'nonseparable', if a reform of the decision rule would alter a member state's utility over the degree of vertical integration or vice versa. This conditionality might go both ways. For example, France might prefer deeper cooperation in justice and security politics only if decision-making in this area will become more efficient by extending majority voting and lowering the voting thresholds. Ireland, on the other hand, might prefer deeper cooperation in the same area only if it retains its veto right. The case where actors prefer more efficient decision rules in reaction to higher de facto transfer of competences is called 'positive complementary'. The case where actors prefer less efficient decision rules in reaction to higher de facto transfer of competences is called 'negative complementary' (see Enelow and Hinich 1984).

Having said that, it appears obvious that the degree and direction of this conditionality varies across governments and across time. This variation might be explained by governments that have alternative power resources. A reform of the decision rule toward majority voting causes a decrease in the importance of voting power relative to other power resources, such as agenda-setting and budgetary and informational power (Bailer 2006: 43). It appears reasonable to assume that large and rich member states possess more of these alternative power resources than do poor member states. Hence, their relative power to avoid heterogeneity costs despite higher preference asymmetry increases when the voting threshold decreases. He who pays the piper calls the tune.

> *Hypothesis 4.1:* Governments from large and rich countries have nonseparable and positive complementary preferences. By contrast, the preferences of poor member states (net receivers) are nonseparable and negative complementary.

The nonseparability between governments' evaluation of the decision rule and their evaluation of the level of integration provides an endogenous explanation for positional change. Governments with positive (negative) complementary preferences will adjust their position on the decision rule toward more (less) majoritarianism if they are confronted by a higher level of vertical integration then they had originally hoped for. For example, let us assume that the Danish government held negative complementary preferences at the time of the Amsterdam IGC. If the Treaty of Amsterdam shifted more competences to the EU level than the Danish government had originally hoped for, it would have been eager to maintain its veto power and would have adjusted its position on reforming the decision rule accordingly. By contrast, let us assume that the French government held positive complementary preferences. Almost certainly, the Treaty of Amsterdam provided for less integration than the French government had originally hoped for. In response, the French government would have adjusted its position on the voting rule in the same direction as the Danish government. However, if the complementarity of the French government's preferences had been negative, which would contradict Hypothesis 4.1, it would have responded to the Treaty of Amsterdam by preferring an even more progressive reform toward majoritarianism. Finally, it is via this mechanism of conditional preferences that domestic actors impact the governmental positions on the decision rule too.

Hypothesis 4.2: A government with nonseparable preferences adjusts its position in response to treaty reforms. The direction of this adjustment depends on the treaty reform relative to the government's previous ideal position, and on whether its nonseparable preferences are positively or negatively complementary.

This section began with a conceptualisation and definition of revealed preferences, followed by an explanation of the difference between preferences on individual reform issues and positions in a lower-dimensional conflict space. It was argued that patterns of intergovernmental conflict can be sufficiently captured by two dimensions that match the two parameters of the model of constitutional choice; namely, the level of integration and the design of the decision rule. Finally, the domestic origins of governmental reform positions were discussed. In particular, it was argued that positions on vertical integration are not an exclusive function of structural, economic or political factors. Instead, they can be explained as result of the domestic preference formation process. More specifically, governmental positions depend on the medium- and short-term positions of the median voter, and the partisan composition of parliament and government. By contrast, positions on the decision rule depend primarily on population size. Finally, the degree and direction of the conditionality in actors' evaluations of both reform dimensions depend on their endowment with alternative power resources, especially the power of the purse.

THE PROCESS AND SET OF RELEVANT ACTORS

In this section, it will be argued that any explanation of European treaty reforms must take into account the governmental positions of all member states. This argument will be accompanied by a short introduction to those concepts applied in the spatial analysis of politics that are necessary to understand the subsequent empirical chapters. Readers familiar with spatial analysis may want to skip these paragraphs. The importance of procedural constraints on intergovernmental negotiations will be discussed in the next section.

RELEVANT ACTORS

Liberal intergovernmentalism is broadly acknowledged as the gold standard in integration research (Moravcsik 1998). It is founded on three widely criticised propositions (Kassim and Dimitrakopoulos 2004; Finke 2009a). First, domestic and supranational actors are irrelevant to our understanding of EU treaty reforms.

Second, analysis of the largest member states sufficiently explains the progress of European integration, which is manifest in treaty reforms. Third, intergovernmental negotiations are subject to no procedural or institutional constraints.

To begin with, the exclusive focus on governments has been criticised by authors claiming that supranational institutions exert a significant influence on the outcome of European treaty reforms. In particular, the Commission and the EP hold agenda-setting powers and influence the drafting of the legal document by their exclusive knowledge of the EU's decision-making mechanisms (Hix 2002; Beach 2006; Maurer 2007: 46). However, compared with the increasing importance of the Commission and the EP in EU legislative politics (Crombez 1996; Moser 1996; Steunenberg 1994; Tsebelis 1994; Kreppel and Tsebelis 1999; Tsebelis and Garrett 2000; König and Pöter 2001; Thomson et al. 2006), neither of the two supranational actors possesses formal agenda setting, voting or even veto rights with regard to treaty revisions. In general, new treaties must be signed by the governments of all member states and ratified according to the national provisions. However, in the exceptional case of the constitutional treaty, the EP has been asked to ratify the text. Furthermore, both supranational actors participated in the Laeken Convention, where they cooperated closely with the Praesidium and provided expertise during the summit negotiations (Tsebelis 2006; Beach 2006). This fact will be returned to when discussing the role of procedural constraints.

Concerning the role of domestic actors, an increasing number of researchers argue that the unitary-actor assumption cannot be upheld because domestic actors are relevant at the bargaining table too. In multiple empirical studies, these researchers have examined the relationship between domestic and European levels and concluded that the unitary-actor assumption is not warranted (e.g. König and Hug 2000; Hug and König 2002; König and Finke 2007a). Their main argument concerns the ratification process, and they maintain that governments can credibly tie their own hands by referring to sceptical domestic ratification actors. Theoretically, these studies elaborate on Schelling's (1960) 'paradox of weakness', which has been prominently discussed in the literature on two-level games (e.g. Pahre 1997; Iida 1993, 1996).

In his path-breaking analysis, Moravcsik argues that treaty reforms from Messina to Maastricht are sufficiently explained by analysing the preferences of the three largest and most powerful member states (Germany, France, UK). If necessary, these large countries will offer either 'financial side payments or symbolic concessions' to the smaller ones to achieve their grand economic bargains (1998: 65f.). However, Moravcsik's original work deals with a maximum of twelve member states since 1986 and with even fewer states before the first Northern and the subsequent Southern enlargements. When the Treaty of Maastricht was negotiated (1991), the total GDP of Germany, France and the UK outweighed that of the remaining nine member states by a factor of 1.8. In terms of population size, this factor was 1.3. Hence, the three largest member states held an economic power almost twice as strong as all the other countries combined.

In contrast, the Northern (1995) and Eastern (2004/7) enlargements added, beside Poland, another fourteen small to medium-sized countries to the EU, the majority of which had relatively weak economies at the time they entered. In 2004, the total economic power of the UK, Germany and France was roughly equal to that of the remaining twenty-four countries, and these three states accounted for only 201 of the 485 million EU inhabitants. Given this shift in the balance of economic power, the making of financial side payments to smaller countries appears to be a less feasible strategy. In addition, the focus of the IGCs since Maastricht has shifted away from economic integration and coordination toward institutional reforms and political integration (Laffan 1997: 289). Against this background, it is not surprising that recent researchers, writing in the tradition of liberal intergovernmentalism, argue that large and small member states are equally important for our understanding of EU treaty reforms (e.g. König and Hug 2006). In his empirical analysis of the Amsterdam IGC, Slapin (2006) found that large member states did not have any more power than the average member state at the bargaining table.

Now this finding is transferred to the spatial analysis of politics. Under the assumption that all actors hold complete and perfect information, bargaining theory expects Pareto efficient and Pareto superior outcomes (Muthoo 2002: 9). An outcome is Pareto superior if it improves at least one actor without making any other actor worse off. An outcome is Pareto efficient if the set of Pareto superior outcomes is empty. Without additional informational limitations, a Pareto efficient outcome provides an equilibrium solution for the bargaining game. Complete information presumes a situation in which actors possess relevant knowledge about all other actors. If it is assumed that the set of relevant actors is limited to national governments, this means that governments know the preferences of all other governments on all reform issues. Perfect information presumes that governments also observe the actions of all other governments. Both assumptions are particularly questionable in highly complex bargaining situations that involve a multitude of actors at different levels of government and with different procedural constraints.

In the spatial analysis of politics, a bargaining outcome is Pareto superior if it is located in the win set of the status quo, and it is Pareto efficient if it is located in the core (Tsebelis 2002: 39). Hence, if the outcome is in the core, the win set of the status quo must be empty. The status quo is defined by the currently binding European treaties. Within this theoretical framework, actors evaluate alternative outcomes by the Euclidean distance to their ideal position. In Chapter 3, the mathematical notation of actors' so-called Euclidean utility loss is presented. For now, the discussion is restricted to the underlying graphical intuitions. It is assumed that all actors must agree on reform, hence the unanimity core and the unanimity win set is analysed. Overall, size and location of the win set and the core can be altered by the following three parameters.

First, the dimensionality of the conflict space might increase or decrease. Figure 2.6 (I) depicts a one-dimensional policy space. The status quo (SQ) is in equilibrium and, accordingly, the win set of the status quo is empty. Figure 2.6 (II) adds a second dimension. On the horizontal dimension, the positions of actors A, B and C equal those in Figure 2.6 (I). Nevertheless, in the two-dimensional picture, the status quo is located outside the unanimity core. As a result, the win set of the status quo is nonempty. It is defined by the intersection of actors' indifference curves through SQ (dashed circles). An actor is indifferent between all points on this curve because they are all equally far away from his ideal position. In Figure 2.6 (II), the boundaries of the win set are defined by actors A and B. Accordingly, theory expects member states to agree on a reform treaty (T) located inside both the core and the win set of the status quo. However, the reform agenda has been relatively stable throughout the post-Maastricht IGCs, and therefore there is no expectation of a change in dimensionality.

Second, comparing Figures 2.6 (II) and 2.6 (III) illustrates that adding or subtracting actors might alter the shape of the win set and the unanimity core. Any additional actor might (e.g. actor D) or might not (e.g. actor E) enlarge the core and reduce the size of the win set. Conversely, the subtraction of any actor might or might not reduce the size of the core and enlarge the win set. For the present analysis, Eastern enlargement has obviously altered the set of actors, though it is up to empirical analysis to determine the extent to which it has reshaped the core or the win set.

Third, comparing Figures 2.6 (III) and 2.6 (IV) illustrates how positional changes might alter the shape of the core and the win set. In this example, the change of D to D' is crucial to reshaping the unanimity core such that the status quo is located outside its boundaries. Accordingly, the expectation that a reform agreement (T') will be located inside the new unanimity core as defined by A', D', B' and E', as well as inside the win set of the status quo as shaped by actors D' and B'.

Overall, to test the extent to which the sequence of European treaty revisions is a function of member states' changing positions, there must be a control for changes of the agenda, the issue space and the number of actors.

According to Moravcsik's original approach, treaty reforms in the win set and core would be expected to be defined by the three largest member states only. This presumes that the status quo ante must be situated outside the core of France, Germany and the UK. If, however, financial side payments are impossible, treaty reforms must adhere to the reform positions of all member states. In other words, the bargaining outcome must be located within the unanimity win set and the unanimity core defined by all member states. However, if this is true, the sequence of intergovernmental reform agreements observed at Amsterdam, Nice and Rome II could only be possible if the status quo had been in disequilibrium, hence outside the unanimity core. As a consequence, the positions of national governments must have changed between one IGC and the next (Caporaso 2007).

> *Hypothesis 5.1:* The history of post-Maastricht European treaty reforms follows a sequence of equilibrium and disequilibrium defined by the changing positions of all national governments.

In particular, Hypothesis 5.1 implies that the Treaty of Maastricht did not define an intergovernmental equilibrium at the time of Amsterdam. Neither did the Treaty of Amsterdam at the time of the Nice Treaty, or the Treaty of Nice at Rome II. However, at all three IGCs, governments should have agreed on a reform located

the conceptual framework | 67

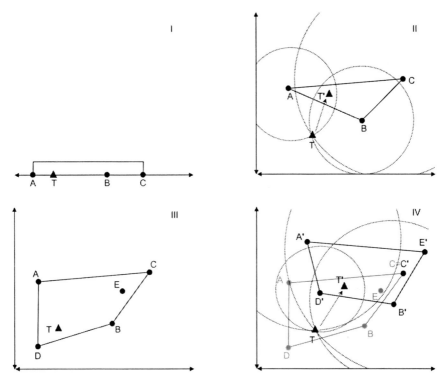

A, B, C, D, E = actors; T = Treaty; solid line = unanimity core; dashed line = actors' indifference curves

Figure 2.6: An illustration of how the subtraction and addition of actors and dimensions as well as the shift of positions may reshape the unanimity core and the win-set of the status quo

inside the unanimity core as defined by member states' preferences at that time. Furthermore, the reforms of Amsterdam and Nice must have improved the governments of all member states. Hence, they should be located within the win set of the status quo as defined by member states' preferences at that time. Therefore, the history of European treaty reforms from Maastricht to Nice can be described as a sequence of equilibrium and disequilibrium. Given the relatively stable agenda described later in the chapter, this presupposes the change of member states' positions from one IGC to the next.

PROCEDURAL CONSTRAINTS

Classic liberal intergovernmentalism claims that bargaining is 'subject to essentially no procedural constraints' (Moravcsik 1998: 61), and thus treaty reforms are a result of pure and unconstrained intergovernmental bargaining. In the post-Maastricht period, this assumption faces three challenges. First, in a Union of six, nine or even twelve governments, such an unconstrained bargaining game might produce efficient outcomes, especially if the table is dominated by the three senior partners of France, Germany and the UK. However, the efficiency of such an unstructured bargaining game decreases with the number of participants. Second, many of the institutional reforms on the post-Maastricht agenda imply a redistribution of political power among member states, most prominently discussed in connection with issues such as the design of voting rules and the composition of the Commission. As a consequence, the nature of intergovernmental conflict shifts from being a coordination problem toward being a mixed motive game, which is substantially more difficult to solve. Third, the Laeken Convention constitutes a procedural innovation that not only prolonged the negotiation process but also left governments with imperfect and incomplete information.

These arguments are well reflected in the theoretical literature. First, and most obviously, the number of participating actors raises the transaction costs of international negotiations (e.g. Cross 1969). Second, without any procedural constraints on the agenda, neither multidimensional spatial voting models (McKelvey 1976) nor multilateral strategic bargaining models identify unique subgame-perfect equilibrium (Muthoo 2002: 300). Theoretically, the problem of multiple equilibria can be circumvented with a restriction of the bargaining protocol (e.g. Chae and Yang 1994; Baliga and Serrano 1995; Krishna and Serrano 1996).[38] In other words, both the social choice and the bargaining literatures would identify a unique equilibrium in multilateral negotiations only if process matters.

Traditionally, bargaining at IGCs is restricted by the following procedural rules. First, the Council Presidents perform the crucial tasks of preparing political agreements and organising the IGC itself. Therefore, it has been argued that the President holds a certain degree of agenda-setting power (Elgström 2002). Usually, the President prepares the IGCs via bilateral shuttle diplomacy to settle the less important issues on the agenda (which are identified a priori by an expert committee). The more important and contentious issues are saved for the decisive summit, where it is the President's responsibility to set the agenda and propose a political compromise. By contrast, the Constitutional Treaty was prepared by a novel method; namely, the Convention on the Future of Europe. At the Convention, the President (Giscard D'Estaing) held considerable agenda-setting powers (Tsebelis 2008; Tsebelis and Proksch 2007).[39] For this book, the more important question is the extent to which the Convention draft predetermined the outcome of the IGC. In the end, the IGC adopted the Convention draft almost without modification – but where did the Convention's de facto agenda-setting power come from?

The key to answering this question lies in softening the perfect and complete information assumption. In the case where there is a maximum of twelve unitary governmental actors representing stable national economic interests, the information assumption may appear justifiable. However, once the set of relevant actors is

---

38. Another assumption that allows for unique subgame-perfect equilibria in multilateral bargaining games is that of stationary strategies (e.g. Merlo and Wilson 1995; Banks and Duggan 2000).

39. He could pick and choose among amendments suggested by the working group, alter the rules of the game during the procedure, and iterate the agenda *ad libitum* – and he did not intend an explicit vote on the complete draft.

expanded to twenty-seven member states with (coalition) governments that represent heterogeneous domestic interests, plus parliamentary or even popular ratification actors, the information assumption appears very demanding.

The effect of imperfect information was evident in the case of the Convention, the importance of which was unclear in the beginning and the success of which was critically dependent upon its President, Giscard d'Estaing (Norman 2005; Tsebelis 2008). Furthermore, the Convention intermingled the domestic coordination and the international negotiation phases (Göler and Marhold 2003; König and Slapin 2006). Indeed, the analysis by Tsebelis and Proksch (2007) shows that the President availed himself of private information in his approach to managing the Convention; i.e. he left the delegates with imperfect information on the rules of the game. Nevertheless, national governments had installed the Convention and committed to its outcome to go beyond the modest reforms agreed to at Nice. Unfortunately, the governments at Laeken did not expect the Convention to produce a coherent draft constitution; they expected a report of more or less nonbinding recommendations and suggestions.

During the Convention, member states increasingly faced a dilemma. Either they had to disempower the Convention via intergovernmental overrule (which would tarnish both international and domestic reputations) or they could play along with the Convention and its President by enhancing the status of their delegations. Note that the second strategy (upgrade) dominates the first (disempower) in the sense that a disempowerment of the Convention would have required collective action, which was unlikely as some member states, most notably France and Germany, realised that the president was largely promoting their goals. Accordingly, member states with different preferences were forced to counterbalance their power in the Convention at the expense of upgrading the committee's power. Beginning with the engagement of Joschka Fischer and Dominique de Villepin, almost all governments decided to send top-level officials to the Convention during the final stage (Norman 2005: 155). This upgrade raised the reputation costs of disregarding the Convention draft. Finally, the Laeken declaration prescribed a clear timeline for the entire process, which would end with elections to the European Parliament in June 2004. This fixed deadline provided additional pressure to keep the box closed and renegotiate only the most controversial issues.

Governments were uncertain about the choices that their own and other member states' parliamentary or popular ratification actors would make in the future. Indeed, the power of governments to use Euro-sceptical domestic principals to their advantage critically depends on this uncertainty (Pahre 1997; Milner 1997). In particular, there is uncertainty because voters' preferences are partly formed in future referendum campaigns or because voting depends on issues other than European ones anyhow ('second-order voting'; Binzer-Hobolt 2006: 154). As a consequence, governments may announce referenda during the negotiation stage, even though they may lack the necessary popular support at the subsequent ratification stage. The negative French and Dutch referenda in 2005 may be good examples of such an 'involuntary defection' (Iida 1996; Finke and König 2009).

As a result, it is expected that procedural constraints will be more important for explaining Rome II than earlier IGCs. In particular, given the Convention President's power to shape the outcome, his putatively prointegrationist reform position and the Convention's de facto agenda-setting power, a more progressive treaty reform is the expectation, one that moves beyond the minimal compromise of previous IGCs.

> *Hypothesis 5.2:* The treaty reforms agreed to at Amsterdam and Nice constitute Pareto efficient and Pareto superior compromises, respectively, among all governments. The Constitutional Treaty constitutes a Pareto efficient, progressive reform, which might be Pareto inferior for some governments.

In this section, expectations are formulated regarding the outcome of intergovernmental treaty negotiations. In particular, the expectation that there will be reforms to improve the governments of all member states, and European integration no longer to be driven by a few large, senior partners. Furthermore, I expect the history of European treaty reforms to follow a sequence of equilibrium and disequilibrium. Finally, I argue that because of the increased number of member states, the changing nature of the conflict space and the invocation of the Convention, intergovernmental bargaining is subject to procedural constraints.

SUMMARY

In the wake of Maastricht, the EU confronted three challenges: political integration, decision-making efficiency and democratic legitimacy. The impending Eastern enlargement provided additional pressure to act. In the first section of this chapter, a two-parameter model of constitutional choice is presented. Specifically, it is argued that a government's cost-benefit calculation over alternative constitutional designs is a function of the vertical level of integration and the design of the decision rule. The former comprises institutional aspects of political integration and the division of competences, whereas the latter deals with the design of the decision rule and its implication for member states' relative power. The post-Maastricht reform agenda along both dimensions is discussed, using the empirical and theoretical literature on the political and economic systems of the EU. The discussion illustrates that most reform issues that promise to boost democratic legitimacy can be subsumed under the dimension of vertical integration.

A conceptual definition of preferences is explored, on the assumption of being sincere, stable, intransitive, comparable and realistic, followed by a discussion of the possibilities for reducing governments' preferences on the multitude of individual issues to a few crucial dimensions of intergovernmental conflict. In contrast to previous studies, the argument here is that the conflict over vertical integration and the conflict over the decision rule cannot be reduced any further. Instead, there is an expectation of a truly two-dimensional intergovernmental conflict space. In the long run, governmental positions are restricted by the corridor of country-specific socio-economic characteristics. However, in the short and medium terms, changes of governmental positions are best conceived of as resulting from domestic politics involving voters, parties and parliaments. Finally, the conditionality between the choice of decision rule and the choice of vertical integration is discussed, in particular, the expectation that the intensity and direction of such complementary preferences vary according to member states' economic power.

The focus on governmental positions is justified. In contrast to previous studies, it is argued that treaty reforms must be to the benefit of all governments. The history of post-Maastricht treaty revisions are reviewed as a sequence of equilibrium and disequilibrium, whilst the importance of procedural constraints for the post-Maastricht treaty revisions are examined. In particular, it is argued that because of the increased number of member states, the changing nature of the conflict space and the invocation of the Convention, intergovernmental bargaining is subject to procedural constraints.

In the remainder of this book, empirical proof will be provided for my hypotheses about intergovernmental conflict space, the domestic origins of governmental positions and an explanation for the observed treaty revisions.

chapter three | patterns of intergovernmental conflict

EMPIRICAL METHODOLOGY

In this section, the relevant methodological issues in the empirical derivation of policy spaces are briefly discussed, in particular, the idea underlying spatial utility functions and its relationship to the subsequent statistical model. Next, the available data on governments' reform preferences at the IGCs of Amsterdam, Nice and Rome II, as well as data on the preferences of the governmental delegates at the Convention on the Future of Europe is presented, followed by a discussion of the validity of the data and a justification of the chosen methodology.

SPATIAL MODELS

Politicians who belong to the same coalition of interests tend to stick their heads together in one corner of the conference room. It appears that thinking of politics in terms of space is almost natural. Acknowledging this observation, Aristotle long ago knew that 'you will be safest in the middle' (Hinich and Munger 1997: 21). In modern political science and economics, the idea of spatial competition was revived by Hotelling (1929), but the final breakthrough did not come until Downs wrote *An Economic Theory of Democracy* (1957) and Black proposed the Median Voter Theorem (1958). After that, it took another twenty years for spatial theory to become an inherent part of political science (Riker 1980; Schofield and McKelvey 1986; McKelvey 1976).

The increasing popularity of spatial models raised the question of how to determine the relevant number of dimensions in a political system. Essentially, this is the question of how the researcher can reduce actors' preferences to an ideal position in a lower-dimensional latent political space, a strategy discussed in Chapter 2. However, as soon as researchers began aggregating observed political behaviours for theoretical analysis, they confronted a set of methodological concerns. How do the decisions of one actor relate to those of another in a meaningful way to produce a strategy? Can coalitions of actors be identified with similar interests or typical conflicts among actors? These problems are apparent regardless of the data source for actors' preferences – texts, voting behaviours, interviews, or even secondary socio-economic data.

A helpful starting point is the question of how the relevant actors themselves perceive dimensionality. What beliefs do they hold about their own and other actors' positions, strategies and voting decisions? The cognitive abilities of individuals reduce the number of feasible dimensions. Furthermore, procedural and institutional constraints, such as party groups and committees, lead actors to subdivide their decision in lower dimensional issue spaces (Shepsle 1979). Accordingly, a common presumption holds that the real issue space is of very high dimensionality, but the ideal points of political actors can be captured in a lower-dimensional space (Ordeshook 1976; Hinich and Pollard 1981). It is beyond question that higher-dimensional models explain a larger share of the observed variance, but this additional explanatory power comes at the price of increasing complexity, which is reflected in a higher number of parameters (Box 1976: 792).[1]

As a convention, a government's utility loss is specified as the distance between its ideal position, vector X, and a policy vector ω. More specifically, in the two-dimensional model outlined in Chapter 2, the ideal position of government i would be $X_i = \{K_i^*; E_i^*\}$, henceforth $X_i = \{x_{i1}; x_{i2}\}$. As far as policies are concerned, we are particularly interested in two vectors: the status quo of European integration, $\omega = \{sq_1; sq_2\}$, henceforth sq; and the outcome of any treaty reform, $\omega = \{o_1; o_2\}$, henceforth o. Accordingly, the utility under reform o of governments $i = 1, 2, 3 \ldots n$ across the dimensions $j = 1, 2$ is equivalent to:

$$U_i(o, sq) = \sqrt{(x_i - sq)(x_i - sq)} - \sqrt{(x_i - o)(x_i - o)} \qquad \text{Equation 3.1}$$

The theoretical discussion in Chapter 2 leads to an expectation that there are two intergovernmental conflict dimensions. One centres on the level of vertical integration and the other on the choice of the decision rule. It is reasonable to suspect that governmental preferences are nonseparable across the two dimensions. Furthermore, actors may regard different issue dimensions as more or less salient. On the one hand, this raises questions about the correct aggregation rule to use to determine an actor's overall utility. On the other hand, the matter of salience has implications for the explanatory model. If, for example, actors attach different levels of salience to different dimensions, they might agree on package deals across dimensions (Stokman and Van Oosten 1994). Besides, conflict dimensions can have varying degrees of importance for different member states.

To account for the potential conditionality between the two dimensions and for salience, the above utility function can be extended by a positive semidefinite 2 × 2 matrix A. In the main diagonal of A ($a_{11}, a_{22} \geq 0$), we find the salience that government i attaches to each of the two dimensions. The higher the value, the more important the dimension for the government's utility calculation. Accordingly, the elements a_{12} and a_{21} capture the conditionality in the government's utility calculation over both dimensions. However, the standard statistical model of ideal point estimation assumes that the dimensions are equally salient and separable, hence it assumes that $A = \begin{bmatrix} 1 & 0 \\ 0 & 1 \end{bmatrix}$

$$U_i(o, sq) = \sqrt{(x_i - sq) A_i (x_i - sq)} - \sqrt{(x_i - o) A_i (x_i - o)} \qquad \text{Equation 3.2}$$

In Chapter 6, this standard model is explored further to account for the possibil-

---

1. Technically, an additional dimension can be treated as just another hyperparameter in the explanatory statistical model (Jackman 2001: 231).

ity of nonseparable preferences. The next section describes the available data on governments' reform preferences as expressed at Amsterdam, Nice, the European Convention and Rome III, followed by a brief discussion of the statistical method of choice.

DATA

In December 1995, the so-called Reflection Group (created by the member states) presented a set of issues to be covered at the subsequent *Amsterdam* IGC. In response to this action by the member states, the EP formed its own Task Force to analyse possible reform proposals and make recommendations. For this purpose, it collected the preferences of all seventeen delegations to the IGC and presented these preferences for comparison to the status quo.[2] The Task Force emphasised that, despite their provisional nature, the tables of policy preferences 'offer a reasonably reliable summary of the present situation as regards the IGC and should improve understanding of the Conference' (JF/bo/290/97: 1). The initial set covers 228 single issues.[3] However, König and Hug (2002) examined this data set and identified a set of ninety-seven contentious and important issues (Hug and König 2002: 458).

In addition, Thurner *et al.* (2002) compiled a second data set on governmental positions via expert interviews. They developed a questionnaire by first analysing the *fiches* provided by the Services Juridiques in preparation for the Westendorp report[4] (2002: 25). The questionnaire comprises forty-six questions, which were put to 124 top-level bureaucrats (roughly 20 per cent of member states' positions are missing). The forty-six questions cover six categories: 1) legal status and rights; 2) common foreign and defence policy; 3) justice and home affairs; 4) decision-making institutions; 5) the role of European and national parliaments; and 6) other policy areas (e.g. employment, environment) (2002: 169). The issues dealing with the decision-making institutions comprised the composition and accountability of the European Commission, the election and composition of the EP, the decision-making rule in the Council, and the possibilities for Enhanced Cooperation. Unfortunately, the data were not gathered until the period between

---

2. The data used here were published by the EP under the following reference: European Parliament (1997). Summary of the Positions of the Member States and the European Parliament on the 1996 Intergovernmental Conference, JF/bo/290/97, Luxembourg, 12 May.

3. The headings of the report are: 1.1. Citizenship and Fundamental Rights; 1.2 Third Pillar; 1.3 Employment; 1.4 Overseas Territories; 1.5 Environment; 1.6 Subsidiarity; 1.7 Transparency and Simplification; 2.1 The European Parliament; 2.2 National Parliaments; 2.3 The Council; 2.4 The Commission; 2.5 The Court of Auditors; 2.6 The European Court of Justice; 2.7 Fight against Fraud; 2.8 Differentiated Integration and Flexibility; 2.9 The Committee of Regions; 2.10 Hierarchy of Legal Acts and Budgetary Matters; 2.11 New Policy Areas; 2.12 The Economic and Monetary Union; 3.1 The Common Foreign and Defence Policy; 3.2 The Defence Policy and the WEU.

4. The Westendorp report was the outcome of an intergovernmental reflection group chaired by the Spanish President (Carlos Westendorp). It was presented at the Council of Madrid in December 1995.

May 2000 and March 2001 (2002: 23).

Slapin (2006: 12) cross-validated both data sources, and he was able to match seventy-four of the 249 issues mentioned in the EP task force report using the information in Thurner *et al.*'s data. He found 959 actor positions present in both data sets, 84 per cent of which are identical. Given this high level of cross-validity, the subsequent analysis is restricted to the survey data provided by Thurner *et al.* (2002). To facilitate interpretation, Thurner *et al.*'s forty-six questions have been recoded such that the smallest value indicates the least integrationist position.[5] The polytomous variables provide between two and seven categories.

Governments' positions at *Nice* were gathered via an expert survey conducted during November and December 2000 at the University of Constance (König and Luetgert 2003). The research team developed questions by systematic document analysis. In addition, they conducted a pretest to ensure that the questionnaire covered the entire issue space. Most interviews were conducted via telephone, some were online, and only a very few were face to face. About 70 per cent of the interviewees were employed by the governments of the member states, while the rest were working in, or associated with, academia. Finally, each country was represented by a minimum of one and a maximum of four interviews.[6] The data show relatively high cross-expert validity (about 90 per cent).

The survey asked thirteen more-or-less institutional questions, covering nineteen policy areas. The institutional questions referred to the organisation of the Commission, the composition of the ECJ, Court of Auditors, Committee of Regions and Economic and Social Committee, the European Public Prosecutor, the accountability of the Commission, seat allocation in the EP, weighting of votes, principles of QMV, application of legislative procedures, and closer cooperation. The answer categories were generated systematically via document analysis and validated in a pretest. In addition, the experts were asked whether their respective governments thought the following policy areas should be domestic competences, EU competences with the unanimity voting rule, or EU competences with the qualified majority voting rule: defence, environment, currency, cooperation with developing countries, health and social welfare, basic rules for media and press, workers' rights, immigration policy, fundamental human rights, the fight against unemployment, agriculture and fishing, support for economically-depressed regions, education, technological research, value added tax, foreign policy, cultural policy, and the fight against drugs. The response categories were ordered such that the smallest value indicates the least integrationist or, more generally, reformist position. The polytomous variables in the final data set have between two and four categories. The final missing data count amounts to less than 2 per cent.

The same research group conducted interviews to gather the positions repre-

---

5. Here 'least integrationist' means limited transfer of powers or competences to the EU, and limited departure from the principles of equality and consensus, which guarantees member states' individual veto power.

6. Furthermore, the data set contains information on four candidate countries (Slovenia, Slovakia, Bulgaria, Malta).

sented by the delegates of the *Convention on the Future of Europe*. However, this time, they primarily used mail instead of online interviews. The questionnaire was sent to the 102 delegates of the Convention, sixty-eight of whom responded, covering each of the fifteen member states as well as the ten accession states (König et al. 2006: 27).

The issue space of the questionnaire was developed by analysing the very first documents published by the Convention. The policy areas covered are CFSP, cooperation with developing countries, immigration and asylum, human rights, justice, the fight against drugs, health, social policy, taxes and economic policy, unemployment, workers' rights, agriculture and fishery, education, research, consumer protection, traffic and infrastructure, basic rules for the media, data protection, and industry. Institutional issues included the division of competences, voting rules in the council, voting weights, the role of parliament, qualified majority voting, the number and division of seats in EP, the election of the EP, the organisation and election/nomination of the Commission, the role of national parliaments, the right of initiative, the application of legislative procedures, the organisation of council work, the council presidency, and the number of Commissioners. The same coding rule was applied as for Amsterdam and Nice. In total, the data set comprises forty-eight polytomous variables with a maximum of five categories.

Finally, an international research group working together in the Domestic Structures and European Integration (DOSEI) project gathered information on governmental positions expressed at Rome II (König and Hug 2006). To identify the issue space, the group used the Convention documents, especially the amendments, from which they extracted a first set of contested issues.[7] The criteria to determine the final set of sixty-five issues for the DOSEI questionnaire were: a) thematic classification (synthesis), b) number of proposed amendments (prominence), and c) the number of proposed alternatives (thematic variety) (König and Hug 2006: 10). In total, they interviewed eighty-two experts, forty-seven (57 per cent) of whom were from inside government. They finished the majority of these interviews before Christmas 2003 (83 per cent). They completed the remaining interviews by February 2004, with the notable exception of three additional interviews conducted in May 2004 to gather the position of the new Spanish government. The adjusted cross-validity of the experts was about 85 per cent, and missing data amounted to 3.3 per cent[8] (for details, see König and Hug 2006: 5). A broader classification lists twenty-five issues as substantial, and another forty issues as institutional topics that cover the following policy areas: agriculture, structure and cohesion, area of freedom, security and justice, foreign and defence, social, health, environmental, education, research, fiscal, monetary, economic, and employment.

---

7. The construct validity of the questionnaire listing these issues and alternatives was examined in a pretest done with the German scientific adviser of a German Convention member, Professor Oppermann.

8. The experts mentioned a total of 110 relevant domestic actors; seventy-three (67 per cent) were governmental actors, and the remaining actors were members of parliamentary committees and interest groups.

The validity of the DOSEI data has been extensively tested (see König et al. 2006; König and Hug 2006: 5). Nevertheless, I conducted an additional cross-check, analysing the EP Task Force Report compiled by the Committee on Constitutional and Foreign Affairs just before the IGC. However, the information in this report is at a higher level of aggregation. Using its nineteen issues, I could match seventeen of the sixty-five issues in the DOSEI data. Within these seventeen issues, there are 340 actor positions present in both data sets, 87 per cent of which are in agreement.

MODEL

In recent years, the statistical modeling of ideal point estimation has experienced significant progress. This development has its roots in the increasing calculation power of computers, which allows for the estimation of Bayesian models (e.g. Clinton et al. 2004; Jackman 2001; Martin and Quinn 2002). These models have been most frequently used to examine roll call votes in the US Congress (e.g. Poole and Rosenthal 2000; Clinton et al. 2004), in the US Supreme Court (Martin and Quinn 2002), in the UN General Assembly (Voeten 2005; Kim and Russett 1996), in the EP (Han 2007; Hix et al. 2007), and in the Council of Ministers (Hoyland and Hagemann 2008). Currently, the most frequently used model resembles the two-parametric item response model, which was developed in psychometrics. Its direct correspondence to the Euclidean utility-loss function is a primary advantage over other techniques, such as multidimensional scaling, standard factor analysis, principal components analysis, or correspondence analysis. This model assumes that each legislator has an ideal point and chooses the alternative closest to this ideal point. Moreover, each issue (or item) is assumed to have a difficulty parameter, α_j, and a discrimination parameter, β_j. The former captures the overall difficulty across all actors to agree to a reform proposal on issue j, and the latter captures the extent to which issue j discriminates between the latent dimensions of conflict in a given proposal space.[9] Theoretically, the two-parameter item response model corresponds to the Euclidean voting model as follows. Let the d-dimensional conflict space be defined by the choices of $i = 1, 2, ..., n$ actors over $j = 1, 2, ..., m$ issues, and let an actor's preference on an alternative follow a quadratic utility function. Then, his observed choice $Y^*_{i,j}$ follows the latent utility calculation:

$$Y^*_{i,j} = U_i(sq_i) - U_i(o_j) = \sqrt{(x-sq)'(x-sq)} + \eta_{i,j} - \sqrt{(x} \quad \text{Equation 3.3}$$

$$= 2(o_j - sq_j)'x_i - o_j'o_j + sq_j'sq_j + \eta_{i,j} - v_{i,j} \quad \text{Equation 3.4}$$

$$= -\alpha_j + \beta_j'x_i + \varepsilon_{i,j} \quad \text{Equation 3.5}$$

---

9. In a one-dimensional conflict space, $-\frac{\alpha_j}{\beta_j}$ defines the cut point; i.e. the ideal point of an actor who is indifferent between the status quo and the reform proposal. In multidimensional spaces, this formula extends to cutting lines or hyper planes, respectively (Clinton et al. 2004).

where O_j denotes the reform proposal and sq_j the status quo on issue j;[10] $v_{i,j}$ and $\eta_{i,j}$ are the error terms of the utility calculation. More precisely, the parameters correspond as follows (Clinton *et al.* 2004):

$$\beta_j = 2(o_j - sq_j); \; -\alpha_j = o_j'o_j + sq_j'sq_j \, ; \varepsilon_{i,j} = \eta_{i,j} + v_{i,j}$$

The application of this model to the research question in this book is somewhat complicated by the fact that we are interested in the comparison of governmental positions across time; i.e. across IGCs. To solve this problem, the literature suggests that item or person parameters must be constrained (Bailey 2007). For example, if actors from different institutions or IGCs are confronted with an identical choice (same set of alternatives for the same issue), the corresponding item parameters may be constrained to be identical. In other words, one question can only have one meaning for the common issue space of all three IGCs. Hence, a direct comparison is only possible if at least two surveys contained questions that were identical and offered the same answer and reference categories. This criterion is only met by a minority of the variables in our data sets. The majority of questions on similar issues used different wordings and different answer categories. The following example illustrates the problem. The Dutch government preferred more EU competences in the area of employment at Amsterdam but was satisfied with the EU's competences in the same policy area at Nice. Two explanations are possible. First, the different answers might be due to the reforms agreed to under the Treaty of Amsterdam. Second, the Dutch might have changed their position on this issue. However, we cannot know which of these explanations is true. Fortunately, this ambiguity is not present in all questions. The Appendix provides a list of those questions in which a direct comparison between different data sets is possible (Finke 2009a). These questions, henceforth called item-level 'bridgers', were asked in at least two of (and some of them in all) three surveys.

Bailey (2007) discusses indirect constraints on item parameters as another method to enable cross-institutional comparison. This option exists when the set of answer categories is not identical but can be rank ordered across IGCs. The simplest implementation of such constraints would be to recode two similar variables into one new variable (Uebersax 1991). However, there are only a few possibilities for such item-level constraints in the present data, and in any case, the number of bridgers allows for sufficient matching of items across the three data sets.

Finally, cross-IGC comparison could benefit from the fact that the same actors participate in more than one IGC. Accordingly, we might want to constrain the position of this actor to be similar in both rounds of intergovernmental bargaining. However, given that I am interested in positional change, it seems counterintuitive to constrain member states' positions to be constant in the first place. Therefore, I assume that member states' positions are independent across IGCs. Martin and Quinn (2002) discuss the possibility of explicitly modelling the interdependency or dynamics of actors' ideal points across time. Fortunately, and in contrast to

---

10. The extension to more than two alternatives is straightforward (Johnson and Albert 1999: 182).

Martin and Quinn's examination of the US Supreme Court,[11] the present estimation does not require loosening the independence assumption.

The European treaties were coded as additional cases in the data sets. Both the ToA and the ToN serve a double purpose. The ToA served as the outcome of the Amsterdam IGC and as the status quo for the Nice IGC. Accordingly, it is contained as a case in both data sets. The ToN was the outcome of the Nice IGC and the status quo for Rome II as well as for the preceding Convention. It, too, is contained as a case in both data sets. The parameters of both treaties are constrained to be identical across IGCs.

RESULTS

Before turning to the results, it is worth briefly describing the most important points of the estimation strategy. The item response model described in Equation 3.1 is fitted using a probit link. The model is globally identified by normalising the latent trait; i.e. mean = zero, and variance = unity (Rivers 2003). Finally, identification is ensured by an *ex post procruste* transformation of the ideal points.[12] The algorithm was implemented in GAUSS 9.0. The subsequent estimates rely on the following survey data.[13] For Amsterdam, the matrix includes information on fifteen national positions plus the ToA for forty-three issues. For Nice, it has information on fifteen national positions plus the ToA and the ToN for thirty-two issues. For Rome II, it includes information on twenty-five national positions plus the ToN for sixty-three issues. Accordingly, the data matrix used for estimation has 57×138 ($= 7{,}866$) cells, 4,822 of which are empty. Overall, twelve items had to be excluded from the analysis because their values were constant across actors; i.e. all governments held the same position. To maintain the intergovernmental character of the resulting conflict space, the Treaty of Maastricht, the Constitutional Treaty, the Convention proposal and the positions of the Convention delegates were located in the resulting latent space ex post estimation. Overall, the two-dimensional model estimates 821 parameters[14] for 138 items and 57 cases. Convergence[15]

---

11. Martin and Quinn (2002) analysed roll call votes of the US Supreme Court. They developed their dynamic ideal point estimator to allow for some change of judges' positions across time. However, their data set does not provide for any item-level bridgers. This would only be needed if a judicial case repeated itself.
12. Essentially, this procedure rotates the entire posterior distribution according to an exogenously given criterion. In this case, I chose the logic underlying standard principal component analysis.
13. To increase the number of unambiguous bridgers, the analysis adds information from the EP Task Force Reports. For details please consult the appendix.
14. There were 138 item difficulty parameters, 276 item discrimination parameters, 114 person parameters and 293 cutoff parameters.
15. I validated the convergence according to three criteria. First, visual inspections of the trace plots. Second, reestimation of the model to see whether the results could be reproduced and were independent of the starting values. Both analytical steps lead to satisfactory results. Third, the algorithm appears to be reasonably efficient, with acceptance rates for the cutoff parameters varying between a minimum of 0.49 and a maximum of 0.83, with a mean of 0.61 (Johnson and Albert 1999: 54).

was reached after a burn-in period of approximately 10,000 iterations. The subsequent analysis is based on another 15,000 draws from the posterior distribution.[16]

Table 3.1 summarises the model's predictive power relative to the null model (chance) and a one-dimensional model. The two-dimensional model predicts roughly 74 per cent of the cases correctly, and according to the log-likelihood and Akaike's Information Criterion (AIC),[17] it performs better than the one-dimensional and the null model. However, adding a third dimension would not cause a significant increase in the model's explanatory power. In other words, the optimal number of latent dimensions is indeed two, which supports my Hypothesis 1.1.

Table 3.1: Model comparison: predictive power of the one- and two-dimensional model as compared to chance

	2-D	1-D	Chance
% correct predictions	73.6	63.4	38.4
log-likelihood	-814.6	-997.2	-1311.5
AIC	5485.5	5772.2	5901.6

In the next section, the estimated ideal points and their changes across the three IGCs are discussed, followed by an analysis of the substantial meaning of the latent conflict space.

GOVERNMENTAL POSITIONS

To begin with, the estimates of governmental positions for each of the two dimensions are discussed separately. In particular, I am interested in whether or not these positions have changed from one IGC to the next. For now, there is an assumption that one dimension represents vertical integration and the second dimension represents the reform of the decision rule. Indeed, the discussion of the item parameters later will prove this to be true.

Figure 3.1 depicts the national positions on European integration as revealed at the IGCs of Amsterdam (dot),[18] Nice (diamond) and Rome II (triangle). A comparison of the Euro-sceptical Danish with the prointegrationist Italian position revealed at Amsterdam illustrates the scope of the cross-country variation. On the side of the integration sceptics, we find Denmark and Ireland at all three IGCs, the UK, Sweden and Portugal at Amsterdam, and Hungary, Poland and Estonia at Rome II. By contrast, the most integration-friendly governments came from six founding members plus Spain at Amsterdam, the Benelux countries plus Portugal, Spain and Greece at Nice, and Greece and Belgium at Rome II.

The Italian case is also a good example of change across time. At Amsterdam,

---

16. The chain has been thinned, using every 10th value only.

17. $AIC = 2k - 2ln(L)$, where k denotes the number of parameters and L denotes the likelihood (Akaike 1974).

18. For the Amsterdam IGC, the results are highly correlated (Pearson's $r > 0.7$) with positions used by Aspinwall (2007). However, Aspinwall simply sums governments' positions across all issues contained in the data set.

the first Prodi government maintained an extremely prointegrationist course. By contrast, the succeeding government of D'Alema, and especially the first Berlusconi government, turned out to be significantly less integrationist. Furthermore, the estimates locate the New Labour government in Britain to the right of its conservative predecessor, and the Schröder-run German government was significantly less integrationist at Nice than the Kohl government was at Amsterdam. Thus, on first glance, Figure 3.1 supports my critical reevaluation of the unitary actor assumption: if governments are the representatives of nonunitary member states, their positions will change in response to domestic changes, such as a new partisan composition of government or parliament. However, not all positional changes correspond to shifts in the partisan composition of the government. For example, the Swedish government was dominated by the Social Democrats throughout the period of observation. Nevertheless, Figure 3.1 indicates significant differences between the Swedish positions at Amsterdam, Nice and Rome II. In addition, Figure 3.1 contains the 95 per cent confidence intervals. This information allows us to judge whether two positions are significantly different, as in the Swedish example, or not, as in the case of the Austrian position, which has been remarkably stable.

Figure 3.1 also depicts the results of a second model, which constrains each member states' ideal point to be stable across all three IGCs. This model predicts only 63 per cent of the cases correctly. In addition, the insufficiency of this stability assumption becomes apparent when the location of the treaties is considered. According to the original model, which allowed for positional change, the post-Maastricht treaty revisions resemble a steady increase in integration. This picture reflects our knowledge about the Treaties of Amsterdam and Nice, as well as the Constitutional Convention and the Lisbon Treaty. By contrast, when we assume stable positions, the estimates can no longer discriminate between the Treaties of Amsterdam and Nice.

Figure 3.2 depicts the estimates for the second dimension, which contributes only half as much to the overall explanation as the first dimension. It shows the national positions on the decision rule revealed at the IGCs of Amsterdam (dot),[19] Nice (diamond) and Rome II (triangle). Governments markedly rejecting any reforms toward an increase in majoritarianism were Austria, Greece, Belgium, Portugal, Denmark, Ireland and Luxembourg at Amsterdam; the Netherlands, Luxembourg and Sweden at Nice; and the Slovak, Czech and Danish governments at Rome II. Again, it comes as no surprise that governments from smaller states dislike reforms of the decision rule, as most proposals contained elements of proportional representation. Accordingly, the opposing coalition forms around the governments from larger member states: France and the UK at Amsterdam; Italy, Germany, France and the UK at Nice; Italy, Germany, France and Spain at Rome II.

---

19. For the Amsterdam IGC, the results are highly correlated (Pearson's $r > 0.7$) with positions used by Aspinwall (2007).

patterns of intergovernmental conflict | 83

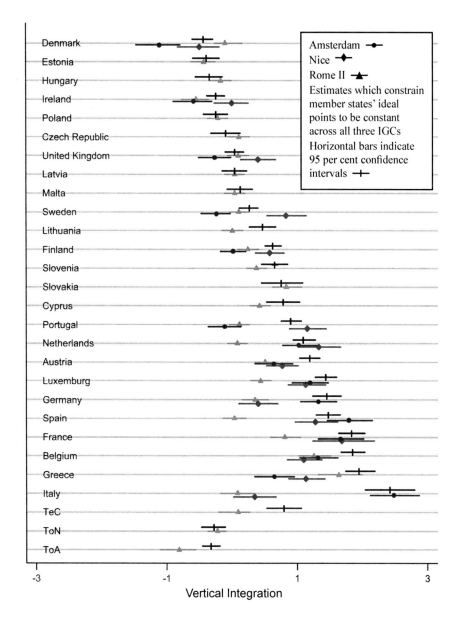

Figure 3.1: Governmental positions on European integration at Amsterdam, Nice and Rome II

Hence, the more interesting questions centre on the positional changes of individual member states. Why, for example, did the Italian government reject reforms of the decision rule at Amsterdam but back the most drastic reform proposals at Nice and Rome II? How do these changes correspond to the changes in government from Prodi to D'Alema and Berlusconi? A similar sequence of positional changes can be observed for Germany, whereas the French position on the decision rule was relatively stable. Finally, the British position moved in the opposite direction, demanding less progressive reforms at Rome II than it did previously at Amsterdam and Nice. On the other hand, the Austrian position, which had been remarkably stable on the first dimension, changed from the most vigorous reform opponent at Amsterdam toward a rather progressive stance at Nice and Rome II. The same is true for Ireland, Belgium, Luxembourg and, though less drastically, for Greece and Portugal. By contrast, the Danish position moved toward reform at Nice but back again at Rome II, whereas the Dutch became even more reform sceptical at Nice, only to jump toward a very progressive position at Rome II.

Overall, the 95 per cent confidence intervals are larger in comparison with those on the first dimension. However, this just reflects the lower explanatory power of this dimension. As for the first dimension, Figure 3.2 also depicts the model that restricts governmental positions to be stable across IGCs. Again, the treaty locations estimated by this model are inconsistent with our prior knowledge. It suggests that the ToN brought reforms toward unanimity voting and consensus, whereas the locations of the ToA and the TeC do not significantly differ.

SUBSTANTIAL INTERPRETATION

This section provides a substantial interpretation of the estimated conflict space. Please note that Chapter 4 is devoted to a more extensive discussion of each individual IGC. In Chapter 2, the proposals on the post-Maastricht reform agenda with respect to their potential costs and benefits was discussed, especially their effect on decision-making efficiency, legitimacy and economics of scale and scope. For the *dimension* depicted in Figure 3.2, the most relevant issues are the compositions of the Commission; the design and extension of QMV; the extension of, and rules for, Enhanced Cooperation; the duration, rotation and composition of the Council presidency and the allocation of seats in the EP, the Committee of Regions and the ESC; and the allocation of judges in the ECJ and the ECA. Crucial issues for *vertical integration* are the extension of competences (including the extended applicability of Enhanced Cooperation); the strength of individual legal rights (especially fundamental and human rights); the objectives of the EU; the empowerment of domestic actors such as national parliaments, regions and social partners; the empowerment of the EP (especially the extension of the codecision procedure); the financial and personal endowments of the ECA and ECJ; and all measures that increase the accessibility of information (e.g. public documents, public meetings) and the political accountability of EU-level actors (e.g. Minister of Foreign Affairs, long-term Council presidency).

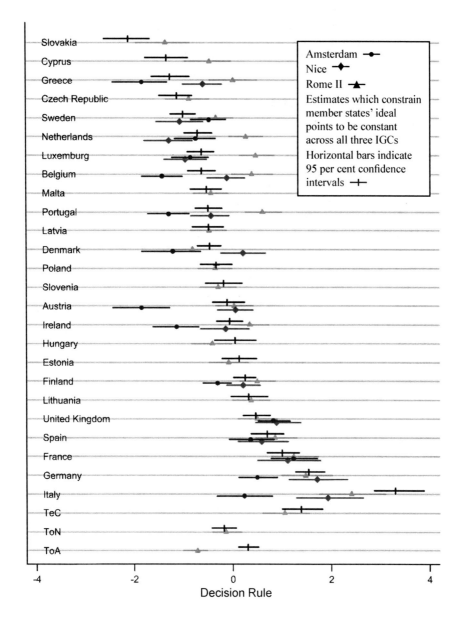

Figure 3.2: Governmental positions on reforming the decision rule at Amsterdam, Nice and Rome II

In Table 3.2, thirty-one of the 138 issues in the data set are assigned exclusively to the horizontal dimension. Another fifty-six issues are assigned to the vertical dimension, forty-five issues refer to both dimensions, and six do not fit into the theoretical framework at all.[20] Unfortunately, the Nice data include a battery of variables that link information on the preferred level of competence and the decision rule for nineteen policy areas.[21] Overall, the item discrimination parameters depicted in Table 3.2 reflect my theoretical expectations.

For those issues that theory assigns to the vertical dimension, there was an expectation of positive parameters because all variables have been coded such that large values indicate 'more integration', and indeed, Table 3.2 reveals large positive parameters for issues that refer to the EU's *political mandate*. This is especially true with respect to the division of competences in the second and third pillars, plus several so-called new policy areas (especially employment, health and social policy). Furthermore, large positive values can be found for the applicability of Enhanced or Closer Cooperation. Considering the fact that the discussion on Enhanced Cooperation focused on its extension to the area of CFSP, this is rather unsurprising. Other issues that would redefine the EU's political mandate reveal large positive values too. Examples are the employment objective, EU citizenship and the legal status of fundamental rights. In addition, issues that deal with the *empowerment of domestic actors* at the EU level reveal large positive parameters; in particular, the empowerment of the EP in the budgetary procedure and the extended applicability of the codecision procedure. Finally, Table 3.2 reveals significant and positive estimates for reform issues that strengthen *political accountability*, such as the election of the Council President and reform of the EU's external representation. Overall, the model was statistically significant for ninety-three of the ninety-seven issues assigned to the vertical dimension.

For the second *horizontal dimension*, the model returns significant parameters for the issues concerning the composition of the Commission and the applicability of Enhanced Cooperation, including the related areas of security and defence, and migration and asylum (see Table 3.2). With respect to Enhanced Cooperation, the minimum number of participants and the rules for initiation were hotly-contested issues. Furthermore, the extension of QMV and the design of the voting threshold and weights reveal significant and positive estimates on the horizontal dimension. Finally, for the Nice IGC, the allocation of seats in the EP and the number of judges in the ECA return significant values, too. Overall, the model turns out statistically significant for thirty-one of the forty-three issues that theory assigns to the horizontal dimension.

---

20. The following issues can hardly be attributed to either of the two dimensions: inclusion of a religious reference, right of withdrawal, the legal personality of the EU, exception from SEM strict environmental rules, and the internal hierarchy of the Commission (see Table 3.3).

21. The interviewee could choose between 'domestic competence', 'EU competence, but unanimity' and 'EU competence and QMV'. However, I recoded each of these variables into two dichotomous variables, the first one indicating whether or not the government preferred the EU level, and the second one differentiating between unanimity and QMV. I then reestimated the model, but the results do not differ significantly.

Table 3.2: Item discrimination and difficulty parameters, labels, theoretical assignment to either of the two conflict dimensions and short descriptions for 138 issues

Question	Short Description	Assignment	Disc.1	Disc.2	Diff.	Question	Short Description	Assignment	Disc.1	Disc.2	Diff.
A_1.1	Citizenship of the Union	vertical	-0.336	1.611*	-0.304	A_4.1	EP (allocation of seats)	horizontal	0.588*	1.406*	-0.442
A_1.3	Fundamental Rights (introduction)	vertical	-0.350	0.684*	-1.136*	A_4.2	EP (introduction of uniform electoral procedures)	vertical	-0.005	1.596*	-0.120
A_1.4	Fundamental Rights (monitoring)	vertical	0.070	1.406*	-1.225*	A_4.3	QMV (extension)	horizontal	-0.453*	0.818*	-1.091*
A_1.5	Principle of Subsidiarity (introduction)	vertical	0.092	-0.089*	-0.326	A_4.4	QMV (threshold)	horizontal	-1.054*	0.706*	-0.688*
A_1.6	Principle of Subsidiarity (monitoring)	vertical	-0.686*	1.651*	0.160	A_4.5	QMV (voting weights)	horizontal	1.024*	1.358*	0.489
A_1.7	Transparency of Council meetings	vertical	-0.441*	0.660*	0.053	A_4.6	QMV (dual majority)	horizontal	0.682*	0.938*	-0.149
A_1.8	Legal Personality of the Union	vertical	-0.018	1.767*	0.071	A_4.7	Commission (composition)	horizontal	1.927*	1.133*	0.506
A_2.1	CFSP (planning and preparation)	vertical	-0.402*	1.374*	0.489	A_4.8	Enhanced Cooperation (flexibility clause)	horizontal/vertical	1.263*	1.488*	-1.174*
A_2.2	CFSP (application of QMV)	horizontal	-0.976*	1.703*	-1.358*	A_4.9	Enhanced Cooperation (conditions for flexibility: application of QMV)	horizontal	0.284	0.593*	0.288

Question	Short Description	Assignment	Disc.1	Disc.2	Diff.	Question	Short Description	Assignment	Disc.1	Disc.2	Diff.
A_2.3	CFSP (implementation and ext. representation)	vertical	-0.426*	1.254*	-0.820*	A_5.2	EP (application and reform of procedures)	vertical	-0.291	1.444*	-0.982*
A_2.4	CFSP (financing)	horizontal	-1.500*	0.407	-0.839*	A_5.3	EP (scope of co-decision and assent)	vertical	-0.442*	0.729*	-0.622*
A_2.5	Common Defence Policy	vertical	-0.367*	1.556*	0.004	A_5.4	Commission (role of EP in nomination)	vertical	-0.017	0.890*	-0.044
A_2.6	Relations with WEU	vertical	-0.285*	1.180*	-0.922*	A_5.5	EP (budgetary powers)	vertical	0.329	1.759*	-0.089
A_2.7	Common Armament Policy	vertical	0.061	2.176*	-0.504	A_5.6	National Parliaments (powers in legislative process)	vertical	-0.068	0.263	-0.713*
A_3.1	JHA (EU competences)	vertical	0.447	2.326*	0.346	A_5.7	Commission (powers in legislative process)	horizontal/ vertical	-1.078*	1.455*	-0.810*
A_3.2	JHA (applicability of EC method)	vertical	-0.578*	0.636*	-0.786*	A_5.8	ECJ (jurisdiction)	vertical	0.013	1.607*	-0.091
A_3.3	JHA (application of QMV)	horizontal	-0.713*	0.729*	-0.260	A_5.9	Committee of Regions (areas of consultation & inst. autonomy)	vertical	-0.843*	1.216*	-0.085
A_3.4	JHA (democratic control)	vertical	-1.263*	1.408*	-0.427	A_5.10	ESC (areas of consultation & inst. autonomy)	vertical	-0.275	0.939*	-0.092

patterns of intergovernmental conflict | 89

Question	Short Description	Assignment	Disc.1	Disc.2	Diff.	Question	Short Description	Assignment	Disc.1	Disc.2	Diff.
A_3.5	JHA (judicial control)	vertical	-0.603*	1.030*	-0.981*	A_6.1	Employment (chapter and objective)	vertical	-1.321*	1.502*	-0.582
A_6.2	Employment (monitoring committee)	vertical	-1.411*	0.625*	-0.272	N_II7	Closer cooperation	horizontal/vertical	1.343*	1.556*	-0.821*
A_6.3	Environment (EU competences & role of EP)	vertical	-0.629*	0.238	-1.511*	N_III1	Level of competence & voting rule: defence	vertical/(horizontal)	0.537*	1.780*	0.057
A_6.4	Environment (exception from SEM)	—	0.223	-0.402	-1.740*	N_III2	Level of competence & voting rule: environmental protection	vertical/(horizontal)	-0.182*	0.530*	-1.271*
A_6.5	New Policy Areas (EU competences)	vertical	-0.322*	0.808*	0.301	N_III3	Level of competence & voting rule: monetary	vertical/(horizontal)	-0.465*	0.987*	-1.046*
A_6.6	External economic relations (EU competences)	vertical	-0.371	1.677*	0.108	N_III4	Level of competence & voting rule: cooperation with developing countries	vertical/(horizontal)	-0.696*	1.364*	-1.219*
N_I1	Number of Commissioners	horizontal	1.604*	1.352*	-1.489*	N_III5	Level of competence & voting rule: health and social welfare	vertical/(horizontal)	-0.748*	2.022*	-0.355

Question	Short Description	Assignment	Disc.1	Disc.2	Diff.	Question	Short Description	Assignment	Disc.1	Disc.2	Diff.
N_I2.1	ECJ (composition)	horizontal	*0.073*	0.587*	1.108*	N_III6	Level of competence & voting rule: basic rules for media and press	vertical/ (horizontal)	-0.267*	0.759*	-0.173
N_I2.2	ECA (composition)	horizontal	0.908*	0.880*	1.056*	N_III7	Level of competence & voting rule: workers' rights vis-a-vis their employers	vertical/ (horizontal)	-0.156	1.252*	-0.534*
N_I2.3	Ctte. of Regions (composition)	horizontal	*-0.101*	0.265	0.182	N_III8	Level of competence & voting rule: Immigration policy	vertical/ (horizontal)	0.014	0.903*	-0.911*
N_I2.4	Economic and Social Committee (composition)	horizontal	*-0.110*	0.278	0.178	N_III9	Level of competence & voting rule: Fundamental Human Rights	vertical/ (horizontal)	-0.335*	1.683*	-0.518*
N_I3	European Public Prosecutor	vertical	0.154	0.586*	0.483*	N_III10	Level of competence & voting rule: fight against unemployment	vertical/ (horizontal)	-1.871*	1.930*	0.395
N_II1	Commission (internal hierarchy/ organisation)	—	-0.024	0.627*	-0.472*	N_III11	Level of competence & voting rule: agriculture and fishing	vertical/ (horizontal)	-0.111	*0.262*	-1.193*

Question	Short Description	Assignment	Disc.1	Disc.2	Diff.	Question	Short Description	Assignment	Disc.1	Disc.2	Diff.
N_I12	Commission (political accountability towards EP)	vertical	0.317*	0.711*	-0.800*	N_II12	Level of competence & voting rule: support for economically depressed regions	vertical/(horizontal)	-0.187*	0.325*	-1.193*
N_I13	EP (allocation of seats)	horizontal	0.719*	0.697*	0.706*	N_II13	Level of competence & voting rule: education	vertical/(horizontal)	-1.496*	1.412*	0.680*
N_I14	QMV (voting weights)	horizontal	1.020*	0.939*	0.043	N_II14	Level of competence & voting rule: technological research	vertical/(horizontal)	-0.673*	1.108*	-1.239*
N_I15	QMV (principle or case wise extension)	horizontal	0.681*	0.578*	-0.195	N_II15	Level of competence & voting rule: value added tax rates	vertical/(horizontal)	0.187	1.010*	-0.689*
N_I16	Co-decision (extension)	vertical	0.370	0.500*	-0.317	N_II16	Level of competence & voting rule: foreign policy towards non-EU countries	vertical/(horizontal)	-0.124	0.869*	-0.918*
N_II17	Level of competence & voting rule: cultural policy	vertical/(horizontal)	-0.968*	1.271*	0.273	R_13.a	Minister of Foreign Affairs (role of Commission in appointment)	vertical	0.187	1.334*	-1.188*

Question	Short Description	Assignment	Disc.1	Disc.2	Diff.	Question	Short Description	Assignment	Disc.1	Disc.2	Diff.
N_II18	Level of competence & voting rule: political asylum	vertical/ (horizontal)	0.175	0.637*	-0.985*	R_13.b	Minister of Foreign Affairs (role of EP in appointment)	vertical	-0.319*	-0.403*	0.267*
N_II19	Level of competence & voting rule: fight against drugs	vertical/ (horizontal)	-0.246*	1.436*	-0.572*	R_14	ECJ Jurisdiction	vertical	-0.479*	0.915*	-0.852*
R_1	Charter of Fundamental Rights	vertical	-0.182	1.444*	-0.807*	R_15.B	Legislative initiative for European Parliament	vertical	-0.374*	*0.210*	1.481*
R_2	Subsidiarity	vertical	-0.405*	0.615*	1.344*	R_15.C	Legislative initiative for Council	vertical	0.169	*0.183*	1.220*
R_3	Religious reference	—	0.010	0.745*	-0.137	R_15.E	Legislative initiative for citizens	vertical	0.388*	0.873*	0.725*
R_4	Right to withdraw from the Union	—	0.247*	0.751*	-0.350*	R_16	Enhanced cooperation	horizontal/ vertical	1.322*	1.828*	-1.621*
R_5.A	Economic objectives : market economy	vertical	0.643*	0.764*	-0.294*	R_17.1	Level of competence for Agriculture	vertical	-0.557*	1.044*	-1.119*
R_5.B	Economic objectives : employment	vertical	-0.206	1.483*	-1.477*	R_17.2	Level of competence for Structural and cohesion politics	vertical	-0.906*	1.240*	1.414*

patterns of intergovernmental conflict | 93

Question	Short Description	Assignment	Disc.1	Disc.2	Diff.	Question	Short Description	Assignment	Disc.1	Disc.2	Diff.
R_5.C	Economic objectives : competitiveness	vertical	-0.345	0.176	1.353*	R_17.3	Level of competence for the Area of Freedom, Security and Justice	vertical	0.445*	1.613*	-1.547*
R_6	Presidency of the European Council (organisation)	horizontal	0.192	1.267*	-0.699*	R_17.4	Level of competence for Foreign Policy	vertical	0.524*	1.726*	0.198
R_7	Presidency of the European Council (nomination)	vertical	-0.523*	0.329	0.661*	R_17.5	Level of competence for Economic Policy	vertical	-0.195	1.661*	0.631*
R_8	QMV	horizontal	0.508*	1.230*	-0.344*	R_17.6	Level of competence for Tax harmonisation	vertical	-0.015	0.709*	0.624*
R_9	Number of commissioners	horizontal	1.830*	0.718*	1.166*	R_17.7	Level of competence for Employment Policy	vertical	-0.922*	1.571*	0.871*
R_10	Appointment of Commission President (role of Council. EP or nat. parliaments)	vertical	-0.050	0.073	0.975*	R_17.8	Level of competence for Social Policy	vertical	-0.223	1.812*	0.937*
R_11	Appointment of Commissioners (role of EP)	vertical	0.319*	1.571*	0.363*	R_17.9	Level of competence for Health Policy	vertical	-0.032	1.232*	0.452*
R_12	External representation	vertical	0.159	1.271*	-0.512*	R_17.10	Level of competence for Environment Policy	vertical	-1.065*	1.444*	1.016*

Question	Short Description	Assignment	Disc.1	Disc.2	Diff.	Question	Short Description	Assignment	Disc.1	Disc.2	Diff.
R_17.11	Level of competence for Education Policy	vertical	-0.563*	1.200*	1.201*	R_18.B5	Decision rule (EP) for Tax harmonisation	vertical	0.111	1.967*	0.920*
R_17.12	Level of competence for research, technological development & space	vertical	0.103	1.819*	0.063	R_18.B6	Decision rule (EP) for Monetary policy	vertical	-0.723*	1.384*	0.157
R_18.A2	Voting rule (Council) for Structural and cohesion politics	horizontal	-0.170	0.947*	-1.123*	R_18.B7	Decision rule (EP) for Economic Policy	vertical	-0.860*	1.251*	0.259
R_18.A3	Voting rule (Council) for Area of Freedom, Security and Justice	horizontal	0.603*	0.322	-0.105	R_18.B8	Decision rule (EP) for Employment Policy	vertical	-0.360*	1.811*	-0.236
R_18.A5	Voting rule (Council) for Tax harmonisation	horizontal	1.299*	1.383*	0.790*	R_18.B9	Decision rule (EP) for Social Policy	vertical	0.000	1.057*	-0.458*
R_18.A6	Voting rule (Council) for Monetary policy	horizontal	0.086	1.848*	-0.583*	R_18.B10	Decision rule (EP) for Social security rights	vertical	-0.251	1.390*	0.605*
R_18.A7	Voting rule (Council) for Economic Policy	horizontal	-0.006	1.499*	-0.169	R_18.B11	Decision rule (EP) for Common Foreign Policy	vertical	-0.425*	1.156*	1.568*
R_18.A8	Voting rule (Council) for Employment Policy	horizontal	0.596*	0.304	-0.778*	R_18.B12	Decision rule (EP) for Defence Policy	vertical	-0.460*	1.175*	1.546*

Question	Short Description	Assignment	Disc.1	Disc.2	Diff.	Question	Short Description	Assignment	Disc.1	Disc.2	Diff.
R_18.A9	Voting rule (Council) for Social Policy	horizontal	1.055*	1.469*	-0.604*	R_19	Rights of EP in the adoption of the budget	vertical	0.015	0.631*	-0.272*
R_18.A10	Voting rule (Council) for Social Security rights	horizontal	0.242	1.543*	0.368*	R_20	SGP I (flexibility)	—	-0.223	0.416*	0.406*
R_18.A11	Voting rule (Council) for Common Foreign Policy	horizontal	1.667*	1.539*	0.423*	R_21	SGP II (debt/ GDP criterion)	—	0.140	0.866*	-0.230
R_18.A12	Voting rule (Council) for Defence Policy	horizontal	0.860*	2.134*	1.197*	R_22	Defence Cooperation	vertical	1.449*	2.252*	-0.289
R_18.B1	Decision rule (EP) for Agriculture	vertical	-0.379*	0.710*	-0.361*	R_23	External borders (management)	v/(h)	0.279	1.033*	-0.658*
R_18.B2	Decision rule (EP) for Structural and cohesion politics	vertical	-0.564*	1.287*	-1.064*	R_24	Migration and Asylum	v/(h)	1.103*	1.325*	-0.684*
R_18.B3	Decision rule (EP) for Area of Freedom, Security and Justice	vertical	-0.119	1.429*	-0.095	R_T1	Level of competence for Education Policy	vertical	-0.274	0.798*	0.312*
R_18.B4	Decision rule (EP) for Internal market	vertical	-0.815*	1.453*	-1.227*						

Note: * = 90 % confidence interval does include zero; Disc. 1= Item Discrimination Parameter Dimension 1; Disc. 2= Item Discrimination Parameter Dimension 2; Diff. = Item Difficulty Parameter; 'A_' refers to Amsterdam data; 'N_' refers to Nice data; 'R_' refers to data on Constitutional IGC; *Bold numbers are consistent with theoretical expectations.* Underlined numbers are not consistent with theoretical expectations.

Laursen (2006: 10) observes that the most prominent and salient issues at Nice, as compared with Amsterdam, centred on institutional design; i.e. on the horizontal distribution of power. Table 3.3 supports this observation. It reveals a smaller mean item discrimination parameter for the horizontal dimension at Amsterdam, whereas it reveals a smaller mean item discrimination parameter for the vertical dimension at Nice. It appears that only Rome II reveals equally intense conflict on both dimensions.

The item difficulty parameter α contains information on how contentious an issue is. If, for example, two out of fifteen governments favoured reform and the remaining thirteen opposed it, the item difficulty parameter would show large positive numbers. In contrast, if thirteen governments favoured reform and the remaining two were opposed, it would show large negative numbers. However, the interpretation is more interesting the better a particular item discriminates between actors' ideal points within the estimated latent space. Therefore, the large mean item difficulty parameter of Rome II (see Table 3.3) leads us to expect that Eastern enlargement increased the number of Euro-sceptical governments. This argument is confirmed by governmental positions discussed above.

Table 3.3: Means and standard deviation of the estimated item and person parameters

	Mean at Amsterdam (Std. Dev.)	Mean at Nice (Std. Dev.)	Mean at Rome II (Std. Dev.)
Item Discrimination β_1	-0.245 (0.698)	-0.021 (0.732)	0.057 (0.637)
Item Discrimination β_2	1.122 (0.575)	0.972 (0.496)	1.142 (0.551)
Item Difficulty α	-0.427 (0.576)	-0.367 (0.722)	0.091 (0.862)
Position x_1	0.653 (0.969)	0.775 (0.550)	0.251 (0.473)
Position x_2	-0.535 (0.941)	0.141 (0.937)	0.142 (0.796)

SUMMARY

In this chapter, the rich data collected on governmental preferences for each of the three IGCs and for the Convention is described. A statistical model is presented that corresponds to the Euclidean utility-loss function, which is crucial for the spatial analysis of politics. The model was applied to the data, and, by and large, the empirical results confirmed the theoretical expectations formulated in Chapter 2. The optimal number of dimensions is two, where one dimension represents conflict over the decision rule and the second dimension corresponds to vertical integration. Furthermore, the variance of the estimated parameters across member states and across time confirms existing qualitative studies on individual IGCs (e.g. Laursen 2006, 2002; Moravcsik and Nicolaïdis 1999) and the potential impact of enlargement (e.g. Heinemann 2003; König and Hug 2006). Next, the constellation of governmental positions within this two-dimensional conflict space will be discussed, and the implications for the observed treaty revisions at Amsterdam, Nice and Rome II.

chapter four | a short history of eu treaty negotiations

In this chapter, the statistical results *vis-à-vis* previous research on European treaty revisions are examined, in particular, how far the empirical results support the claim that the history of European treaty revisions can be described as a sequence of equilibrium and disequilibrium defined by national governments' reform positions. For this purpose, a brief summary is given of the reform agenda and governments' positions observed at all three IGCs. But where the IGCs at Amsterdam and Nice confirm the theory, the events at Rome II adhered to a slightly different logic. Especially, the ToN was more or less in equilibrium as defined by governments' positions in spring 2004. Nevertheless, the heads of state and government signed a progressive reform, namely the Treaty Establishing a Constitution for Europe. This raises the question of why some member states signed the reform treaty even though they preferred the Treaty of Nice. This section is concluded by discussing one possible answer: the procedural innovation presented by the European Convention.

AMSTERDAM

The so-called Amsterdam IGC was officially opened in Turin in April 1996 and concluded at the Amsterdam summit, April 16–17, 1997. It was the first IGC to take up the challenges of Europe's constitutional quandary, namely to ensure legitimacy, efficiency and integration against the background of Eastern European enlargement. Member states had included a revision clause in the Maastricht Treaty (Article N) demanding 'to examine those provisions of this treaty for which revision is provided, including those provisions dealing with defence and other aspects of CFSP, the continuation of the pillar structure, the scope of the codecision procedure, the hierarchy of the Union's legislative acts and the possibility of specific clauses in the areas of civil protection, energy and tourism'. In other words, governments strived for three goals: first, to enhance the simplicity and efficiency of the Union's decision-making procedures; second, to check the implementation of the Maastricht Treaty in practice; and third, to analyse the extent to which further integration in the above mentioned new policy areas would be both sensible and politically feasible.

In the mid 1990s Europe faced a growing economic crisis affecting the political efficiency and the integration goal. Against this background, an internal paper of the Christian-Democratic faction in the German Bundestag argued that economic developments might cause renationalisation tendencies (Lamers and Schäuble 1994; see also Pijpers and Edwards 1997: 3). At the Corfu Council in March 1994, the heads of government established a so-called reflection group mandated to prepare an IGC. The group included participants from the Commission, the EP and the member states. It was chaired by the Spanish presidency in the person of Carlos Westendorp. It was to preselect the most urgent reform tasks and elaborate realistic reform proposals. The Council of Madrid (December 1995) agreed that the 'Westendorp report'[1] should be the agenda of the upcoming IGC. It subdivided the issues to be discussed at Amsterdam into three areas: a) 'citizens and the Union', b) 'an effective and democratic Union' and c) 'external action of the Union'. The subsequent Irish presidency[2] as well as the draft of the ToA itself follow this subdivision, except for splitting the first block, 'Citizens and the Union', into a more general part with the same heading, and a second one with the heading 'Area of Freedom Security and Justice' (Stoiber 2003: 132).[3]

With respect to the two dimensions of constitutional choice established in Chapter 2, the Amsterdam IGC discussed the following issues of relevance to *vertical integration*.

Among the most well-known innovations of the ToA is the so-called Area of Freedom Security and Justice (AFSJ). This term primarily refers to classic internal affairs policies such as judicial and police cooperation, especially the fight against drugs and organised crime as well as civil protection in the case of catastrophe. Most prominently, though unresolved, the AFSJ comprises the establishment of a European public prosecutor and arrest warrant. Visa, immigration and asylum policy can be likewise considered part of the AFSJ. In this area, most governments preferred a limited increase in European policy competences, exceptions being the UK and Ireland. Due to its unique geographical position and colonial history, the UK was especially reluctant with regard to visas, immigration, asylum and other policies related to free movement. Against this background, a protocol attached to the Treaty guaranteed both countries a de facto opt-out/opt-in[4] with regard to these policy areas (Monar 2001). However, only Germany,[5] Austria, Spain and the Benelux countries were in favour of the more radical proposals such as the European public prosecutor. In the end, member states agreed on a time frame and aims con-

---

1. SN 520/1/95/REV1
2. CONF 4000/97
3. Numerous books contain qualitative summaries of the reforms agreed at Amsterdam, such as Laursen (2002); Monar and Wessels (2001) or Stubb (2002).
4. The opt-out rules provide for the following: a) once a proposal for legislation in this area is presented, the UK and Ireland have three months to decide whether to participate in discussions; b) if either the UK or Ireland (or both) do not wish to participate, discussion then continues between the other member states, which can adopt the proposal with UK and/or Irish participation; c) if the UK or Ireland (or both) do wish to participate, discussion goes on with their full participation; but if British and/or Irish objections hold back adoption of the proposal, then it could ultimately be adopted by the member states without their participation; d) after adoption of legislation in this area without UK and/or Irish participation, the UK and/or Ireland could opt-in to that legislation later if they change their minds, with the approval of the European Commission.
5. However, it has been reported that the German government was somewhat reluctant with regard to police cooperation because police and crime prevention belong to the most important competences of the *Länder*, which impact the formation of the national position (Stoiber 2003: 279).

cerning asylum, refugees and displaced persons (Art. 62, 63 TEC; Niemann 2007).

Employment policy, respectively the fight against unemployment, has been another prominent issue. Here, member states are traditionally reluctant to delegate competences to the European-level either because of the redistributive effects (Majone 1996) or because of the potentially high adaption costs implied by reforming the employment administration and crucial elements of the social security systems (Treib 2005: 11). With regard to minimum standards for working hours, income, social security or labour safety, both member states with relatively high standards – especially Scandinavian governments – as well as states with relatively low standards – especially the British and Irish governments – rejected additional EU competences. In contrast, the governments of continental welfare states such as Germany, France, Austria, Belgium and to a lesser extent some of the Mediterranean governments, were willing to go furthest. Results of the Amsterdam IGC were the European Social Chapter, signed in 1997, and the new Title VI, added to the TEC. The European Social Chapter limits the role of the EU to a few minimum standards (Padoan 1997: 209). Title VI includes policy objectives and the demand for a coordinated strategy, which *inter alia* requires the Council to elaborate annual guidelines that member states should consider when deciding upon their national employment policies. Furthermore, governments agreed on introducing the open method of coordination[6] in the field of employment policy.

As far as the CFSP is concerned, major issues were: i) the extent to which a quasi automatic military assistance clause should be introduced, ii) whether some of the West European Union's (WEU) functions could be overtaken by the EU, iii) how an EU with enhanced military capabilities and competences would define its relationship to NATO and iv) which role the neutral states[7] would play in such an overhauled European security structure (Mahncke 1997: 233). The UK, because of its transatlantic ties, and Greece, because of its special regional interest,[8] were the two governments most explicitly opposed to further harmonisation in foreign policy. On the other hand, the French government was in favour of strengthening both foreign and defence cooperation, but on the condition of not losing its unilateral privileges such as its permanent seat on the UN Security Council. Likewise, the French proposed an independent representative for the CFSP ("Mr. CFSP"), who would replace the Commissioner in this field and become the unique representative of the Union for foreign policy matters, nominated by the national

---

6. The open method of coordination, or OMC, is a relatively new and intergovernmental means of governance in the European Union, based on the voluntary cooperation of its member states. It primarily rests on benchmarking and best practice (e.g. Zeitlin 2005).

7. Austria, Finland, Ireland and Sweden.

8. The special relationship of Greece to Turkey is the dominant issue of the official governmental position; e.g. Greece stresses twice 'that all future members must respect the principles of democracy and human rights'. Source: 'Towards a Citizens' Europe – Democracy and Development: memorandum for the 1996 IGC', prepared by the Greek government, published online: www.europarl.eu.int/igc1996/pos-el_en.htm#doc, (accessed October 12, 2005).

governments. The German government opposed this idea and favoured a High Representative attached to and embedded in the Commission instead (Moravcsik and Nicolaïdis 1999: 72). Moreover, the governments of the Nordic countries and Austria remained reluctant to any extension of the CFSP because of their neutral legacy. In the end, governments agreed on a bundle of new decision-making and coordination procedures. The ToA categorised the decision-making procedures available in the CFSP in 'principles and general guidelines, which the European Council (Heads of State and Government decides [...] common strategies, decided by the Council of Ministers, [...] joint actions, decided by the Council of Ministers, [...] common positions, also decided by the Council of Ministers' (Mahncke 1997: 237; Art. 12 TEC). As a general rule, all decisions are taken by unanimity (Art. 23 TEC). The most visible reforms agreed to under the ToA are the creation of the High Representative for the CFSP (Art.18 TEC) and the policy-planning and early warning unit, also known as the Political and Security Committee (Art. 25 TEC).

With regard to defence policy, the governments of France, Germany, the Benelux countries, Greece, Spain and Portugal explicitly demanded the incorporation of the WEU into the institutional structures of the EU or, as the official Italian statement formulated, to 'turn the WEU into the defence arm of the EU'.[9] Though only the Belgian government favoured a common European army, most others were willing to create so-called double-hatted EU-NATO battle groups, exceptions being governments of the UK,[10] Ireland and the group of neutral states. In particular, the Austrian, Danish, Irish and Swedish governments explicitly excluded the option for EU defence cooperation for the sake of territorial defence, but not for peacekeeping and humanitarian missions (Petersberg Tasks[11]). In the area of defence cooperation, the results of Amsterdam were limited (Title V TEC). Any military action of the EU would continue to require the agreement of either NATO and/or WEU.

The governments of the Scandinavian states stressed the necessity to strengthen the common environmental policies. Others were less explicit; for example the Greek, Spanish, Belgian and Finnish governments pointed out that the internal market should be supplemented by other policy areas to correct for externalities and market failures. A great success of the ToA has been the inclusion of environmental protection and sustainable development (Art. 2 TEC, Art. 6 TEC). Other, but unsuccessful, reform proposals included the right of national governments to

---

9. Italian government statement of February 23, 1995, on foreign policy guidelines, published online: www.europarl.europa.eu/igc1996/pos-it_en.htm#feb, (accessed October 12, 2005).

10. Summary of 'The United Kingdom Government's Memorandum of 2 March 1995 on the treatment of European defence issues at the 1996 Intergovernmental Conference', published online: www.europarl.europa.eu/igc1996/pos-en_en.htm, (accessed October 12, 2005).

11. The Petersberg tasks are the military tasks of a humanitarian, peacekeeping and peacemaking nature that were defined in June 1992 at the Hotel Petersberg near Bonn at a meeting of the Council of the WEU, where the member states agreed to deploy their troops and resources from across the whole spectrum of the military under the authority of the WEU. As a part of the partial merger of the WEU with the European Union, according to the ToA, these tasks today form a part of the European Security and Defence Policy.

enforce stricter environmental protection laws in case they contradict EU common market directives. In addition, a report issued by the EP in preparation of the IGC lists so-called new policy areas, in particular a common energy, consumer protection and tourism policy, as well as the harmonisation of selected taxes and a declaration on sport. Here, the German and Austrian governments stressed the necessity for increased European competences with regard to energy policies and – a view shared by the Spanish government – the foundation of a European Energy authority. However, at Amsterdam, governments could not agree on any significant integration of these areas.

With regard to citizens' rights, the IGC discussed the recognition of the European Charter of Fundamental Rights, the extension of social and economic rights and the status of EU citizenship. Here, the Anglo-Saxon governments were most outspokenly against far-reaching reforms. In the end, governments refined the right of European citizenship (Art. 17 and Art. 21 TEC) and strengthened the right of non-discrimination (Art. 13 TEC).[12] In addition, governments discussed various general policy objectives such as the protection of the environment, subsidiarity and transparency. However, in the end it only included the high level of employment as a general objective of the EU (Art. 2 TEC), whereas economic competitiveness was not incorporated until the Lisbon summit in March 2000.

To strengthen the democratic representation within the EU, the IGC discussed the empowerment of the EP in legislation, budgeting and nomination. Except for the UK, most governments preferred an extension and reform of the codecision procedure. The governments of Portugal, Austria and Ireland argued that the link between codecision and QMV should remain in place. The Benelux governments furthermore demanded extended rights of the EP in the budgetary procedure and in the nomination of individual Commissioners. Accordingly, one of the major institutional reforms under the ToA concerned the simplification and extension of the codecision procedure (Art. 251 TEC) to areas of social exclusion, public health and the fight against fraud as well as the introduction of subsidiarity as a general norm (Art. 5 TEC; Protocol 30[13]). Furthermore, according to the ToA, the president of the European Commission must be approved by the EP (Art. 214 TEC). Though intensively discussed, the IGC did not extend the codecision procedure to decisions on the EU's budget, nor did the governments reform the electoral period or procedures. However, governments agreed to dispose of the third reading for the sake of efficiency (Crombez 1999). The empowerment of the joint conference between MPs and MEPs (COSAC[14]) and the extension of information and

---

12. As an immediate consequence thereof, every citizen of the EU can write to the one of EU institutions in one of the twelve languages of the treaties and must receive an answer in the same language.
13. Protocol on the application of the principles of subsidiarity and proportionality.
14. The Conference of Community and European Affairs Committees of Parliaments of the European Union (COSAC) is a conference of MEPs and MPs who must be delegates of the parliamentary committees responsible for European Union affairs.

consultation rights for national parliaments were partially successful[15] (Nentwich and Falkner 1997: 10). With regard to the Committee of Regions and the ESC, the governments agreed to strengthen both institutions' autonomy and extend the areas of compulsory (according to Art. 262 TEC, only the Committee of Regions) and optional consultation.

As for the *reform of the decision rule*, the two most prominent issues were the compositions of the Commission and the design of the QMV rule, in particular the voting weights and thresholds. However, the Amsterdam IGC could not agree on significant reforms. Governments of smaller member states were unwilling to sacrifice 'their' Commissioner for the sake of the efficiency gains implied by a smaller overall college of Commissioners. The Greek government explicitly argued that 'the large member states are excessively favoured by having two commissioners'.[16] Only the Luxembourger and Dutch were willing to reduce the size of the Commission below fifteen, but on the basis of strict equality between all member states. The governments of Germany, France, the UK and Italy held the opinion that, in view of enlargement, the size of the Commission should be reduced, but they were not willing to give up their second Commissioner without the guarantee of at least one permanent Commissioner. Finally, the Spanish government laboured in being recognised as a 'large member state'.

Furthermore, governments from larger states explicitly favoured a reform of the QMV rules toward lowering the voting threshold and redistributing the voting weight so it would become more proportional to population size. By contrast, governments from smaller states favoured the rules under the status quo, which guaranteed them a relatively high blocking power.[17] Regarding the distribution of voting power, the Spanish government linked the issue to the future composition of the Commission. In case it received more voting weight, it would have been willing to give up the second Commissioner. In addition, it favoured 'sectoral' blocking minorities, i.e. establishing different weighting arrangements in accordance with the subjects or policies voted on, following the precedents'[18] – a proposal that would have thwarted any transparency efforts.

But then the real impact of QMV depends on its extension to new policy ar-

---

15. National parliaments must get all consultation documents such as the White and Green Books of the European Commission. In addition, the ToA grants national parliaments a minimum time for consultation of the documents during the drafting stage. Furthermore, they must be informed before Council meetings (Protocol 9 annexed to the TEU).

16. Summary of 'Memorandum of the Greek Government of January 24, 1996, on the IGC: Greece's Positions and Comments,' published online: www.europarl.eu.int/igc1996/pos-el_en.htm#doc, (accessed October 12, 2005).

17. Since the 1995 enlargement, a majority required sixty-two of eighty-seven "yes" votes to come from at least eight member states. Allocation of the votes was as follows: ten for Germany, UK, France and Italy; eight for Spain; five for Belgium, the Netherlands, Greece and Portugal; four for Austria and Sweden; three for Denmark, Finland and Ireland; two for Luxembourg.

18. Summary of document issues by the Spanish government, document of March 2, 1995: 'The 1996 Intergovernmental Conference: Starting Points for a Discussion,' published online: http://europa.eu.int/en/agenda/igc-home/ms-doc/state-es/discussn.html, (accessed 12 October 2005).

eas. The Amsterdam IGC agreed on a case-wise extension and moved or introduced an additional twenty-four articles to QMV (Miller 2004: 14). For most issues, this extension has been rather uncontroversial, e.g. public health, openness, countering fraud, statistics, data protection, supporting the outermost regions and customs protection. The more controversial issues included equal opportunity for men and women as well as research and development framework programmes, both with extensive exceptions (Moravcsik and Nicolaïdis 1999: 77). The Belgian, Luxembourger, Greek and Italian governments were willing to make QMV the general rule, but only if the voting rules were designed according to their preferences. The governments of Germany, France, Austria, Portugal, Ireland and the Netherlands favoured vast extensions, but with specific exceptions accounting for each member state's vital interests (e.g. France for cultural policy and education, Germany for police cooperation). The remaining states favoured a rather careful and selective extension of QMV, often excluding areas which imply high costs of adaptation or potential redistribution of wealth, for example for social programmes, employment and defence. Far-reaching extension of QMV to the CFSP was not a realistic option for any government, with the exceptions of the Belgian, Luxembourger and German governments.

Furthermore, the semi-annual rotation scheme for the Council presidency has been criticised as being unable to provide for the necessary continuity, especially as far as external representation is concerned (Devuyst 2002: 4). In particular, Denmark and Sweden suggested a long-term team presidency – a view shared by the French government, which favoured a general upgrading of the Council. In the end, governments could not agree on any reforms. Moreover, they discussed the allocation of seats in the EP, the Committee of Regions and the ESC as well as the allocation of judges in the ECJ and the ECA. With regard to all five institutions, the debate focused on a proposal to strengthen proportional representation. As regards the EP, the Amsterdam IGC agreed on a ceiling of 700 MEPs (Art. 189 TEC), but did not alter the overall distribution of seats.[19] Neither did it provide for changes of the seat allocation in the ECA, the Committee of Regions or the ESC.

Under the label Enhanced Cooperation (Title VII TEU), governments discussed the possibility of an avant-garde to go ahead and cooperate in additional policy areas. Here, the major conflicts centred on the areas to which Enhanced Cooperation should be applicable, the rules of initiation as well as the possibility for laggards to join in later. The German and French governments had a strong preference in favour of extension, while most governments from smaller states such as Denmark, Portugal, Ireland and Greece were afraid to be excluded by any future avant-garde. In the end, governments agree to enable Enhanced Cooperation in the first and in the second pillar, retaining the possibility for constructive abstention within the

---

19. For Art. 47 TEU, the ToA adds a new subparagraph: 'In the event of amendments to this paragraph, the number of representatives elected in each Member State must ensure appropriate representation of the peoples of the States brought together in the Community'. However, it does not add any concrete interpretation to this declaration of intent (Nentwich and Falkner 1997: 9).

latter (Art. 27 TEU, Art. 40 TEU).[20]

Overall, the limited reforms of decision-rules and institutions became known as the infamous 'Amsterdam leftovers', referring to the compositions of the institutions, especially the size of the Commission, the weighting of votes in the Council and the extension of qualified majority voting and the codecision procedure (Yataganas 2001: 5; Laursen 2006: 5). Regarding vertical integration, governments agreed on decisive reforms, in particular when compared to the results of Nice. This impression is supported by Figure 4.1, which depicts my estimates of governmental reform positions, the ToM and the ToA in the two-dimensional latent conflict space.

Table 3.2 suggests that the following Amsterdam-issues strongly contribute to the positions on the vertical dimension: EU competences in external economic relations; the inclusion of an employment section and a general employment objective; EU competences in JHA as well as a common armament and defence policy; the extended applicability of Enhanced Cooperation to the second and third pillars; the empowerment of the EP in the budgetary procedure; the extension of the codecision procedure; the introduction of a uniform election procedure; strengthening the role of national parliaments as monitors of the subsidiarity principle. To determine how far the latent dimension reflects theory, the ratio is calculated between those issues that theory assigns to the vertical dimension and the remaining issues. This factor equals 1.42.[21] Overall, the governmental positions in Figure 4.1 reflect the above discussion. Governments with many national provisos against additional EU competences such as Ireland, Denmark and the UK are located at the lower end, whereas Italy, Belgium, Spain and France are located at the top.

Moreover, Table 3.2 suggests that the following Amsterdam-issues strongly contribute to the positions on the horizontal: the composition of the Commission; Enhanced Cooperation; voting weights and voting threshold in the Council of Ministers; the application of QMV in the area of CFSP, in particular to the budgetary decision. Overall, the item parameters of those issues that theory assigns to the horizontal dimension outperform the parameters of the remaining issues by a factor of 2.23. With the exception of Luxembourg and Austria, governmental positions almost perfectly correspond to member states' population sizes.

Within spatial theory, the unanimity core comprises the set of Pareto-efficient alternatives defined by the positions of all relevant actors. Once a treaty is located within the core, further reform becomes impossible, as the win-set to such a treaty would be empty (see Chapter 2). In other words: whenever an existing treaty is located in the core, it is in equilibrium. By contrast, a treaty that is located outside the core is in disequilibrium and theory expects a reform that moves the treaty

---

20. Although the official voting rule for closer cooperation in the first and third pillar was qualified majority voting, each member state could nonetheless veto closer cooperation for vital domestic reasons, as under the Luxembourg compromise (Schoutheete 2001: 162).

21. This refers to the ratio of the summed absolute item discrimination parameters. One way to interpret this factor suggests that theoretically assigned issues have 1.4-times the impact on the dimension than other issues.

a short history of eu treaty negotiations | 105

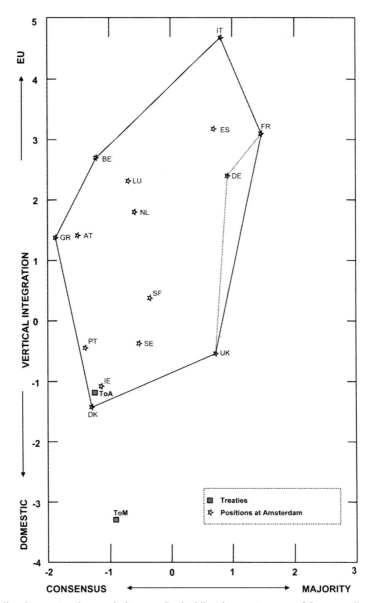

Solid line demarcates the unanimity core. Dashed line demarcates core of Germany, France and the United Kingdom
AT: Austria; BE: Belgium; DE: Germany; DK: Denmark; ES: Spain; FR: France; GR: Greece; IE: Ireland; IT: Italy; NL: The Netherlands; PT: Portugal; SF: Finland; SE: Sweden; LU: Luxembourg; UK: United Kingdom; ToM: Treaty of Maastricht; ToA: Treaty of Amsterdam

Figure 4.1: Governments' positions at Amsterdam (n=15) in two-dimensional conflict space

inside the core (Tsebelis 2002: 39). More precisely, such a reform should be located within the win-set of the status quo, as defined by the positions of all relevant actors.

However, scholars disagree over the set of relevant actors. For the pre-Maastricht era classic liberal intergovernmentalists expect the outcome to be located within the core of the three largest member states (Moravcsik 1998). For the Amsterdam IGC, the empirical findings do not support this proposition. Governments agreed on an outcome (ToA) far away from the boundaries of the core defined by Germany, France and the United Kingdom. The picture would not change once Italy and Spain are added to the group of relevant, large member states. By contrast, other scholars advanced Moravcsik's argument and expect that all member states are equally important in explaining the outcome (e.g., König and Hug 2006; Slapin 2006). As discussed in Chapter 2, the reasons to broaden the set of relevant actors are the new agenda of the post-Maastricht era and the reduced power of the large countries in a Union of fifteen or even twenty-five member states. According to Figure 4.1, the ToM was in disequilibrium at the time of Amsterdam and governments agreed on an outcome, namely the ToA, within the unanimity core of all fifteen national governments. Being situated close to the margin of the unanimity core and within the unanimity win-set of the status quo, the ToA resembles a minimum compromise located way off from the positions of Germany, France and the UK. The relevant lower-left margin of the unanimity core is defined by Denmark and Greece on the horizontal, as well as Denmark and the UK on the vertical dimension.

NICE

The Westendorp report issued in 1995 had defined three goals for the Amsterdam IGC: 1) making Europe more relevant to its citizens; 2) enabling the Union to work better and preparing it for enlargement; 3) giving the Union greater capacity for external action. When evaluating the final compromise, most governments acknowledged that not all of these goals had been achieved as planned. In particular, they noted potential shortcomings with respect to the institutional design of the Union. Therefore, they attached a protocol on institutions to the ToA demanding a 'comprehensive review of the provisions of the Treaties on the composition and functioning of the institutions [...] at least one year before the membership of the European Union exceeds twenty'. The protocol itself envisaged a two-stage reform. The first stage should prepare the Union's institutional set-up for enlargement. In particular, this stage should deal with the Amsterdam leftovers (Yataganas 2001: 5; Laursen 2006: 5). The second stage should enhance democratic legitimacy and strengthen the instruments for external policy, security and quality of life as stressed during the Cardiff Summit in June 1998.[22] Practically, the two stages describe yet another attempt to solve Europe's post-Maastricht constitutional quandary.

---

22. Presidency Conclusion of the Cardiff Summit, June 18–19, 1998, published online: http://ue.eu.int/ueDocs/cms_Data/docs/pressData/en/ec/54315.pdf.

The Nice IGC was officially inaugurated under the Portuguese presidency on February 14, 2000, and finished under the French presidency on December 11, 2000, at the Nice European Council. Approaching Eastern enlargement forced governments to agree on a rigid deadline, set for the end of December 2000. Against this background, governments were in dispute over the extent of the agenda.

> Some Member States argue that the IGC only has enough time to address the issues remaining from Amsterdam. These countries believe that the size of the Commission, the weighting of votes and majority decision-making are such sensitive issues that all available time should be spent on them. [...] For many Member States, fears that enlargement would be delayed are another important reason to keep the IGC agenda short. These countries believe that if the IGC takes on too many difficult questions, it will be almost impossible to finish before the deadline of the end of 2000.[23]

As a consequence, the discussions at Nice had a focus on reforming the institutional issues and reforms of the decision rule (Laursen 2006: 10). However, issues of *vertical integration* remained on the agenda, though less prominently.

As regards the CFSP, the integration of the WEU and the EU remained high on the agenda. Meanwhile, most governments agreed on a more or less complete dissolution of the WEU, most explicitly demanded by the governments of the Benelux countries, Germany, France, Italy and Greece.[24] The German, French, Italian, Spanish and Benelux governments demanded that the EU should have its own crisis management capabilities. In contrast, the Irish and the Scandinavian delegations held the opinion that the development of effective crisis management capabilities does not require institutional reforms. The general approach of the British government was to strengthen the European role within NATO on the basis of the existing treaties. The Spanish, German and French expressed the greatest interest in further enhancing European cooperation in research and the development of arms. This matches the importance the European Aeronautic Defence and Space Company (EADS), founded in June 2000, would have for these countries.[25] Other issues included the strengthening of the European role within NATO, the development of European crisis management capabilities as well as cooperation in the field of armament research, development and production (Rynning 2006; Algieri 2001). In some cases, positional changes are visible even within the official position papers. For example, the Austrian government [26] stepped away from its neutrality doctrine and the UK signalled its willingness to partly extend

---

23. Available in digital document archive attached to Weidenfeld (ed.) (2001).
24. Joint contribution CONFER 4788/00, published online in the archive of the European Council: http://register.consilium.eu.int, (accessed 10 October 2006).
25. EADS was founded in July 2000 by a merger of the German company DASA (DaimlerChrysler Aerospace), the French Aérospatiale-Matra and the Spanish company CASA (Construcciones Aeronáuticas S.A.).
26. In December 2001 the Austrian parliament adopted a new security and defence doctrine, shifting away from a permanently neutral to a non-allied country (Blanck 2006: 36).

Enhanced Cooperation to the third pillar. On the other hand, the Spanish position paper expressed explicit reluctance toward additional EU competences. Overall, the Nice IGC did not agree on far-reaching reforms.[27] A notable exception is the extension of Enhanced Cooperation to CFSP (Art. 27A-E TEU).

With regard to the AFSJ, judicial cooperation, immigration, asylum as well as the fight against drugs and organised crime remained on the agenda. In particular, the French government explicitly preferred the enhancement of judicial cooperation accompanied by a reform of the EU's judicial system. The governments of Ireland and France highlighted the fight against drugs, while counterparts in Germany, France, Denmark and Austria stressed the importance of fostering cooperation in immigration policy. Again, the ToN does not provide for any new EU competences in the AFSJ.

The issues of employment and social policy took a backseat, not least because many issues had been successfully solved at Amsterdam. However, the Belgian government suggested establishing a committee for the coordination of national social policies. Moreover, Laursen (2006: 61) observes that the Danish government did prefer a stronger emphasis on social, employment and consumer protection policies in order to gain legitimacy among their domestic constituencies. Furthermore, governments discussed the EU's future role in so-called new policy areas, such as consumer protection, tourism, education and research, commercial policy as well as economic, financial and technical cooperation with Third World countries. However, most governmental position papers remain silent on these issues. Exceptions are the Greek government, which suggested strengthening EU competences in all areas 'close to the citizens' such as 'sports, society and economy of knowledge, consumer protection (food safety), protection from natural disasters and enhanced provisions for employment' (Yataganas 2001: 27). However, the Nice IGC did not agree on any significant changes in these areas either (Feus 2001: 27).

At the same time, the governments raised the issue of how the common agricultural and regional policies should be financed and organised after enlargement. In combination with proposals on the EU's role in taxation, these reform talks created a strained atmosphere. In particular, the governments of Austria, Belgium and Italy explicitly demanded more EU competences in direct and indirect taxation. The German and French governments likewise preferred an extension of EU competences plus a careful extension of QMV.[28] The Danish, Swedish, Irish and Greek governments suggested more competences for the EU to coordinate the VAT rates. However, especially the governments of Ireland and the UK opposed any additional EU competences in taxation. In effect, governments did not agree to

---

27. In Art. 17 TEU it added a provision to clarify the relationship between the WEU and the EU. Furthermore, it provided some detailed regulations on the functioning of the Political and Security Council established at Amsterdam.

28. Joint position of the French and German delegation, CONFER 4808/00, 'IGC 2000: Extension of Qualified Majority Voting in Taxation (Article 93)' published online in the archive of the European Council: http://register.consilium.eu.int, (accessed 10 October 2006).

incorporate any changes of any of these issues into the ToN. Instead, the common agricultural and regional policies were reformed by a separate intergovernmental treaty, namely the 'Agenda 2000' agreed at the Berlin summit in December 1999.[29]

With regard to the Union's objectives, governments discussed the goal of economic competitiveness, the final geographical borders of the EU and, most prominently, the status of the Charter of Fundamental Rights. With respect to the latter, the opposition was led by the British government and supported by their counterparts in Finland, Ireland and Denmark. By contrast, the six founding members explicitly favoured the incorporation. However, neither of these reform proposals made it into the final treaty. Furthermore, governments dealt with the fragmentation, internal organisation and specialisation of the ECJ. Here, they established the possibility of creating additional, area-specific judicial panels (Art. 236 TEC; Giering 2001: 122).

As regards the extension of the codecision procedure, the British, Italian, Austrian, Danish and Finnish position papers suggested an extension to all areas under QMV. Moreover, the length of this wish-list differed among members, with the UK at one extreme and Benelux at the other. In the end, they agreed to extend the codecision procedure to nine additional areas: namely anti-discrimination action (Art. 13 (II) TEC); judicial cooperation (Art. 67 (IV) TEC; Art. 63 TEC); asylum and refugees (Art. 76 TEC; Art. 63 TEC); AFSJ (Art. 251 TEC and all factual issues under Title IV); social policy (Art. 137 TEC); industrial policy (Art. 157 TEC); structural policy (Art. 159 TEC); and the establishment of European parties (Art. 191 (II) TEC) (Giering 2001: 117). The issue of subsidiarity and the role of national parliaments has been less prominent on the agenda. However, governments attached the 'Declaration on the Future of the Union (No. 23)' to the ToN, which calls for further debate on the future role of national parliaments (Rittberger 2005: 178).

With regard to the *decision-rules and institutions*, the compositions of the Commission and the design of the QMV rule remained the most contentious issues on the agenda. As regards the Commission, governments from larger member states signalled their general willingness to give up their second Commissioner if the smaller countries would forgo their permanent Commissioner. However, with the exception of Austria, none of the smaller member states was willing to agree on a rotation system, not even on an equal basis, as suggested by the Italian government. The German and French governments proposed two alternatives: first, an upper limit to the number of Commissioners, with one permanent Commissioner for the large member states and either rotation for all others or the introduction of so-called Junior Commissioners who would not be granted budget competences; second, they suggested compensation via an enlarged and longer presidency with a nomination process favourable to the larger states. Most governments of smaller

---

29. The three major aspects of the Agenda 2000 are: a) the reduced payment of and applicable criteria for the common agricultural policy, b) the inclusion of the accession countries into the common regional and structural policy and c) the financial framework 2000–2006. For more details please visit: http://ec.europa.eu/agenda2000/index_en.htm, (accessed 10 November 2006).

member states could agree on a stronger presidency, but stressed that the principle of equality in the nomination of the president was sacrosanct. In the end, governments agreed on a ceiling to the number of Commissioners to be applied at a later date, while retaining the status quo until 2005[30] (Protocol on Enlargement, Art. 4).

After enlargement, the existing rules would have resulted in a situation in which a qualified majority decision represented less than 50 per cent of the EU-27 population. Against this background, even governments of smaller states felt that 'a model must be found that strikes a balance between (proportionally) over-representation of smaller member states in the decision-making process – the integration aspect – and consideration of population size – the democratic aspect'.[31] Technically, member states discussed two options: first, a double-majority system. The Belgian and Luxembourger governments favoured a simple double majority, whereas the Greek government favoured a qualified double majority, which should require 60 per cent of member states and 60 per cent of the EU population. Second, they discussed the re-weighting of votes within the current system. Most governments had no explicit preferences for either of the two techniques.

Interestingly, governments of rather similar-sized countries began to compare themselves with each other. For example, the Dutch argued that, due to their larger population size, they should be granted more votes than Belgium. Another example was the French government, which on the one hand preferred re-weighting according to population size, but on the other hand was unwilling to agree to any solution that would undermine its power parity with Germany. In the end, governments maintained the infamous voting weights with a triple-majority threshold (Protocol on Enlargement, Art. 3). The re-weighting of votes benefited Spain and, since May 2004, Poland, but made no distinction between Germany and the other large member states. The rather complex triple-majority threshold requires between 71 per cent and 74 per cent of necessary weighted yes-votes, depending on the state of enlargement, plus a majority of member states and, if a member requests, 62 per cent of the total EU population.[32]

As for the extension of majority voting, the German,[33] Benelux,[34] Italian, Spanish and Portuguese governments, and to a certain extent the Finnish and

---

30. From 2005 onward, the large member states (Germany, the UK, Spain, Italy and France) had to give up their second Commissioner, whereas all member states will have one Commissioner until the number of member states exceeds twenty-seven. In that case, rotation on an equal basis will take place (Yataganas 2001:37).

31. 'Basic Principles of Austria's Position', CONFER 4712/00, published online in the archive of the European Council: http://register.consilium.eu.int, (accessed 10 October 2006).

32. This criterion grants Germany greater blocking power and was suggested by the German delegation (Moberg 2002: 259).

33. However, while the German government was generally in favour of QMV, the *Länder* were more reluctant and formulated a list of seven key treaty articles that should remain under unanimity including anti-discrimination actions, professional training, cultural support, specific actions outside structural funds, environmental provisions and measures) (Engel 2006: 102, fn 24).

34. However, Luxembourg had reservations with respect to taxation, social security, and military deployment (Mackel 2006: 223).

Austrian governments, preferred to make QMV the general rule and to define clear criteria that justify exceptions to this rule. The list of exceptions comprised ratification and implementation hurdles, defence and national security issues, constitutional constraints, provisions derogating from the *acquis communautaire* and, as far as the Austrian and Finnish[35] are concerned, 'particularly sensitive areas such as water resources, regional planning, land use and choice of energy sources'.[36] In particular, the otherwise supportive Belgian government had rejected QMV in taxation because it faced a critical public debate over this issue (Kerremans 2006: 53). As a result, governments generally supportive of QMV were at odds with each other about the exclusion list.

By contrast, a second group preferred a more careful and limited extension in the first place. The Danish government favoured an extension to the first pillar only. Interestingly, the members of the two major oppositions parties, namely the Unity List and the Peoples' Party, attempted to restrict the government's negotiation mandate such that it could not agree to any extension of QMV (Laursen 2006: 65). The British, Greek, Finnish, Austrian and Italian governments demanded to link the codecision procedure and QMV in the sense that any extension of QMV would require an extension of the codecision procedure. The British government insisted on unanimity for treaty change, accession, taxation, border controls, social security, defence and the EU budget, at least as far as own resources are concerned. The French government's list of exceptions included culture, lesser-developed countries, and economic and social cohesion policy. However, neither the official position papers nor the survey data confirms Yataganas' (2001) observation 'that all member states are ultimately more in favour of the extension of qualified majority voting in the Council than a parallel extension of the codecision procedure' (Yataganas 2001: 26).[37]

In the end, the Nice IGC agreed on a case-wise extension of QMV (Baldwin *et al*. 2001: 10). All in all, seventy-five legal provisions existed that still required unanimity decision – fifty of which the French presidency suggested that QMV might be introduced. In the end, only twenty-seven rather less significant provisions came under QMV, spread across many of the areas just mentioned, except for taxation and social security policies (Baldwin *et al*. 2001: 10).[38]

Moreover, governments negotiated the allocation of seats in the EP, the

---

35. Finland expressed reservations with respect to amendments to the treaties, changes to common institutional systems, division of competences, budgetary decisions, and defence policy (Antola 2006: 125). Austria expressed reservations with respect to water resources, regional planning, land use and choice of energy sources (Blanck 2006: 30).

36. 'Basic Principles of Austria's Position', CONFER 4712/00, published online in the archive of the European Council: http://register.consilium.eu.int, (accessed 10 October 2006).

37. Yataganas (2001: 26) argues that this pattern emerges because member states 'have greater confidence (at least as regards matters of vital national interest) in quasi-intergovernmental negotiations (despite the progressive removal of the veto) than in a supranational process which is partly out of their control'.

38. Laursen (2006: 8) applies a different categorisation. According to him the presidential proposal included thirty-nine 'areas' and in the end QMV was extended to eight of these areas.

Committee of Regions and the ESC as well as the allocation of judges in the ECJ and the ECA. Here, the major dispute centred on equal versus proportional representation. While Benelux, Denmark, Finland and the UK preferred that the number of MEPs should not exceed 700, governments agreed on a marginally higher ceiling of 732, where only Luxembourg and Germany maintained all their previous seats (Protocol on Enlargement, Art. 2). In effect, this reform rendered the distribution of seats increasingly proportional to population size. Likewise, governments agreed that the ESC and the Committee of Regions cannot exceed 350 members (Art. 258 TEC; Art. 263 TEC), but they maintained the relative allocation among member states raging from five delegates from Malta to twenty-four delegates from Germany, France, Italy and the UK. Pertaining to personal and financial endowments as well as the competences, governments enhanced the political responsibility of the Committee of Regions toward the regional and local authorities (see Art. 257 TEC).[39] As regards the ECJ and the ECA, the Nice IGC reinforced the principle of 'one judge per member state'.

With respect to Enhanced Cooperation, the Benelux governments turned out to be most progressive when they suggested lowering the minimum number of participating member states, extending the mechanism to all three pillars and allowing QMV for certain aspects of CFSP. The governments of the six founding members and Spain preferred an extension of Enhanced Cooperation to all three pillars, with the Italian and German governments willing to go furthest.[40] The French government was less enthusiastic about the introduction of QMV. The governments of Finland, Denmark, Sweden and the UK explicitly preferred the status quo. Interestingly, the Greek government shifted its position on Enhanced Cooperation after it became clear that they would join the EMU. From that moment the Greek government no longer favoured the status quo, though it insisted on a participation of at least half of the member states (Yataganas 2001: 27). Yataganas argues that the Greek government, once it joined the EMU, expected to belong to the group of front-runners and not to those left behind (2001: 27). In the end, governments lowered the minimum number of participating states for Enhanced Cooperation to eight (Art. 43 TEC) and, with few exceptions, abolished the veto right for matters under the first and third pillars (Art. 27E TEC; Art. 40B TEC; Janning 2001: 146).

In comparison to Amsterdam, the centre of intergovernmental conflict had moved, but not its intensity. In particular, governments of smaller states appeared more compromising with regard to the extension and design of QMV rules. By contrast, governments from large member states felt increasingly pressured to agree on progressive reforms before Eastern enlargement doubled the number of small member states. In their official positions papers, many governments link different issues of the decision-rules and institutions. For example, the Finnish

---

39. The 'committee is to consist of representatives of the various economic and social components of organised civil life' (Art. 257 TEC).
40. 'IGC 2000: Enhanced Cooperation – Position Paper from Germany and Italy', CONFER 4783/00, published online in the archive of the European Council: http://register.consilium.eu.int, (accessed 10 October 2006).

'government can accept changes to the weighting of votes in the Council provided that satisfactory results are achieved in other institutional issues'.[41]

Overall, the Nice IGC agreed on significant institutional reforms beyond the principles of equality and consensus toward the principles of proportionality and majoritarianism. Outstanding changes of relevance for vertical integration were the extension of Enhanced Cooperation, the possibility for a future empowerment of national parliaments and the strengthening of the ECJ.[42] Overall, these changes appear small when compared to Amsterdam. This impression matches with the location of the ToA and the ToN in Figure 4.2.

Table 3.4 suggests that the following Nice-issues strongly contribute to the estimated positions on the vertical dimension: the extension of EU competences in the areas of defence, cooperation with developing countries, education as well as the fight against drugs and unemployment; inclusion of fundamental human rights into the EU's legal system; the extended applicability of Enhanced Cooperation. The item parameters of those issues that theory assigns to the vertical dimension outperform the parameters of the remaining issues by a factor of 1.55.[43]

As for the horizontal dimension, Table 3.4 suggests that the three single-most important issues are the composition of the European Commission, the voting weights for QMV and the extension of Enhanced Cooperation. Overall, the parameters of those issues that theory assigns to the horizontal dimension outperform the parameters of the remaining issues by a factor of 2.6.

The cursory qualitative discussion of official governmental statements matches with the positions in Figure 4.2. The horizontal dimension confronts the smaller with the larger member states. On the vertical dimension, we find Denmark and Ireland located at the lower end, whereas France, the Benelux countries, Spain, Portugal and Greece are at the upper end of the scale. In comparison to Amsterdam, the positions of the UK, Germany and Italy converged somewhere in between. As

---

41. 'IGC 2000: Contribution from the Finnish Government: Background and Objectives in the IGC 2000', CONFER 4723/00, published online in the archive of the European Council: http://register.consilium.eu.int, (accessed October 10, 2006). The German government made a similar statement: 'Die endgültige Zustimmung zur Ausweitung von Mehrheitsentscheidungen steht unter dem Vorbehalt, dass auch in den anderen Bereichen der Regierungskonferenz (z.B. Stimmgewichtung) für die Bundesregierung befriedigende Ergebnisse erzielt werden. Außerdem sind etwaige Bezüge zum institutionellen Gefüge zu berücksichtigen'. ('IGC 2000: Policy Document of the Federal Republic of Germany on the Intergovernmental Conference on Institutional Reform', CONFER 4733/00, published online in the archive of the European Council: http://register.consilium.eu.int, (accessed 10 October 2006).)

42. In a Protocol annexed to the Treaty of Nice, the Statute of the ECJ, incl. the Court of First Instance, was revised, whereby the CFI becomes the ordinary court for all direct actions. A new judicial body, the 'European Civil Service Tribunal' has been set up to adjudicate in disputes between the European Union and its civil service. In addition, the Treaty of Nice created specialised judicial panels to hear cases in specific areas. This reform allowed for specialised EU tribunals to deal with disputes in the field of employment and industrial relations.

43. This refers to the ratio of the summed absolute item discrimination parameters. One way to interpret this factor suggests that theoretically assigned issues have 1.6-times the impact on the dimension than other issues.

114 | european integration and its limits

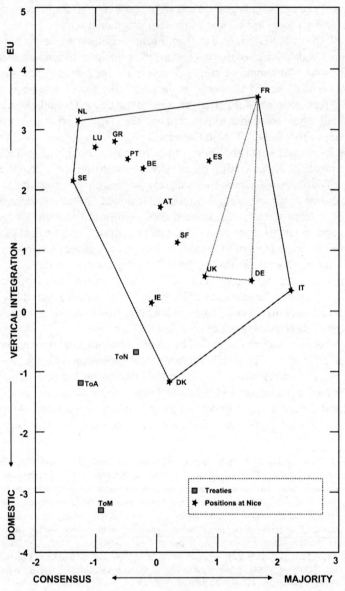

Solid line demarcates the unanimity core. Dashed line demarcates core of Germany, France and the United Kingdom
AT: Austria; BE: Belgium; DE: Germany; DK: Denmark; ES: Spain; FR: France; GR: Greece; IE: Ireland; IT: Italy; NL: The Netherlands; PT: Portugal; SF: Finland; SE: Sweden; LU: Luxembourg; UK: United Kingdom, ToM: Treaty of Maastricht; ToA: Treaty of Amsterdam

Figure 4.2: Governments' positions at Nice (n=15) in two-dimensional conflict space

far as the UK is concerned, this upward move is an unsurprising consequence of the new Labour government. The main difference between Labour and the Tories can be found in the former's openness toward the extension of QMV and toward incorporation of the WEU into the EU (Laursen 2006: 314). In Germany the Social Democrats turned out to be less integration friendly than the former Christian-Democratic government led by Helmut Kohl. It preferred a more pragmatic, case-by-case approach to future integration. Furthermore, the German government proposed to strictly limit the agenda to the necessary institutional reforms (Engel 2006: 92). Most striking is the huge downwards shift of the Italian position. The Amsterdam position was prepared under the leadership of Romano Prodi, the latter president of the European Commission, whereas the Nice position was prepared under the leadership of Massimo D'Alema from the PDS. Partisan composition of government hardly accounts for this surprisingly strong shift because both prime ministers led a centre-left coalition primarily composed of parties from the Olive Tree. In Chapter 5, there is a systematic discussion of alternative explanations for positional change.

How does the positional configuration match with my hypothesis on treaty change derived in Chapter 2? Please remember that the Amsterdam IGC had moved the European treaty framework inside the unanimity core, i.e. the treaties were in equilibrium. However, three years later, governmental positions have changed. Especially the rightward changes of the Danish, Irish, Portuguese, Austrian, and Swedish governments has led to a rightward shift of the unanimity core. As a consequence, the ToA was in disequilibrium and the Nice IGC could agree to shift Europe's decision-rule away from consensus rule toward majoritarianism. As a result, the ToN defines yet another compromise at the least common denominator. It is situated close to the margin of member states' unanimity core at the time of Nice, and within the unanimity win-set of the status quo. However, this time the reforms do not even pass the boundary of the core. Hence, the outcome must be considered suboptimal, which reflects the dissatisfaction expressed by politician's right after the concluding Nice summit. Finally, the reform is located way off the core, as defined by the three largest member states. In other words, the treaty revision can hardly be considered as a deal brokered by the big member states, as found by Moravcsik (1998) for treaty revision of the pre-Maastricht era.

ROME II

At the time the Nice summit held its concluding press conference, the governmental delegates seemed to have known that they failed to agree on the reforms necessary for an efficient, effective and democratic Union of twenty-five or more member states. Considering the location of the ToN just outside the unanimity core in Figure 4.2, this evaluation is rather unsurprising. Tony Blair summarised the generally pessimistic appraisal as follows: 'As far as Europe is concerned we cannot do business like this in the future' (BBC News, December 11, 2000). One year later, the European Council at Laeken suggested an encompassing revision of the ToN (Giering 2003: 6). Governments agreed that the previous two IGCs failed to provide the necessary institutional reforms. Therefore, the Council suggested a novel method of preparing the next IGC and invoked the Convention on the Future of Europe. The plan was to overcome the constitutional quandary by broadening the social and political discussion and involving representatives of national parliaments, the EP, elder statesmen and academics. The Laeken Council identified three major tasks that again mirror the conflicting goals discussed in Chapter 1: the 'simplification of the Union's instruments'; the improvement of the 'division and definition of competencies' and the enhancement of 'democracy, transparency and efficiency'.[44] Officially, the Convention mandate was to agree on recommendable reform proposals before the next IGC scheduled to start in fall 2003. However, the mandate did not specify whether the final documents should be a more or less loose collection of individual proposals or a concrete and coherent draft proposal for a new treaty.

The Convention started its deliberations in February 2002 and it proposed a coherent draft treaty in June 2003 in Thessaloniki. It comprised delegates from twenty-eight national governments and parliaments from member states and candidate countries. However, delegates from candidate countries were not granted official voting rights. Toward the end of the Convention, it became clear that some of the more salient issues – such as the extension of voting thresholds under QMV, the presidency of the Council and the Commission as well as the extension of Enhanced Cooperation – would be at the centre of the subsequent IGC (Dinan 2004: 40 ; Giering 2003: 13). Technically, the 'Masters of the Treaty' could have altered each and every treaty article, de facto the IGC agreed on a very short list of modifications. It lifted the QMV threshold from 50 per cent of the member states and 60 per cent of the EU's population to 55 per cent and 65 per cent respectively.[45] It delayed the reduction of the number of Commissioners to the year 2014 instead of 2009. It agreed to postpone the application of the codecision procedure and of QMV for the first provisions on the Structural and Cohesion Funds until after the Constitutional Treaty has entered into force and it refined the definition of Enhanced Cooperation among the Euro-group (Milton et al. 2005: 51; König et al. 2008).

In this section, the agenda and governmental positions at the IGC are summarised and the most important reforms are described, followed by a scrutiny of the role of the Convention as a de facto agenda setter. Please note that Rome II will be examined in more detail in Chapter 6, which discusses the role of sequential decision-making. The ten accession countries, which were to enter in May 2004, participated in the IGC on an equal footing with the old member states. While official governmental position papers remain a valuable source with respect to the prominent issues – in particular the presidency of the European Council and

---

44. The Laeken Declaration, December 2001. Available online at: http://europa.eu/futurum/documents/offtext/ declaration_nl.pdf; (accessed 6 July , 2006).

45. The draft constitution suggested 50 per cent of the member states and 60 per cent of the EU's population.

the CFSP[46] – they contain less information than was the case for earlier IGCs. Many governments, including the Benelux, French, German and the Swedish governments, explicitly represented the position to keep the Convention proposal in place, hence they did not engage in drafting additional position papers (Milton *et al.* 2005: 87). Therefore, the subsequent discussion resorts to information found in secondary sources, in particular the information presented in a report of the EP's Committee on Constitutional Affairs,[47] the information collected by the European Policy Institutes Networks (EPIN)[48] and the country-wise, qualitative discussion of the national positions gathered in the DOSEI project presented in a volume by König and Hug (2006).

As regards *vertical integration*, CFSP, AFSJ, taxation, fiscal and social policies were central to the negotiations. As for CFSP, the main issues were the applicability of Enhanced Cooperation as well as the extension of EU competences in general, starting from cooperation in research and development up to mutual assistance or even a common European army. The governments of Belgium, France, Germany, Greece, Hungary, Luxembourg, Portugal, Spain, the UK and Italy preferred an increase in European competences. By contrast, their Baltic, Czech and Polish counterparts opposed any such plans. Furthermore, the Convention and the IGC discussed the proposal to establish an EU Foreign Office (Algieri and Bauer 2005). Except for the Polish and Czech governments, most favoured the establishment of such a post, though the Greek, Austrian and British governments preferred a very restrictive political mandate. The governments of Sweden, the Netherlands and Spain favoured the new post to be responsible to Commission and Council; all others preferred a strictly intergovernmental accountability. In the end, governments agreed on a Foreign Office that would simply merge the tasks of the existing High Representative for the Common Foreign and Security Policy and the External Relations Commissioner. Furthermore, the overall objective has been extended to comprise a common defence strategy (Algieri 2005: 210; Piris 2006: 145).

With regard to the AFSJ, governments discussed the more general issues of enhancing judicial and police cooperation as well as three more specific issues, namely the introduction of a public prosecutor, external border protection and the EU's competences in the area of migration and asylum (Hagedorn 2005). The Irish and British governments intensely opposed the idea of a public prosecutor because they feared that the office would be at odds with the principle of common law. The

---

46. Most governments replied to the questionnaire on the 'Legislative Function, the Formations of the Council and the Presidency of the Council of Ministers', (CIG 9/03) which was sent out by the Italian presidency. Available online at: http://europa.eu/scadplus/cig2004/negociations1_de.htm, (accessed 10 June 2007).

47. DV\512456EN.doc; available online: www.europarl.eu.int, (accessed 6 November 2003).

48. The EPIN provides information on the positions of seventeen member states on eighteen primarily institutional issues. The data is based on expert knowledge from the research institutes that take part in the network. The information is published online at: www.epin.org/national/debate.html, (accessed 10 October 2006).

Italian government opposed the idea at the beginning, but changed its mind during the heyday of its presidency. The Scandinavian governments explicated their scepticism, but did not reject the idea altogether (Hagedorn 2005: 196 f.).

As regards border protection, the governments of the UK, Spain, Italy and Greece promoted the idea of a common management system, including a European frontiers guard corps. With the notable exception of the Swedish and Baltic governments, all other countries preferred the common management of external borders, but without a European frontiers guard. Pertaining to asylum and migration policies, the Danish government was eager to keep the Danish Maastricht opt-outs in place (Dorussen and Lenz 2006: 117). The British, Czech, Slovak, and Slovenian governments preferred minimum standards, whereas the Belgian, German, Greek, Italian, Dutch and Swedish governments preferred EU-wide harmonisation for all three sub-areas. Finally, the governments of France, Spain, Luxembourg, Cyprus, Malta, Lithuania, Estonia and Ireland preferred EU-wide harmonisation of asylum regulations, but minimum standards in all other areas. In general, the governments of Denmark, Austria, Ireland, the Netherlands, Poland and Hungary opposed any extension of EU competences, as regards the AFSJ. In addition, the German government was sceptical, as many of these competences belong to the German *Länder* (Euobserver, Sept. 19, 2006).

In the end, governments agreed to strengthen the common instruments. They introduced a general right of initiative for the Commission, mutual recognition[49] in the areas of civil and criminal law, further development of Europol, the common European border patrol and the step-wise development of Eurojust, including a European public prosecutor that the Council may install by unanimity (Hagedorn 2005: 199 ; Piris 2006: 164).

As regards fiscal policy and taxation, a prominent issue was whether or not the Euro-group should be granted special rights to coordinate their fiscal policies within the institutional framework of the EU. Naturally, this idea was supported by members of the Eurogroup, but fiercely rejected by all others. Pertaining to tax policy, the coordination of VAT remained high on the agenda with positions of the old member states unchanged. The governments of Cyprus, the Czech Republic and the Slovak Republic supported an additional harmonisation of taxes, but only if decided by unanimity. As far as fiscal coordination was concerned, Lithuania, Latvia and Slovenia appeared to be most favourable. In the end, the governments did not agree on any substantial reforms.

Furthermore, governments negotiated the potential coordination and standards in social and social security policy. Here, the rather complex discussion primarily referred to the direct effects of the common labour market, such as equal opportunity employment, occupational health and safety, minimum wage, coordination and compatibility of national health and social insurance systems. In the end, governments agreed on no substantial changes, except that social justice, protection and cohesion would be listed as official objectives of the Union (Art. I–3 Constitutional Treaty).

---

49. A mutual recognition describes a principle whereby two or more countries agree to recognise one another's legal and administrative standards, i.e. conformity assessments.

With regard to individual rights, the British and Irish governments were the only ones in favour of keeping the Charter of Fundamental Rights non-binding. Most other governments preferred to integrate the Charter into the constitutional framework, but as only partially binding for the EU institutions. The Constitutional Treaty includes the Charter as a legally binding provision (Art. I–7 Constitutional Treaty). Furthermore, governments agreed on a list of objectives such as full employment and competitiveness, which had been hotly discussed during the Convention (Art. I–4 Constitutional Treaty).

As was the case at Amsterdam and Nice, the extension of codecision procedure ranked high on the Constitutional agenda, with governments now being surprisingly supportive. Most hotly contested were extensions to the areas of CFSP, AFSJ, taxation and fiscal policy. In the end, governments agreed to add a limited number of provisions concerning agricultural policy and further aspects of home affairs, now calling codecision procedures the 'ordinary legislative procedure' (Art. 302 Constitutional Treaty). In addition, the governments of Spain, Luxembourg, Greece, Germany, Belgium and Austria preferred the extension of the EP decision rights for both the annual budget and the multi-annual financial framework – an idea rejected by the governments of Finland, Sweden, Portugal and the UK. Most other countries preferred somewhat more rights for the EP in the annual budgeting procedure, but no veto power. In the end, they agreed to strengthen the EP's say in the annual and multi-annual budgeting process, including agriculture (Art. 53–55 Constitutional Treaty). The codecision procedure would now cover approximately 95 per cent of all EU law-making activities (Piris 2006: 90).

During the Convention, the suggestions for strengthening national parliaments were multifarious, comprising the empowerment of COSAC,[50] enhancing national parliaments' information and control rights during the drafting stage, the rights to summon and question the Commission, the control of the principle of subsidiarity by national parliaments ('subsidiarity watchdog'), the right of legislative initiative for national parliaments and even creating a second chamber of the EP representing national parliaments (Rittberger 2005: 189). Governments agreed to the Convention proposal of setting up a 'subsidiarity early warning system'. According to the early warning mechanism for subsidiarity control, the European Commission would transmit proposals directly to the national parliaments, and they would have the right to claim within six weeks that there has been a violation of the subsidiarity principle. If more than one-third of the national parliaments were to do so, the European Commission would then be obliged to reconsider its proposal.[51] In addition, governments agreed to the Convention's proposal of a popular initiative, requiring the subscription of at least one million EU citizens to initiate a legislative process (Art. 46(4) Constitutional Treaty).

As regards a stronger personalisation and accountability of European politics, the German and Dutch governments explicitly preferred a stronger role for the

---

50. COSAC = Conference of Community and European Affairs Committees of Parliaments of the European Union.

51. Protocol on the Application of the Principles of Subsidiarity and Proportionality.

EP in nominating individual Commissioners. However, their British and Swedish counterparts opposed this idea. In addition, the governments of Finland, Ireland, Portugal, Cyprus, the Czech Republic, Estonia, Hungary, Malta and Slovenia explicitly suggested that the EU foreign minister should be subject to the approval of the EP. The Convention proposed the election of the Commission president by the EP and the synchronisation of both institutions' electoral periods (Art. 26(1) Constitutional Treaty). The governments rejected this proposal, but agreed on establishing the EU Minister of Foreign Affairs, responsible to the Council and acting as vice president of the European Commission (Art. 27 Constitutional Treaty). Furthermore, they introduced a long-term president of the European Council, elected for two and a half years, renewable once (Art. 21 Constitutional Treaty). Both reforms were intended to strengthen the personalisation and hence the accountability of EU politics.

As regards the *decision-rules and institutions*, the most prominent issues remained the same as for the preceding IGCs, namely the compositions of the European Commission and the design of the voting rule. As before, governments from smaller member states perceived their representative in a powerful Commission as a safeguard against unfavourable decisions by larger member states. However, the Benelux, Swedish and Danish governments were ready to compromise on the number of Commissioners. Governments of large states demanded a smaller Commission, but only under the premise that they would be granted a permanent Commissioner or preferential treatment with regard to the Commission presidency. In the end, governments agreed on one Commissioner per member state until 2014, thereafter the number of Commissioners would be reduced to two-thirds of the number of member states (including both its president and the EU Minister for Foreign Affairs), chosen on the basis of equal rotation (Art. 25 Constitutional Treaty). The Convention had proposed the same reforms, but five years earlier.

As regards the voting rules, governments discussed either a double- or even a triple-majority threshold or a re-weighting of votes. In general, the dividing line between large and small countries remained in place. In order to balance the system, governments debated whether weights and thresholds should be based on population size. The governments of Germany, Denmark and France suggested a simple majority of member states plus three-fifths of the population. Interestingly, the French government this time accepted that the new system would favour Germany. The Greek and Belgian governments preferred a simple majority of member states and population. The Irish and Spanish governments favoured the maintenance of Nice or a similar system (Chari and Egea-de Haro 2006: 344). In the end, governments agreed to abandon the voting weights and set the threshold at 55 per cent (with at least fifteen member states) that would represent at least 65 per cent of the EU's population[52] (Art. 24 Constitutional Treaty). In comparison,

---

52. However, Council members representing at least three-quarters of a blocking minority (either at the level of member states or the level of population) can demand that the Council should further discuss the issue.

the Convention had proposed a threshold at 50 per cent and 60 per cent respectively.

Pertaining to the extension of QMV, governments presented a country-specific wish list (Collignon 2002: 125). Most hotly contested were the extensions to taxation, fiscal matters and selected areas of the CFSP and the AFSJ. The governments of Germany, France, Belgium and Greece explicitly preferred further EU competences in fiscal policy matters, supported by the Austrian, Finnish, Italian, Dutch, Portuguese and Swedish governments with regard to taxation. Most of these governments suggested expanding QMV to a newly introduced soft-coordination scheme for VAT and fiscal policy guidelines, but only the above four were willing to go further. However, the governments of the UK, Ireland, Luxembourg, Spain and Denmark as well as their counterparts in the new member states opposed any extension of QMV. As for foreign and defence policy, only the Austrian, Belgian, French, Greek, Italian and Portuguese governments favoured a limited extension of QMV. The governments of Finland, Germany, Spain, Sweden and Luxembourg supported this group with regard to foreign policy. For the British government, the maintenance of unanimity was an absolute red line and would have been a reason to deny its signature (Benedetto 2006: 241). In the end, the UK position prevailed and governments agreed on a limited extension of QMV, most notably in areas such as asylum, immigration and judicial cooperation in criminal matters. Unanimity remained in place for more sensitive areas, in particular for tax, social security, foreign policy and defence. However, so-called emergency brakes were introduced, allowing a member state to appeal to the European Council if it feels that its national interests are at stake. As a rule, unanimity will continue to apply to the field of taxation and, partially, to the field of social as well as to foreign, security and defence policy. Furthermore, laws on a country's own resources, financial perspectives and, as a matter of course, the future revisions of the Constitution itself will have to be adopted unanimously (Piris 2006: 94).

However, the UK victory is limited, as governments agreed that Enhanced Cooperation can now be achieved by QMV, including taxation and fiscal policy coordination among the Euro-group (Piris 2006: 173). Furthermore, they established the 'Permanent Structured Cooperation', which allows for Enhanced Cooperation in security and defence matters, but has to be agreed by unanimity in the European Council.

Likewise, governments from small and large states negotiated the allocation of seats in the EP, the Committee of Regions, and the ESC as well as the allocation of judges in the ECJ and the ECA. In the end, they did not alter the principles of allocation, but instead agreed on a minimal increase in the number of available seats. In particular, the maximum number of seats in the EP was raised to 750, with a minimum number of six seats and a maximum number of ninety-six seats per country.[53]

Critics argued that the semi-annual rotation scheme of the Council presidency

---

53. Protocol on the Representation of Citizens in the European Parliament and the Weighting of Votes in the European Council and the Council of Ministers.

has proven unable to provide the necessary continuity, especially as far as external representation is concerned (Devuyst 2002: 4). However, for the governments of smaller states, it was very important to take over the Council presidency on a regular basis.[54] Therefore, they demanded to keep the rotating presidency, while the governments of the UK, Germany, France, Spain and Sweden favoured a long-standing presidency. Even more progressive, a joint proposal issued by Chirac and Schröder in January 2003 suggested a co-presidency of the Commission and the Council (Schulz 2006: 179). In the end, governments agreed that a team of three member states would preside over the Council for eighteen months. Each member of the team will hold the presidency for a period of six months, while being assisted by the other two states on the basis of a common work programme. The reform would have formalised the ongoing practice of cooperation among succeeding presidencies. Governments stepped above this de facto status quo by deciding that the General Affairs Council would be chaired by the foreign minister[55] (Art. 23 Constitutional Treaty) and that the European Council would be chaired by a president appointed for two and a half years, renewable once (Art. 21 Constitutional Treaty).

Overall, the Constitutional Treaty provided significant reforms on both levels – in particular, the reform of the voting rules, the Council presidency and the compositions of the Commission-settled institutional issues, which have been on the agenda since Maastricht. At the same time, the extension of the codecision procedure, the empowerment of the EP in the budget procedure, the introduction of a Minister of Foreign Affairs and Permanent Structured Cooperation, the empowerment of national parliaments as subsidiarity watchdogs, the introduction of political objectives and the popular initiative meant a significant increase in vertical integration. The estimated treaty locations in Figure 4.3 support this qualitative evaluation.

Table 3.4 suggests that the following Rome-II-issues strongly contribute to the estimated positions on the vertical dimension: the extension of the EU's mandate in the areas of AFSJ (including migration and asylum), CFSP, economic, social, employment and environmental policy; the extension of the codecision procedure to AFSJ, taxation, internal market, employment and social security policies; the empowerment of the EP in the appointment of the Minister of Foreign Affairs; the inclusion of an employment objective. The estimated governmental positions in Figure 4.3 provide a consistent summary of the qualitative discussion that, as

---

54. The so-called *Athen 16* group of small member states drafted a common position paper presented to the Convention in March 2003. One of its core proposals was that in case the rotating Council presidency could not be maintained, every member state should have at least one Commissioner. 'The main principles of the document include preserving and strengthening the Community Method, maintaining the existing institutional balance, and ensuring the equality of all member states' (Veebel and Ehin 2003: 41). *Athen 16* included all small member states except the Benelux countries (Austria, Denmark, Finland, Ireland, Estonia, Cyprus, Czech Republic, Greece, Hungary, Lithuania, Latvia, Malta, Portugal, Slovenia, Slovakia, Sweden).

55. However, considering the close cooperation current and past presidencies have established with their predecessors and successors, this reform more or less reinforces the current practice.

the number of states increases, becomes increasingly complex. Among the old member states, the Danish, Irish and British governments remain the least integrationist, whereas the Belgian, Greek and French governments are estimated as being most integrationist. Overall, the governments of the new member states are located closer to the status quo, i.e. the ToN. Especially the Estonian, Polish and Hungarian governments appear to be integration-sceptical. With regard to the very integration-friendly Slovak government, the analysis of Schulz and Chabrekova (2006: 321) suggests that 'troublesome years under the problematic government of Mečiar' is one reason that Slovakia thereafter 'had become the model child of eastern enlargement and European integration'. The item parameters of those issues, which theory assigns to the vertical dimension, outperform the remaining issues by a scant factor of 1.2.[56]

Table 3.4 suggests that the following Rome-II-issues strongly contribute to the positions on the horizontal dimension: the composition of the Commission; the extended applicability of Enhanced Cooperation; the extension of QMV to taxation, social, employment, foreign and defence policy. Again, the estimated positions, depicted in Figure 4.3, match with the above discussion. Interestingly, the correlation to population size is far weaker than was the case at Amsterdam and Nice. In particular, the three smallest member states, namely Cyprus, Malta and Luxembourg, are located further right than expected. In contrast, the UK and Poland prefer less majoritarian reforms than suggested by their population sizes. Furthermore, Figure 4.3 reflects the other face of the Slovak government: although preferring far-reaching EU competences, it fiercely promoted the equal distribution of decision-making powers among member states. The item parameters of those issues, which theory assigns to the horizontal dimension, outperform the parameters of the remaining issues by a factor of 1.86.

How does Figure 4.3 relate to my theoretical explanations for European treaty revisions as discussed in Chapter 2? Comparing governmental positions at Rome II to those at Nice, only the Danish position causes a minor shift in the lower margin of the unanimity core. As compared to its social-democratic-led predecessor, the new conservative-liberal government opposed further changes toward majoritarianism, but preferred slightly more EU powers. As a consequence, the lower-left margin of the unanimity core moved slightly leftward, now defined by the positions of the Irish, Estonian and Danish governments on the vertical, and the Irish and Italian governments on the horizontal dimension. Interestingly, Eastern enlargement had remarkably little impact on the overall shape of the unanimity core. As a consequence, the ToN has been situated very close to its lower-left margin. Accordingly, the win-set of the status quo was almost empty. Nevertheless, the draft proposed by the Convention and the Constitutional Treaty contained significant reforms on both dimensions. In Figure 4.3, both treaties can be found to the northeast of the ToN. Obviously, both reform treaties would be especially

---

56. This refers to the ratio of the summed absolute item discrimination parameters. One way to interpret this factor suggests that theoretically assigned issues have 1.2-times the impact on the dimension than other issues.

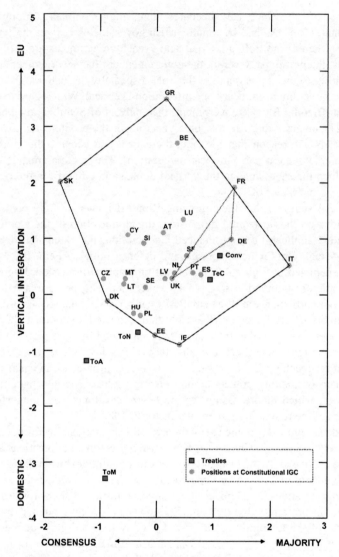

Solid line demarcates the unanimity core. Dashed line demarcates core of Germany, France and the United Kingdom

AT: Austria; BE: Belgium; CY: Cyprus; CZ: Czech Republic; DE: Germany; DK: Denmark; EE: Estonia; ES: Spain; FR: France; GR: Greece; HU: Hungary; IE: Ireland; IT: Italy; NL: The Netherlands; PT: Portugal; SF: Finland; SE: Sweden; SK: Slovak Republic; SI: Slovenia; LU: Luxembourg; LT: Latvia; LI: Lithuania; MT: Malta; PL: Poland; UK: United Kingdom; ToM: Treaty of Maastricht; ToA: Treaty of Amsterdam; ToN: Treaty of Nice; TeC: Constitutional Treaty; Conv: Draft Proposal by the Convention

Figure 4.3: Governments' ideal positions at Rome II (n=25) in two-dimensional conflict space

welcomed by the old, large member states, especially Italy, Germany, France, and Spain. Indeed, the treaties' location close to the margin of the core defined by the five largest countries seems to resemble the logic of European treaty revisions before Maastricht. By contrast, the governments of Estonia, Denmark, Czech Republic, Hungary, Lithuania, Malta and Sweden would have preferred the status quo over the Constitutional Treaty.[57] This raises the question of why some governments signed the Constitutional Treaty, although they preferred the status quo.

In Chapter 2 it is argued that the post-Maastricht intergovernmental treaty negotiations cannot be considered an unconstrained bargaining game. Following strategic bargaining theory, the higher number of member states and the procedural innovation may cause a Pareto-inefficient and/or Pareto-inferior outcome. In particular, the argument that governments held incomplete and imperfect information when installing the Convention is highlighted. As a consequence the Convention (and its Presidium) enjoyed a significantly higher level of agenda-setting power if compared to the Council presidencies organising previous IGCs. In addition, the Convention may have derived additional powers from its legitimate mandate forcing a certain degree of commitment on behalf of the national governments. However, with regard to procedural legitimacy, Luxembourg's prime minister and delegate to the Convention, Jean-Claude Juncker, called the assembly 'the darkest of all darkrooms'. A critical perspective that has been shared in the literature (Göler and Marhold 2005; Tsebelis and Proksch 2007).

As for the IGCs at Amsterdam and Nice, the Council presidency settled the majority of less conflictive issues via bilateral-shuttle diplomacy, and only the most conflictive issues were postponed until the final summit. As a result, the reforms at Amsterdam and Nice were more or less Pareto-efficient and Pareto-superior, but constituted a compromise at the lowest common denominator.

By contrast, the Constitutional Treaty cannot be considered as a minimum compromise. Indeed some governments signed the Treaty, although, according to my empirical analysis, it left them worse off. Furthermore, the small difference[58] between the Convention draft and the agreement of the subsequent IGC points toward the agenda-setting power of the Convention (König and Finke 2007a). This picture supports the logic of my explanation. Member states installed the Convention as a committee, a procedural innovation meant to overcome the inefficiency of previous IGCs. At that time, most governments hardly expected such a powerful president who dominated the Convention and delivered a coherent draft constitution. Once governments realised the importance of the Convention,

---

57. König and Finke (2007) find that all member states but Ireland would have preferred the Constitutional Treaty over the status quo (ToN). While using the same data set, the authors recode the data such that a '0' indicates a position that equals the status quo and '1' if it does not. As a consequence, their result builds on a dichotomous data set. The authors waste information because they are interested in predicting reforms at the issue-level.

58. The IGC changed the Convention draft with respect to five issues: QMV threshold, number of Commissioners, role of the Commission president in the appointment of the Commissioners and the intermission of the codecision Procedure, and qualified majority voting for the first provisions on the Structural Funds after the Constitutional Treaty has entered into force.

they were unable to disempower it unilaterally, hence their only feasible unilateral strategy was to empower and upgrade their own national delegations. As a consequence, governments exchanged their delegates with high-ranking officials and politicians (Norman 2005: 155). Toward the end, the Convention gained an increasingly intergovernmental character. *De jure* the IGC was free to modify each and every article of the draft proposed by the Convention. But de facto governments accepted most of the Convention draft because revocation of their commitment to, and during the Convention, would have damaged their reputation with both the international partners and the domestic audience.

In other words, when governments installed the Convention, they expected a loose recommendation that, subsequently, they could modify *ad libitum*. However, at the end of the Convention, they confronted a de facto closed rule. A rejection of the Convention draft would have had high costs on reputations. But what explains the location of the Convention draft?

THE CONVENTION

The Convention method was supposed to raise the legitimacy of the integration process itself and to produce results that were better suited to prepare the enlarged EU for the challenges of the 21st century (Norman 2003: 10). The deliberations began in February 2002 and the Convention proposed a draft constitutional treaty in June 2003. Deliberations began with the so-called listening phase. At this stage, the delegates from fifteen member and thirteen accession/candidate states presented their views on how to solve Europe's constitutional quandary. Delegates spent surprisingly little time on discussing the topic of institutional reform (Maurer 2003: 248). In September 2002 the presidency initiated a second phase, named the 'study phase', by establishing a system of eleven working groups. The topics of these groups were subsidiarity, the Charter of Fundamental Rights/European Court of Human Rights, legal personality, national parliaments, complementary competences, economic governance, external action, defence, legal simplification, AFSJ and social Europe. The working groups produced a first set of reform proposals.

In spring 2003, the decisive 'drafting phase' of the Convention began. In the end, the Convention adopted a text that had been primarily drafted by its presidency. Giscard D'Estaing and his vice presidents picked from among the proposals presented by the working groups and added their own ideas *ad libitum*. The final debate took place on June 13, 2003 (Norman 2003: 186). The decision-making rule of the Convention was consensus, meaning that President Giscard D'Estaing at some point decided that all objections were to be heard and accounted for (Tsebelis 2008). By comparing the changes agreed at the Convention to delegates' positions, König and Slapin (2006) argue the de facto voting threshold must have been lower than the unanimity threshold.

The Convention was composed of the president and his two vice-chairmen, fifteen delegates of member states' governments, thirty delegates of member states' national parliaments, sixteen delegates of the EP, two delegates of the Commission as well as thirteen delegates of candidate countries' governments plus twenty-six delegates of candidate countries' national parliaments. Including the alternates, this amounts to 207 delegates.[59] Interestingly, at a later stage of the Convention, many lower-ranking governmental delegates were exchanged for their ministers (Norman 2003: 155). Officially, only the delegates from old member states and from the supranational institutions were entitled to vote. But then this distinction makes little difference, as there was no explicit vote on the final proposal anyway.

The unspecific and open mandate granted by the Laeken Council allowed Giscard D'Estaing to play 'every trick in the book' in order to get the draft treaty he preferred (Tsebelis and Proksch 2007: 2). In particular, he limited the number and area of amendments each delegate was able to draft, he installed a reiterated agenda process that allowed the president to modify unpleasant amendments and he prohibited explicit voting, but instead defined unilaterally whether or not consensus had emerged. However, other observers suggest that 'in reality it was the government representatives rather than he [Giscard] who had decided what was meant by consensus' (Milton *et al.* 2005: 83). This argument suggests that the agenda-setting power of the president has been limited by the shadow of the subsequent IGC. Ultimately, this logic provokes the question of how the president perceived the intergovernmental limits of his agenda-setting power. In other words, what did Giscard know about governments' positions and which reactions did he expect from the IGC?

For the president, one way of guessing his discretion *vis-à-vis* the IGC were the positions presented by the governmental delegates to the Convention. However, delegates enjoyed different degrees of freedom to express personal views. In some member states 'there was no concrete mandate but rather a general outline' of the future institutional organisation of the EU (Blavoukos and Pagoulatos 2006: 143). Professional backgrounds suggest that most delegates were more likely to prefer a higher level of integration than their governments (Table 4.1): twelve of the twenty-five delegations were composed of at least one Brussels-based national diplomat, an MEP or a former member of the European Commission, namely Santer and Christophersen. In addition, nine delegations were composed of at least one member who started to work at an EU institution right after the Convention or had been working there before. In addition, Joschka Fischer was discussed as a candidate for the post of European foreign minister. Unsurprisingly, he strongly promoted the establishment of an EU diplomatic corps (Norman 2003: 296). Louis Michel (BE), Danuta Hübner (PL), Peter Balazs (HU) and Sandra Kalniete (LT) served as Commissioners under Romano Prodi. Antti Peltomäki (SF) became head of the European Commission's representation in Finland, Henrik Hololei (EE) became head of cabinet for Commissioner Siim Kallas, and Gijs de Fries (NL) became the EU's anti-terrorism coordinator. Only Austria, Malta, Spain and the UK were represented by governmental delegates and alternates who neither before

---

59. In addition to these 207 individuals, the Economic and Social Committee (three representatives), the Committee of the Regions (six representatives), the social partners (three representatives) and the European Ombudsman were invited to attend the meetings as observers. In sum, 220 persons participated in the deliberations of the Convention.

nor after the Convention worked in either the Brussels-based national diplomacy or any of the EU institutions. Among the most remarkable personalities was the British delegate and Secretary of State for Wales, Peter Hain, who was involved in the drafting of 257 amendments and the seventy-five-year-old former president of Estonia, Lennart Meri. The only two academics among the governmental delegates were Teija Tiilikainen (SF) and Ernani Lopes (PT).

In Chapter 3, the available survey data is summarised on the positions of the Convention delegates. The data presented by König et al. (2006) covers 102 delegates. Table 4.1 identifies the governmental delegates who responded to the survey. Respondents cover all member states except for Cyprus. Overall, the survey asked forty-eight questions, twenty-one of which are directly comparable to questions asked in the DOSEI survey on governmental delegates at the subsequent IGC.[60]

Table 4.1 lists how many of the twenty-one directly comparable issues that the delegates' positions deviated from the national positions. The percentages vary, with a roughly 77 per cent consensus for the Spanish and Slovenian delegations to less than 35 per cent for the Dutch and Italian, with a mean consensus of almost 60 per cent. According to chance, the expectation would be about a 40 per cent consensus. Compared to this number, the observed consensus appears relatively high, which suggests that the delegates differ systematically from the positions of their governments. On the following issues, more than half of the delegations revealed deviating positions: organisation of the Council presidency (13); composition of the Commission (13); EU competences in agricultural (14), employment (15) and education policy (15); EP empowerment in budgetary procedures (15). On other issues, only two or fewer delegations deviated from the official positions of their governments: right of initiative for the EP (1) and EU competences in taxation (1) and health policy (2). As for the issues that theory assigns to the vertical dimension, the majority of deviating delegates demand a higher level of integration than their governments. This finding is confirmed by Figure 4.4. By using the twenty-one bridges, it is possible to plot the positions of the twenty-four interviewed delegates into the two-dimensional intergovernmental issues space.[61] The Estonian position, represented by Lennart Meri, the former Estonian leader of the independence movement, constitutes an 'outlier'. Similar to Peter Hain, he strongly rejected further EU powers, but supported majoritarian decision-making.[62]

Figure 4.4 depicts the unanimity core and the win-set for the EU-25 (solid line) and the EU-15 (dotted line). Considering the EU-25, the ToN was located close to the boundary of the unanimity core. Accordingly, the win-set of the status quo as

---

60. For the technical meaning of 'directly comparable', please consult the definition of 'bridgers' in Chapter 3.

61. This is done by applying the algorithm described in Chapter 3 under the constraint that the item parameters of the twenty-one bridgers are fixed. For a list of the twenty-one bridgers, please see appendix.

62. However, both cases, Hain and Meri, reveal a high number of missing values. Accordingly, the estimates of their ideal positions come with high standard errors.

a short history of eu treaty negotiations | 129

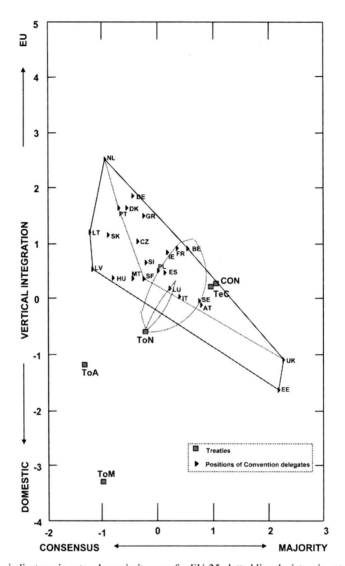

Solid line indicates win-set and unanimity core for EU-25, dotted line depicts win-set and unanimity core for EU-15

AT: Austria; BE: Belgium; CY: Cyprus; CZ: Czech Republic; DE: Germany; DK: Denmark; EE: Estonia; ES: Spain; FR: France; GR: Greece; HU: Hungary; IE: Ireland; IT: Italy; NL: The Netherlands; PT: Portugal; SF: Finland; SE: Sweden; SK: Slovak Republic; SI: Slovenia; LU: Luxembourg; LV: Latvia; LT: Lithuania; MT: Malta; PL: Poland; UK: United Kingdom; ToN: Treaty of Nice; TeC: Constitutional Treaty; CON: Convention draft

Figure 4.4: Positions of the 25 governmental delegations to the European Convention located in the intergovernmental conflict space

defined by Lennart Meri (EE) and Peter Balazs (HU) has been almost empty. This finding does not support my argument that Giscard D'Estaing approximated the reaction of the subsequent IGC by the positions of all twenty-five governmental delegations. However, at the time of the Convention, the new member states were still accession countries without voting rights. While the governments of the old member states did not ignore the newcomers altogether, they might have found it even harder to make their voice heard by the Praesidium than delegations of the old member states. This view is supported by the number of amendments each delegate signed[63] (see Table 4.1). Delegations from old member states participated in an average of 129 amendments, varying between twenty-seven for the Greek delegation and 257 for the British delegation. The ten Eastern European delegations participated in an average of only fifty-three amendments, with a maximum of 117 supported by the Slovenian delegate Dimitrij Rupel and a minimum of twenty-two amendments supported by Cyprus. Considering the high numbers for Luxembourg, Slovenia, Portugal, Ireland and Austria, this difference cannot be explained by population size.

Once the governmental delegates of the ten new member states are ignored, Figure 4.4 locates the ToN further away from the lower margin of the core, now defined by Peter Hain (UK) and Teija Tiilikainen (SF). Accordingly, the size of the win-set of the status quo increases. It is defined by Peter Hain (UK), Gerhard Tusek (AT) and Teija Tiilikainen (SF). The Convention proposal is located at the upper left margin of the EU-15 win-set and directly on the upper margin of the unanimity core.[64]

Unfortunately, the president himself did not answer the questionnaire; hence, it is impossible to know the true position of the agenda-setter. Figure 4.4 suggests that his position should be located somewhere in the upper left corner. In that case he would have located the draft as close to his position as possible, restricted by the win-set of the EU-15. Although speculative, there are at least three good reasons that this might indeed reflect Giscard D'Estaing's true position. First, his biography. He worked together with Mitterrand and was influenced by Jean Monnet, one of the founding fathers of the Europe's federal vision. In an interview shortly before the Convention, he even stated that the EU would develop as a 'union of states with federal competences' (Norman 2003: 29). Second, he might be considered as a representative of the French government, which, as its predecessor, favoured more integration and a reform of decision-rule toward majoritarianism. Third, Giscard wanted to secure his position in the history books. It appears always more appealing to become known as the founding father of the 'European Republic' or the 'United States of Europe' than as the 'Consolidator of Nice'.

---

63. In order to control for the division of labour among delegates and alternates, the mean refers to the partner with the highest number of amendments.
64. Estimating the two-dimensional conflict space only on the basis of DOSEI data (hence without the data for the Amsterdam and Nice IGCs) not only supports this finding, but locates the Constitutional Treaty inside the EU-15 unanimity core.

SUMMARY

In this chapter, a detailed discussion of the positions governments revealed on the most contentious reform issue at each of the three post-Maastricht IGCs is provided, in particular, focussing on the statistical estimates derived in Chapter 3 with information found in official position papers. Five results of this analysis stand out:

First, the statistical estimates match with the qualitative information. However, even my rather cursory discussion illustrates the benefits of the statistical approach. A description of every government's position on all reform issues is far too complex to answer the research questions raised in Chapter 1.

Second, approaching enlargement added pressure to solving Europe's constitutional quandary. As a consequence, governments of small states became increasingly compromising over issues of institutional design. By contrast, governments from larger states felt an increasing pressure to install more proportional decision-rules before the number of small states would increase by another ten to twelve.

Third, governmental positions change from one IGC to the next, even on highly salient issues such as the extension of EU competences to foreign and home affairs. Some of these changes are easily explained by a change in the partisan composition of government, e.g. the New Labour government in Britain and the end of the Kohl era in Germany. However, others are not. The issue of positional change is elaborated on in Chapter 5.

Fourth, the official position papers illustrate that governments thought of treaty revisions as package deals. This was particularly obvious with regard to those reforms of the decision-rule that would have altered the distribution of power among member states, such as the voting rule, the composition of the Commission and the Council presidency. This observation provides further theoretical justification for my methodological approach.

Fifth, official positions illustrate that governmental positions over the level of vertical integration and the decision-rule can hardly be considered separable. By contrast, the statements indicate that a government's decision to delegate is preceded by a careful deliberation about whether the EU would handle the matter efficiently and in their own interest, both aspects depending on the design of decision-rules and institutions. The issue of non-separability is explored further in Chapter 6.

Furthermore, the present chapter discusses in how far the history of European treaty revision can be conceived as a sequence of equilibrium and disequilibrium. In particular, the discussion centres on how far we can uphold the propositions of liberal intergovernmentalism, which proves so powerful in explaining earlier treaty revisions. Two findings stand out:

First, as a consequence of Northern and Southern enlargement, it is impossible for a group of large member states to dominate the intergovernmental bargaining arena as might have been the case during earlier periods of European integration. At both IGCs, the status quo was in disequilibrium (i.e. outside the unanimity core) and the reform left all governments better off (i.e. it was located inside the win-set of the status quo). Moreover, treaty reforms agreed at Amsterdam and Nice are best characterised as compromises at the lowest common denominator. Both reform treaties are situated on the margins of the unanimity core. As a consequence, both reform treaties are a long way off the ideal positions revealed by the governments of large states.

Second, enlargement and the new agenda rendered the unconstrained bargaining game described by Moravcsik (1998) very difficult, if not impossible. Despite lengthy and costly bargaining processes, the reforms agreed at Amsterdam and Nice did not exceed the lowest common denominator. In response, member states decided to increase the efficiency and effectiveness of intergovernmental bargaining by installing a preparatory Committee, namely the Convention. As a matter of fact, the Convention has been strongly advocated by the larger and reformist member states such as France, Germany and Italy. In retrospect, their support appears rather unsurprising. But while this procedural innovation fulfilled its aim and led to a treaty revision beyond the least common denominator, it prolonged the process and created uncertainties along the way. When governments began to realise that the Convention would eventually draft a coherent treaty proposal, they were incapable of unilaterally breaking out. Instead, they upgraded their delegations in order to influence the Convention proposal. Yet the reverse side of this move was that it increased the reputation cost of discarding the Convention proposal in the subsequent IGC.

Inside the Convention, the Praesidium exercised enormous agenda-setting powers (Tsebelis and Proksch 2007), almost exclusively restricted by the president's anticipated reaction of the subsequent IGC. However, one obstacle unforeseen by Giscard D'Estaing was the unique number of ten governments announcing referenda and, in particular, the negative outcome of the plebiscites in France (May 2005) and the Netherlands (June 2005). It took another two years until, in October 2007, the twenty-seven heads of state and government signed a mitigated version of the Constitutional Treaty, now referred to as the Lisbon Treaty. Essentially, it drops any reference to and symbols of a fully fledged constitution. Furthermore, it provides the possibility for opt-outs from the Charter of Fundamental Rights and from Justice and Police Cooperation and delays the reform of the Council voting rules (König *et al.* 2008). However, the Irish voters temporarily stalled the ratification process when they rejected the Lisbon Treaty in June 2008. In the subsequent chapter, it is argued that the importance of voters and parliaments is not restricted to the ratification stage, but extends to the formation of the governmental position.

chapter five | what explains governments' positions on european integration?

In this chapter, official governmental positions are explained using economic and political variables, by scrutinising the assumptions that member states can be treated as unitary actors. In particular, it is argued that government's most preferred level of vertical integration E_i^* is a result of a domestic-preference aggregation process. By contrast, the government's ideal position on reforming the decision-rule K_i^* corresponds to country-specific, structural characteristics, in particular population size. As a consequence, the revealed position on reforming the decision-rule are more stable and shift in lockstep in reaction to a change of context.

In Chapter 2, the discussion rested on public choice literature, which argues that actors' preferences over constitutional design depend on two factors: first, the heterogeneity costs implied by any collectivisation of decision from small, homogeneous to larger, heterogeneous groups; second, the efficiency gains that are realised by the internalisation of externalities and by economics of scale that imply a reduction of unit costs for public policies. Assuming that governments have unlimited foresight, are perfectly informed about future EU politics and the preferences of their domestic principals, the model allows for calculating their expected utility over alternative institutional designs. Unfortunately, this assumption is somewhat unrealistic. First, national governments are, after all, collective actors and representatives of domestic interests. Hence, the question emerges, whose preferences are represented by national governments at European treaty negotiations and whose preferences will be represented by national governments in future EU politics? Second, constitutional choice is always accompanied by a high level of uncertainty with respect to its consequences. This uncertainty is particularly high among individual voters. After all, voters primarily delegate such complex matters to politicians and experts in order to reduce the costs of information-seeking. The problem is that this delegation raises a potential control problem between the principals (voters) and the agents (government). In this chapter, the focus is the analysis of how governments represent the interests of their electorate via intermediary delegates such as political parties and parliaments. The hypotheses derived in Chapter 2 are tested in this analysis.

As regards treaty reforms, prior to Maastricht powerful domestic producer interests were identified as the most relevant origins of governmental positions (Moravcsik 1998). In particular, the arguments referred to the highly competitive industrial producers in northern Europe and the large and powerful agricultural sector in the southern member states, both eager to gain mutual market access – final deals eventually balanced by financial side payments. The SEA and the Maastricht Treaty caused a shift in the focus of the intergovernmental negotiations to the regulatory details of implementing the common market. As a consequence, first doubts turned up as to whether producers are the only relevant domestic actors. 'Regulatory standards may mobilize not just producers, but organised public interest groups and parties that favour particular environmental, consumer, or health and safety regulations. Such matters can generate a powerful electoral response' (Moravcsik 1998: 40). Nevertheless, the key to understanding European integration has long been seen in the mutual benefits of producers in competitive industrial nations as well as in less industrialised nations with large agricultural sectors.

In the wake of Maastricht, the agenda of European treaty reforms shifted away from the common market toward political integration and institutional reform. As regards this new agenda, the role of domestic producer interests remains an open question. Subsequently, it can be argued that for our understanding of the post-Maastricht governmental reform positions, the old, structuralist explanations need revision.

At the same time, the emergence of negative referenda on European reform treaties prove that voters are of increasing importance for our understanding of European treaty reform. Although voters' interest in European politics is low in comparison to domestic politics, it has been steadily increasing during the last decade (Zürn 2006: 224). Political parties respond to this trend by upgrading the attention and resources devoted to European politics. Although European matters cover roughly 4 per cent of national party manifestos, they have been, since the mid 1990s, included in manifestos across member states and political groups (Volkens 2005: 274).

Before Maastricht, governments' representation of domestic producer interests has been silently permitted by the majority of voters who could agree on a common national economic interest (Inglehart 1971). After Maastricht, the future of European integration is increasingly contested at the domestic level. This observation raises the question of how influential different domestic actors are in forming and controlling the governmental reform position. By how much are governmental reform positions a product of a structured domestic-preference formation process? If so, which role do different institutional and procedural provisions of the preference formation process play for the representation of voters by their governments?

The remainder of this chapter is organised into five sections. First, the observed changes in governmental positions on both conflict dimensions are briefly described, followed by possible explanatory variables. Then, the relation between the two most prominent economic factors and governmental reform positions are revisited. Thereafter, the unitary actor assumption is unravelled and the role of voters, parties and parliaments analysed along empirical indicators. Finally, I conduct a multivariate empirical analysis and summarise my results.

THE UNITARY ACTOR ASSUMPTION

Previous empirical studies have been limited to explaining cross-country variation (e.g. Aspinwall 2007; König and Hug 2006; Moravcsik and Nicolaïdis 1999). Such a static approach makes it more or less impossible to unravel the effects of heterogeneous domestic interests within individual countries. Economic, social and political differences between countries are relatively stable. Therefore, it is essential to focus on change in these variables in order to learn about the effect of dynamic and heterogeneous interests within individual countries. Only a longitudinal research design allows for a more explicit test of the unitary actor assumption. If governments are the representatives of heterogeneous domestic interests, their positions will change in response to domestic changes, such as a new partisan composition of government or parliament as well as changes in public opinion. The empirical scope and the longitudinal design of the present study allow for an explicit analysis of such changes. In particular, I argue that structural political characteristics of member states define a more or less stable corridor for the official governmental positions on integration. Within this corridor, the official governmental position is a result of the dynamic political processes of domestic-preference aggregation.

However, this approach is only promising if the observed variation among governmental positions does not completely rest in either time or countries, but in a combination of both.[1] Figure 5.1 depicts member states' changes within the two-dimensional latent space. The triangles that are formed by connecting the three positions at Amsterdam, Nice and Rome II cover a remarkably small part of the overall issue space. In other words, Figure 5.1 suggests that governments' positions do not move randomly through the conflict space. In some countries the cross-temporal transitions appear especially stable. A transition is defined as movement from one IGC to the next. For example, the transition from Nice to Rome II led to almost negligible changes in Austria, Belgium, Italy and Finland, whereas the transition from Amsterdam to Nice led to little change in the national positions of Germany, France, Luxembourg and Spain. Finally, the UK reveals relatively little change for either of the two transitions.

Furthermore, one might suspect that the governmental position in certain countries reflects a higher degree of volatility than in others. Possible reasons for such a pattern could be either the systematically different quality of the data available for some countries or the fact that relevant domestic actors tend to be more stable in some as compared to other member states. However, in absolute numbers, the changes are uncorrelated across the two transitions. Accordingly, it is difficult to identify countries that always tend to move or remain static, or to observe a catch-up process in which a country that was stable at the first transition was more likely to move in the second transition.

Next, it might be the case that the positions of all governments move in parallel from one IGC to the next. Indeed, for the horizontal dimension, Figure 5.1 reveals such a long-term trend. The fifteen old member states moved steadily toward the

---

1. Unfortunately, the ten central European member states that entered the Union in May 2004 are excluded for three reasons. First, most theoretical arguments presume a certain experience in membership on behalf of domestic actors. Second, the availability of data on explanatory variables is limited. Finally, my central methodological innovation is the longitudinal research design, which, unfortunately, cannot be extended to the central European member states because their positions have been measured only for Rome II.

136 | european integration and its limits

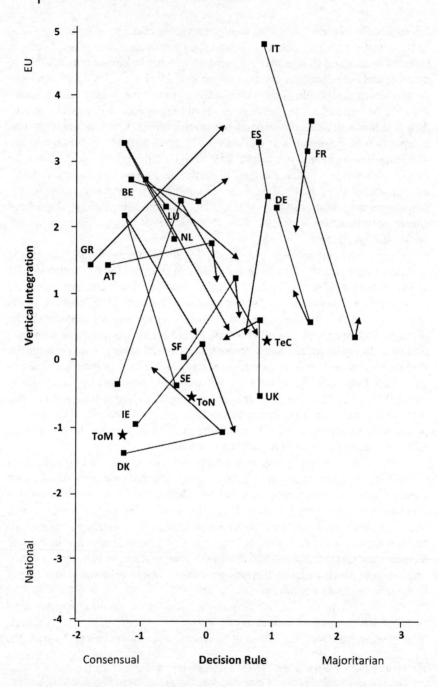

Figure 5.1: The changing reform position of European governments: From Amsterdam (beginning of arrow) over Nice to the Constitutional IGC (end of arrow)

right; i.e. at Amsterdam (mean: -0.39) they favoured less majoritarianism than at Nice (mean: 0.18), when they favoured less majoritarian reforms, as compared to Rome II (mean: 0.51). As regards the first transition, the only exceptions to this rule are Luxembourg, the Netherlands and Sweden; for the second transition, Germany, Denmark, Spain and the UK move in opposition to this general trend. The underlying reason for this trend is discussed in Chapter 4. With Eastern enlargement approaching, all governments became increasingly aware of the necessity for efficiency-enhancing reforms. Hence, we are dealing with a context-level effect. For the vertical dimension, no such trend exists.

At the level of individual member states, positions on vertical integration reveal a higher volatility as compared to those on the decision rule. Given that, at first glance, positions on the decision-rule are related to member states' population sizes, this observation is rather unsurprising. As regards vertical integration, the correlation between governmental positions revealed at different IGCs varies between 0.35 and 0.40 (Pearson's r). By contrast, the correlation for governmental positions on the horizontal dimension is almost twice as strong (Pearson's r ranging between 0.61 to 0.70).

Overall, the observed variation can be systematically decomposed into three components: a time-variant, country-level effect; a time-variant, context-level effect; and a time-invariant effect. Accordingly, a linear regression model, which explains government i's position at any of the three IGCs t, can be presented in the following way:

$$Y_{i,t} = \begin{cases} \sum_{t=1}^{m} \alpha_t & \leftarrow time-variant, context \\ +\beta Y_{i\,t-1} & \leftarrow time-invariant, country \\ +\varepsilon_{i,t} & \leftarrow time-variant, country \end{cases}$$

Table 5.1 summarises the estimates for both dimensions. In order to distinguish between the time-variant and invariant component of governmental reform positions, I conceive the position at time t as a function of the position the same country's government had revealed at the previous IGC (t-1). Unfortunately, this strategy reduces the number of cases to N=30. The results support the previous analysis of variance. The horizontal dimension reveals a large and highly significant effect of the lagged dependent variable, i.e. the time-invariant, country-level effect of the observed variance ($\beta = 0.61$). In other words, consecutive governments from the same member state reveal a similar position on the design of the decision-rule across time. Furthermore, the large and weakly significant positive estimate of $\alpha_{Rome\,II}$ indicates that from Nice to Rome II, all governments shifted toward majoritarianism. However, the estimate of α_{Nice} turns out to be insignificant. Finally, the model indicates that only half of the observed variance can be ascribed to time-variant, country-level effects *(1- R^2=0.55)*. So far, it remains an open question as to which proportion of this unexplained variance can be accounted for by meaningful country-level variables.

By contrast, the vertical dimension reveals no significant context-level effects, though the negative estimate of $\alpha_{Rome\ II}$ comes very close, which might indicate that governments of old member states turned out to be less integrationist than at earlier IGCs. The time-invariant, country-level effect is considerably smaller (β = 0.35), but still statistically significant at the 0.05-level. Moreover, a larger part of the variation rests in the time-variant, country-level effect *(1- R^2=0.67)*. This corresponds to the higher volatility of governmental positions on vertical integration observed in Figure 5.1.

Table 5.1: Analysis of variance of governmental positions at Nice and Rome II (EU15)

N=30	$x_{vertical}$	$x_{dec.rule}$	Analysis of Variance
α_{Nice} (s.e.)	0.07 (0.16)	0.03 (0.25)	time-variant, context level
$\alpha_{Rome\ II}$ (s.e.)	-0.46 (0.18)	0.45 (0.17)	time-variant, context level
β (s.e.)	0.35 (0.12)	0.61 (0.13)	time-invariant, country level
$\varepsilon_{i,t}$ (1- R^2)	0.65	0.55	time-variant, country level

Overall, the average changes on the horizontal dimension are larger than those on the vertical dimension, but governments move in lockstep – a finding that reflects the qualitative discussion in Chapter 4. In other words, the corridor defined by country-specific political, social and economic characteristics is narrower for the horizontal as compared to the vertical dimension. Therefore, the focus of the subsequent analysis is on vertical integration. In the remainder of this chapter, the alleged relationship between structural economic factors and governmental reform positions is first revisited, followed by an analysis as to how far the observed variation of governmental positions can be explained by domestic politics. The second set of hypotheses derived in Chapter 2 are tested here.

THE ECONOMY

Existing research explains the 'national interest' in European integration primarily through politico-economic factors. The majority of these studies focus on different structures of national economies. In particular, they consider reform positions to be a function of producer interests. Countries that stand to benefit from the enhanced trade and competition in the Single European Market are thought to favour a high level of integration (Aspinwall 2007; Moravcsik 1998). According to Aspinwall (2007), the same holds true for member states that receive high net transfer payments out of the EU budget.

Following this branch of the literature, the importance of different economic factors depends on the power of their domestic-level interest representation. According to Moravcsik (1998), the pre-Maastricht era was characterised by increasing economic coordination and the national interest was determined by highly-organised producer groups. Governmental integration policies are 'biased in favour of those actors with concentrated intense and clearly preexisting interests and against those with more diffuse, uncertain, or unrepresented interests. In the latter category belong consumers, taxpayers and third-country producers' (1998: 39).

König and Bräuninger (2004) depart from the existing literature by arguing that EU net payers will have a limited interest in further expanding the EU budget. Therefore, any additional public good provided by the EU implies a reallocation of the EU's scarce financial resources. Accordingly, those who receive high benefits in the status quo should oppose the extended production of public goods by the EU, i.e. further integration.[2] To illustrate this point, König and Bräuninger (2004) deploy Romer and Rosenthal's (1978) taxpayer model to the EU. They demonstrate that, under the assumption of diminishing marginal utilities, net payers will have a limited interest in expanding the EU budget. Against this background, any additional public good provided by the EU implies a reallocation of the scarce financial resources. In a similar way, enlargement threatens the beneficiaries of current transfer payments (Plümper and Schneider 2007).

According to the European Commission's budget report in 2004,[3] the CAP accounts for roughly 43 per cent of the EU's total budget, including the special programmes for rural development. In addition, the structural and cohesion policies account for another 36 per cent of the budget. Considering that the overall EU budget covers about 1.2 per cent of the EU's Gross National Income, the average taxpayer might be relatively unaware of the fact that a small percentage of his taxes are, both directly or indirectly, transferred to and spent by the EU. On the other hand, these programmes have generated a group of beneficiaries whose economic well-being heavily depends on transfer payments by the EU. The most prominent of these stakeholders are farmers and the food industry, small and medium-sized enterprises as well as the citizens and their political representatives in structurally weak regions.[4]

The standard argument expects governments that represent beneficiaries from EU transfer payments to be more favourable toward further integration. Following the logic of König and Bräuninger, the opposite should be true. Yet, Figure 5.2

---

2. This argument assumes that delegation would indeed cause a redistributive effect at the EU level. While this is more likely in areas the EU might be granted a limited budget (e.g. security cooperation, defence policy, external border control, migration (asylum), research policy), it is less likely in areas where EU competences would most likely be restricted to regulatory standards (e.g. environment, tourism, health, social security and social policy).

3. Source: http://europa.eu.int/eur-lex/budget/data/D2005_VOL1/EN/; (accessed 11 January 2007).

4. Between approximately 40 per cent (1996) and 59 per cent (2004) of the payments released under all structural funds were directly entitled to infrastructural projects (European Commission, DG Regio (2002). The Thematic Evaluation of Structural Funds, Appendix I, p. 69, available online at http://ec.europa.eu/regional_policy/sources /docgener/evaluation/ doc/sustainable_annexes.pdf, (accessed 12 October 2006). However, these numbers exclusively refer to public infrastructure (esp. transport and communication) and do not include training and modernisation measures, which are frequently financed under Objectives 1 and 2 and most of which equally benefit companies and employees in Sector Ia).

provides little evidence for any systematic relationship between the two variables.

I shall describe Figure 5.2 in more detail because similar figures will be provided for other explanatory variables, too. Along the vertical axis, it depicts the governmental positions on integration, and along the horizontal axis it depicts the net transfer payments as a percentage of GDP. In doing so, the figure combines three analytical steps. In *step 1*, I separate the observed data along the three IGCs. Thereby, I control for the IGC-specific context (α_t). In *step 2*, I distinguish between the time-variant ($\varepsilon_{i,t}$) and time-invariant ($\beta Y_{i,t-1}$) component of governmental positions at Nice and Rome II. Please note that $\varepsilon_{i,t} + \beta Y_{i,t-1} = Y_{i,t} - \alpha_t$, where α_t is an IGC-specific level-shift, which is controlled for by step 1. In *step 3*, I provide linear predictors for each of the five samples. In short, net transfer payments[5] as percentage of GDP, show little systematic correlation to any component of the observed variance among governmental positions.

Furthermore, the standard economic approach suggests that governments are more integrationist the higher the total benefits of the national economy under the common market. In other words, governments that represent highly competitive economic sectors should reveal a more integrationist position. I operationalise this argument via the balance of Intra-EU trade as a percentage of GDP, which approximates an economy's competitiveness within and the importance of the common market. However, Figure 5.3 provides no evidence that governments representing national economies with a strongly positive balance of trade prefer more integration. If anything, there is weak evidence for the opposite. In particular, the Irish economy heavily benefits from exports to the EU, but the Irish government rejects further integration. In contrast, the Luxembourger and Greek economy spend around 10 per cent of their GDP for imports from other EU states and their governments reveal a very pro-integrationist position.

Overall, the empirical evidence does not support the hypothesis that governments that represent beneficiaries of either the common market or EU transfer payments are systematically more integrationist. While the importance of producer interests used to be a powerful explanation for the treaty revision until Maastricht, it has lost its explanatory power since. The reason is obvious: the new agenda focuses on many issues beyond the common market, which was more or less completed at Maastricht. Instead, the focus is on political integration over an array of different policy areas and on a new separation of power between regional, national and European-level actors. In this debate, governments no longer represent national economic interests, silently supported by a vast majority of voters and parties. Instead, the subsequent analysis reveals that governments represent heterogeneous and multi-layered domestic interests.

---

5. As alternative operationalisation, I used the net transfers *per capita* as well as the gross transfers received as percentage of GDP and per capita. However, the results do not differ.

what explains governments' positions on european integration? | 141

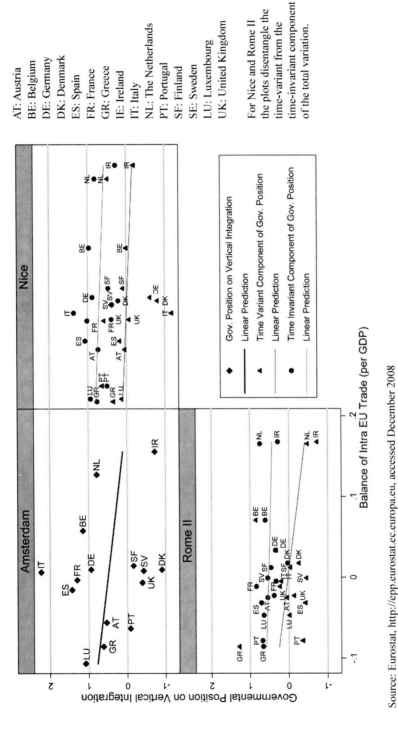

Source: Eurostat, http://epp.eurostat.ec.europa.eu, accessed December 2008

Figure 5.2: Governmental positions plotted against the balance of intra-EU trade as percentage of GDP

142 | european integration and its limits

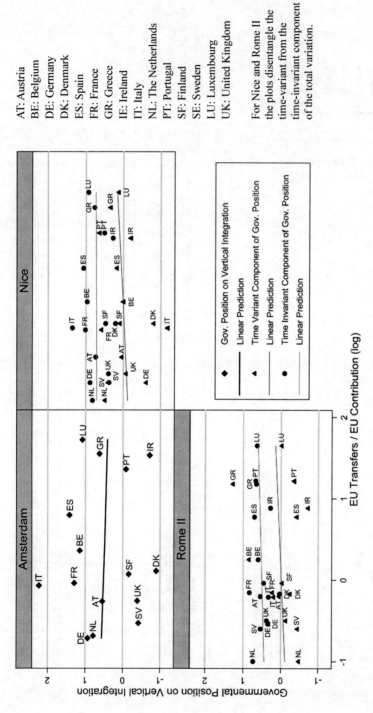

Figure 5.3: Governmental positions plotted against the net payer position measured as the log ratio of received EU transfer to EU contribution in the year preceding each IGC

Source: 'Allocation of 2004 Expenditures by Member State'; http://ec.europa.eu/budget/documents/revenue_expenditure_en.htm, accessed 10 July 2007

THE VOTERS

Next, public opinion is analysed in order to see how far it can explain the observed variation in governmental positions. Public opinion studies find a significant correlation between the evaluation of EU membership, on the one hand, and educational factors as well as sectoral occupation on the other (Gabel 1998). In particular, public opinion responds to those EU legislative activities that are of relevance to their sector of occupation (Luetgert 2007). More recent studies highlight several other mediating and contextual factors, such as ideology and national economic development (e.g. Brinegar and Jolly 2004; Hooghe and Marks 2004). 'Economic theories work best when economic consequences are perceived with some accuracy, are large enough to matter, and when the choice a person makes actually affects the outcome. To the extent that these conditions are not present, group identities are likely to be decisive' (Hooghe and Marks 2004: 2). Empirically, the authors find that the attitudes of party elites and their supporters are highly correlated, as other studies have found (Thomassen and Schmitt 1999; Ray 2003).[6]

Against this background, earlier studies of individual IGCs find a systematic correlation between the position of the median voter and the revealed governmental position (Aspinwall 2007; Finke 2009b). Accordingly, my Hypothesis 2.1 expects governmental positions to correspond to the position of the median voter. In order to test this hypothesis, I operationalise voters' positions on European integration through a set of questions asked on a regular basis in the Eurobarometer surveys.[7] The surveys EB47.1, EB52.0 and EB59.1 asked respondents whether they preferred decisions in a particular policy area to be 'taken by the [national] government or jointly within the European Union'. The surveys have been conducted during the preparatory stage of each IGC. Accordingly, they should reflect governments' knowledge of voters' preferences prior to the decisive summit. All three surveys comprise the following policy areas: defence, protection of the environment, currency, humanitarian aid, health and social welfare, rules for the media, the fight against unemployment, education, scientific research, foreign policy, culture, immigration policy, political asylum and fight against drugs. This selection covers most of the areas on the post-Maastricht reform agenda, with the notable exception of taxation and fiscal policy. Responses are highly correlated across each of the thirteen questions. Using factor analysis, it was possible to re-

---

6. This raises the questions whether elite opinion forms the interests of voters or vice versa. Thomassen and Schmitt (1999) as well as Franklin and Wlezien (1997) present some evidence that the interest formation process is rather bottom-up: the latter authors argue that the direction of interest formation depends on the salience voters attach to a certain policy. For the new eastern European member states, Tucker et al. (2002) find that transition winners reveal more positive attitudes toward the EU as compared to transition losers.

7. The data originates from the following Eurobarometer surveys: 1996: EB46.0 (za2898); 1997: EB47.1 (za2936); 1998: EB49.0 (za3052); 1999: EB52.0 (za3204); 2000: EB53.0 (za3296); 2001: EB56.2 (za3627); 2002 (spring): EB57.1 (za3639); 2002 (fall): EB58.1 (za3693); 2003: EB59.1 (za3904); 2004: EB60.1 (za3938). The data is available at the Zentralarchiv für Empirische Sozialforschung Köln, www.gesis.org/ZA. The identifier for each data set in the Zentralarchiv Köln (ZA) is printed in brackets.

duce the thirteen policy areas to a single underlying factor, which explains almost 64 per cent of the overall variance.[8] Similar results are maintained when using the EB questions on whether or not the respondent is of the opinion that his country's membership in the EU is a 'good thing'.

Figure 5.4 plots the median voters' positions on delegation against the governmental positions. The overall correlation is particularly strong for the Amsterdam IGC, where member states can be roughly classified into three groups: the 'sceptics' (Austria, Finland, UK, Denmark and Sweden); the 'Europeanists' (the six founding states plus Spain) and a middle group composed of Greece, Portugal and Ireland. However, for Nice and Rome II, a decomposition of the observed variation reveals that the correlation remains strong and highly significant for the time-invariant component of the variation. Although a weakly significant and positive correlation exists with regard to the positional changes from Nice to Rome II, there is no such effect for the previous transition from Amsterdam to Nice. In other words, the position of the median voter explains the cross-country variation of governmental reform positions, but not the changes of governmental positions from one IGC to the next.

In Chapter 2, it is argued that, when revealing their positions at the international bargaining table, governments' discretion is restricted by their domestic principals, such as voters and parliaments. Yet the question is which information governments consider relevant for identifying the boundaries of their discretion. In absolute terms, the governing parties are usually far more integrationist than either the opposition parties or their domestic electorate (Schmitt and Thomassen 2000). Therefore, the governmental delegates might be more interested in whether or not the short-term trend in public opinion is favourable toward European integration (Hypothesis 2.3). In order to capture these short-term trends in public opinion, a Eurobarometer question is utilised that asks respondents whether their country's membership in the EU is a 'good' or a 'bad thing'. The advantage of this question is that it has been asked in at least two surveys every year. In order to capture the short-term trend, I subtract the percentage of positive responses ('good thing') at the time the national positions were measured from the percentage of positive responses revealed eighteen months earlier.[9]

Figure 5.5 shows the results. For Amsterdam the effect of the trend variable is zero. Furthermore, there is no effect of the public opinion trend on the time-invariant component of governmental positions. However, Figure 5.5 reveals a positive and significant correlation between the eighteen-month trend in public opinion and the observed changes in governmental position from one IGC to the next. In other words, the cross-country differences in the position of the median voter correspond to the time-invariant cross-country differences of governmental positions. For example, Scandinavian median voters are always less integrationist than their counterparts in France, Spain and Belgium. This matches with the position of their

---

8. As an alternative, I tried an additive index across all policy areas. However, the results remain the same.

9. The results are robust for any time lag between twelve and thirty months.

governments. However, the actual position the Scandinavian governments chose at any particular IGC depends on the short-term trend in public opinion.

Finally, it is argued in Chapter 2 that referenda force the governments to consider the ultimate judgment of the Treaty by the median voter (Hypothesis 2.2). Accordingly, the choice of ratification instrument should reinforce the representation between voters and their governments. In total fifteen member states announced ratification via popular referenda at the three IGCs under examination. At Amsterdam the governments of Denmark, Ireland and Portugal announced referenda. The Irish constitution prescribes a mandatory referendum and the Irish government was the only one to announce a referendum on the Treaty of Nice. Furthermore, an unprecedented, high number of eleven governments, namely Belgium, the Czech Republic, Denmark, France, Ireland, Luxembourg, the Netherlands, Poland, Portugal, Spain and the UK, announced referenda on the Constitutional Treaty. Overall, eleven of the fifteen referenda were announced before the final stage of the respective IGCs, i.e. before the time of measurement (Hug and Schulz 2007: 167).

However, Figure 5.6 provides limited evidence to support my Hypothesis 2.2. On the contrary, it appears as if the correlation between the governmental position $Y_{i,t}$ and the median voter is somewhat stronger in countries without referenda. A closer look reveals that at least for Nice and Rome II, the correlation between the government and the median voter as well as the short-term trend in public opinion is slightly stronger among referendum countries. However, the difference is statistically insignificant by any standard of the discipline. A possible reason for this finding could be that the date governments announced referenda were usually very close to the beginning of the final stage of the IGC. At that time, the domestic-preference formation process might have been completed. Finally, the average position of the government is significantly less integrationist in referendum- as compared to non-referendum countries. Given that representation studies find that governments are usually more integrationist than their voters (Schmitt and Thomassen 1999), this supports the suspicion that referenda are indeed an effective tool to limit governments' discretion. But then the causality might just as well be reversed and only those governments dare to ask their voters whose positions are relatively close.

In short, governmental positions on vertical integration correspond to the integration preferences of their median voters. Most interestingly, governments adjust their positions in reaction to the short-term trends in public opinion. The effect of the chosen ratification instrument appears ambivalent. Next, the focus turns to voters' elected representatives.

146 | european integration and its limits

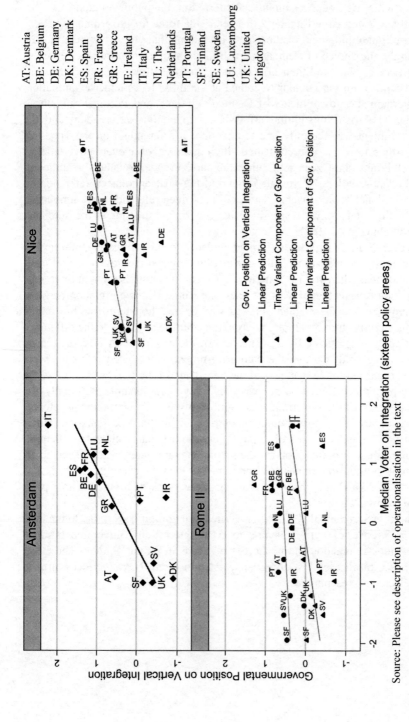

Figure 5.4: *Governmental positions plotted against the median voters' position on European integration. For Nice and Rome II the plots disentangle the time-variant from the time-invariant component of the total variation*

what explains governments' positions on european integration? | 147

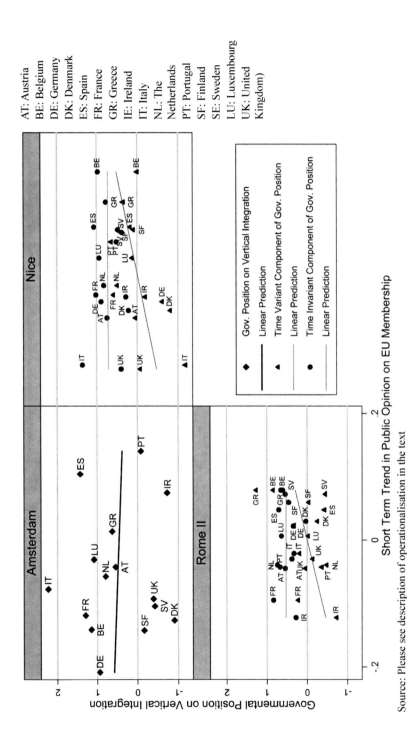

Figure 5.5: Governmental positions plotted against the short-term trend in public opinion on European integration. For Nice and Rome II the plots disentangle the time-variant from the time-invariant component of the total variation

Source: Please see description of operationalisation in the text

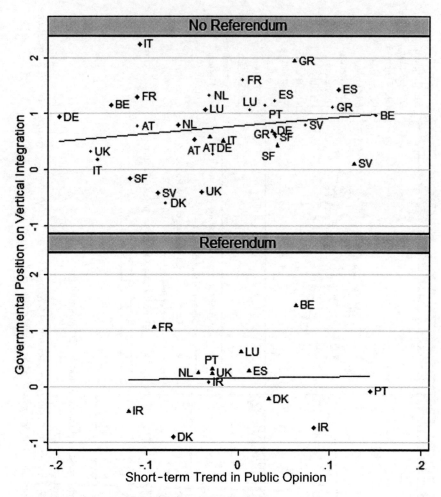

AT: Austria; BE: Belgium; DE: Germany; DK: Denmark; ES: Spain; FR: France; GR: Greece; IE: Ireland; IT: Italy; NL: The Netherlands; PT: Portugal; SF: Finland; SE: Sweden; LU: Luxembourg; UK: United Kingdom

Source: Please see description of operationalisation in the text

Figure 5.6: Governmental positions plotted against the short-term trend in the public opinion on European Integration by ratification instrument

PARTIES AND PARLIAMENT

As regards political parties, the position represented by the government may shift for either of two reasons. First, the position of individual parties may change. Second, the distribution of seats in parliament or the partisan composition of government may change in response to national elections. Please note that it does not take a landslide power shift to cause a crucial change in the partisan positions represented in government or parliament. Even if the composition of parliament remains relatively stable, a minor shift in the distribution of power can cause a significant change in the partisan composition of parliament or government, for example the replacement of the party that provides the median MP or the collapse of the current coalition.

My dependent variable captures governments' official positions revealed before the decisive summit of an IGC. But who represents the government at this stage? For Rome II and Amsterdam, prior empirical research gives a well-grounded answer to this question (König and Hug 2006; Stoiber 2003). First, with few exceptions, the Foreign Ministry takes the lead during the preparatory stage. This applies to both old and new central European member states. In Finland, Spain and Luxembourg, it is the prime minister's office that takes the lead in preparing the official position. In France, interministerial coordination by the Secrétariat Général du Comité Interministériel pour les questions de cooperation économique européenne (SGCI) has a long tradition of preparing IGCs. However, most of the time, the head of the SGCI is the foreign minister (Schulz 2006: 95). Second, during the latter stages of an IGC, the head of government takes the lead, in some countries closely assisted by the Foreign Ministry. In France, dual leadership involving the president and the prime minister is the normal case.

Table 5.2 lists the names and partisan affiliations of all foreign ministers involved in preparing any of the three IGCs. In case the foreign minister has been exchanged during the preparatory stage, Table 5.2 lists both names.[10] Fortunately, such a replacement rarely occurs and never causes ambiguities as regards the partisan affiliation of the ministry. As regards France, I assign the president to be the leader of the decisive summit, whereas the prime and foreign minister are considered to lead the preparatory stage. This decision is particularly relevant, as the IGCs of Amsterdam and Nice fall into periods of cohabitation.

Furthermore, Table 5.2 reveals whether or not the partisan affiliation of the prime and foreign ministers changed between two IGCs. Between the conclusion of the Amsterdam IGC and the decisive stage of Nice, elections were held in all fifteen member states. However, election results altered the partisan composition of government in only five member states. The May 1997 elections in the UK brought New Labour, led to power by Tony Blair, who presented himself as a passionate pro-European. 'Unlike its predecessors, this government is unwaveringly pro-European' (Blair 2000: Foreword). While the Conservatives were dominated

---

10. I define the preparatory stage as the period between the presentation of the agenda by an international task force or committee and the beginning of the decisive negotiation. Usually this takes less than one year (see Chapter 2).

Table 5.2: Partisan Affiliation and position of the heads of government and foreign ministers during the three IGCs

IGC	Country	Head of Government / President	Party	Position	Minister of Foreign Affairs	Party	Position	Median Party (Lower Chamber)	Position
AMST	AT	Vranitzky	SPÖ	7.000	Schüssel	ÖVP	7.000	SPÖ	7.000
AMST	BE	Dehaene	CD&V	6.670	Derycke	SP	6.330	SP	6.330
AMST	DE	Kohl	CDU	6.860	Kinkel	FDP	6.710	FDP	6.710
AMST	DK	P.N. Rasmussen	SD	5.890	Petersen	RV	5.330	SD	5.890
AMST	ES	Aznar	PP	6.310	Matutes	PP	6.310	PP	6.310
AMST	FR	Chirac	RPR	5.250	Juppé / Charette	UDF	6.190	RPR	5.250
AMST	GR	Simits	PASOK	6.700	Papangalos	PASOK	6.700	PASOK	6.700
AMST	IE	Bruton	FG	6.380	Spring	Labour	4.880	FF	5.250
AMST	IT	Prodi	Olive Tree	6.600	Dini	RI	7.000	LN	6.000
AMST	LU	Juncker	CSV	6.308	Poos	LSAP	6.024	CSV	6.308
AMST	NL	Kok	PDvA	5.780	van Mierlo	D66	6.220	PDvA	5.780
AMST	PT	Guterres	PS	6.430	Gama	PS	6.430	PS	6.430
AMST	SF	Lipponen	SDP	6.500	Halonen	SDP	6.500	SDP	6.500
AMST	SV	Persson	SD	6.140	Wallen	SD	6.140	SD	6.140

IGC	Country	Head of Government / President	Party	Position	Minister of Foreign Affairs	Party	Position	Median Party (Lower Chamber)	Position
AMST	UK	Major	Cons	3.500	Rifkind	Cons	3.500	Cons	3.500
NICE	AT	Schüssel	ÖVP	6.780	Schüssel	ÖVP	6.800	SPÖ	6.600
NICE	BE	Verhofstadt	VLD	6.667	Michel	PRL	6.556	PRL	6.556
NICE	DE	Schröder	SPD	6.200	Fischer	GRÜNE	5.667	SPD	6.200
NICE	DK	P.N. Rasmussen	SD	5.143	Petersen	RV	5.330	SD	5.143
NICE	ES	Aznar	PP	6.417	Matutes	PP	6.417	PP	6.417
NICE	FR	Chirac	RPR	5.429	Jospin / Védrin	PS	6.429	RPR	5.429
NICE	GR	Simits	PASOK	7.000	Papandreou	PASOK	7.000	PASOK	7.000
NICE	IE	Ahern	FF	5.833	Andrews	FF	5.833	FF	5.833
NICE	IT	D'Alema	DS	6.667	Dini	RI	6.500	FI	4.833
NICE	LU	Juncker	CSV	6.308	Polfer	DP	6.322	CSV	6.308
NICE	NL	Kok	PDvA	6.545	Aartsen	VVD	5.455	CDA	6.455
NICE	PT	Guterres	PS	7.000	Gama	PS	7.000	PSD	6.600
NICE	SF	Lipponen	SDP	6.600	Halonen	SDP	6.600	RKP/SFP	6.400
NICE	SV	Persson	SD	5.333	Lindh	SD	5.333	SD	5.333

IGC	Country	Head of Government / President	Party	Position	Minister of Foreign Affairs	Party	Position	Median Party (Lower Chamber)	Position
NICE	UK	Blair	Labour	5.385	Cook	Labour	5.385	Labour	5.385
ROME II	AT	Schüssel	ÖVP	6.780	Ferrero-Waldner	ÖVP	6.780	SPÖ	6.380
ROME II	BE	Verhofstadt	VLD	6.540	Michel	MR	6.220	MR	6.220
ROME II	DE	Schröder	SPD	6.110	Fischer	GRÜNE	6.360	GRÜNE	6.360
ROME II	DK	A.F. Rasmussen	V	6.520	Möller	KF	5.440	SD	5.770
ROME II	ES	Aznar / Zapatero	PP/PS	6.230	Palacio	PP	6.230	PS	6.690
ROME II	FR	Chirac	UMP	5.770	Raffarin / de Villepin	UMP	5.770	UMP	5.770
ROME II	IE	Ahern	FF	5.630	Cowen	FF	5.630	FF	5.630
ROME II	IT	Berlusconi	FI	4.987	Frattini	FI	4.987	Pietro	5.000
ROME II	LU	Juncker	CSV	6.308	Polfer	DP	6.322	CSV	6.308
ROME II	NL	Balkenende	CDA	5.780	Scheffer/Bot	CDA	5.780	CDA	5.780
ROME II	PT	Barroso	PSD	6.430	da Cruz / Gouveia	PSD	6.430	PSD	6.430
ROME II	SF	Vanhanen	KESK	5.000	Tuomioja	SDP	6.440	VIHR	5.670

IGC	Country	Head of Government / President	Party	Position	Minister of Foreign Affairs	Party	Position	Median Party (Lower Chamber)	Position
ROME II	SV	Persson	SD	5.500	Freivalds	SD	5.500	SD	5.500
ROME II	UK	Blair	Labour	5.220	Straw	Labour	5.220	Labour	5.220

Note: Party position according to University of Chapel Hill expert surveys (Hooghe *et al.* 2008; Steenbergen and Marks 2007).

(AT: Austria; BE: Belgium; CY: Cyprus; CZ: Czech Republic; DE: Germany; DK: Denmark; EE: Estonia; ES: Spain; FR: France; GR: Greece; HU: Hungary; IE: Ireland; IT: Italy; NL: The Netherlands; PT: Portugal; SF: Finland; SE: Sweden; SK: Slovak Republic; SI: Slovenia; LU: Luxembourg; LT: Latvia; LI: Lithuania; MT: Malta; PL: Poland; UK: United Kingdom).

(CDA: Christian Democratic Appeal; CDU: Christian Democratic Union; CD&V: Christian Democratic and Flemish; Cons: Conservative Party; CSV: Christian Social People's Party; D66: Democrats 66; DS: Democrats of the Left; DP: Democratic Party; FDP: Free Democratic Party; FF: Soldiers of Destiny; FG: Family of the Irish; FI: Forward Italy; GRÜNE: Alliance 90 – The Greens; KESK: Finnish Center Party; KF: Conservative People's Party; Labour: Labour Party; ÖVP: Austrian People's Party; LN: Northern League; MR: Reformist Movement; LSAP: Luxembourg Socialist Workers' Party; PASOK: Panhellenic Socialist Movement; PP: People's Party; PRL: Liberal Reformist Party; PS: Socialist Party; PSD: Social Democratic Party; PvdA: Labour Party; RI: Italian Reneval-Dini List; RKP/SFP: Swedish People's Party; RPR: Rally for the Republic; RV: Radical Left – Social Liberal Party; SD: Social Democrats; SDP: Social Democratic Party of Finland; SP: Socialist Party; SPD: Social Democratic Party of Germany; SPÖ: Social Democratic Party of Austria; SD: Sweden Democrats; UDF: Union for French Democracy; UMP: Union for Popular Movement; V: Venstre, Liberal Party of Denmark; VIHR: Green League; VLD: Flemish Liberals and Democrats; VVD: People's Party for Freedom and Democracy.)

by an intra-party Euro-sceptical minority, the Blair government had no such intra-party opposition (Laursen 2006: 318). Only one month later, President Chirac had to face a leftist, socialist government led by Prime Minister Lionel Jospin. With the victory of the Social Democrats in the German general elections in September 1998, the government of the largest EU member state likewise fell into the hands of leftist parties. Furthermore, Fianna Fail, under the leadership of Bertie Ahern, replaced the Fine Gael-led government in Ireland right after the conclusion of the Amsterdam IGC in June 1997. A different picture appeared in Austria, where the elections held in October 1999 brought the grand coalition government to an end, replaced a coalition of Wolfgang Schüssel's conservative ÖVP with the radical-right Freedom Party, led by populist Jörg Haider. The participation of the Austrian radical rightist party in office caused public outrage and provoked a short-lived political crisis between Brussels and Vienna, lasting until spring 2000. Furthermore, in June 1999 the Belgium general elections resulted in a victory of the Flemish Liberal Party and Guy Verhofstadt became the newly elected Belgian prime minister. Hence, for the first time, Belgium participated in an IGC without the Christian Democrats being in office (Kerremans 2006: 41). In Italy, the soon-to-be president of the European Commission, Romano Prodi, was – after losing a vote of no confidence – replaced by Massimo d'Alema,[11] heading the same centre-left coalition.

Between the Nice summit in December 2000 and the beginning of Rome II in September 2003, almost all member states held general elections. In six member states, the elections led to a change of the governmental coalition. In May 2001 Silvio Berlusconi resumed office as Italian prime minister from socialist Giulio Amato. Earlier that year, Venstre, the Danish liberal party, won the national elections. As a consequence, Anders Fogh Rasmussen became the Danish prime minister and formed a coalition with the conservative People's Party (KF), succeeding the socialist Poul Nyrup Rasmussen. In the Netherlands, Jan Peter Balkenende, leader of the conservative CDA, became prime minister in a coalition with the liberals (VVD) and the right-wing populist List Pim Fortuyn (LPF) after the May 2001 general elections. However, this government collapsed after one year and, as a result of new elections in March 2002, Balkenende formed a coalition with two liberal parties (VVD and D66). In the same month, the social democrats (PDS) won the parliamentary elections in Portugal and today's president Manuel Barroso of the European Commission took over as Portuguese prime minister from the socialist Jorge Sampaio. The June 2002 elections in France brought an end to the cohabitation and Jean-Pierre Raffarin became prime minister. Following the victory of the Finnish centrists (Keskustapuolue) in March 2003, Anneli Jäätteenmäki succeeded the social democrat Paavo Lipponen as Finnish prime minister. Finally, in the shadow of the Madrid terrorist bombings in March 2004, elections in Spain brought the leader of the left-wing alliance PSOE, Jose Luis Zapatero, into the office of the Spanish prime minister, succeeding the conservative Jose Maria Aznar. Overall, and with the exception of Spain, the EU-15 experienced a shift to the right.

---

11. D'Alema was replaced by Amato in April 2000, but this cannot be considered a new government as both the coalition partners and the ministers remained unchanged.

Here, I operationalise party positions through data gathered in expert surveys coordinated at the University of Chapel Hill (Hooghe *et al.* 2008; Steenbergen and Marks 2007). In these surveys, experts were asked to place political parties in their country of expertise on a seven-point Likert scale ranging from '1 = strongly opposed to European integration' to '7 = strongly in favour of European integration'.[12] Subsequently, I use the data from the 1996, 1999 and 2002 surveys. Unfortunately, the 1996 and 1999 surveys do not comprise information on Luxembourg.[13] In previous work, I operationalised party positions through data gathered in the Comparative Manifestos Project (Klingemann *et al.* 2006). However, often parties devote only very short paragraphs to European politics and integration. Anyway, cross-validation revealed a strong correlation between both data sources (Marks *et al.* 2006).

The partisan position of the head of government and the foreign minister are highly correlated (r = 0.75). Given the fact that in twenty-four of the forty-five cases both are members of the same parties, this finding is rather unsurprising. In the remaining twenty-one cases in which the two actors' party memberships differ, the average distance between both parties is approximately 0.5 points, which compares to an average distance of approximately 0.7 points among all heads of government and all foreign ministers. In only five cases is the distance larger than 1 point on the Likert scale. At Amsterdam, the Irish foreign minister was Dick Spring from the Labour Party, which was less integrationist than Fine Gael, the party of the Taoiaseach, Bertie Ahern. At Nice, French President Chirac's UMP was less integrationist than the French Socialist Party of Prime Minister Jospin. Furthermore, the Dutch Prime Minister Wim Kok (PvDA) governed in coalition with the less integration-friendly liberal party (VVD), which provided the foreign minister in the person of Jozias von Aartsen. At Rome II the Danish foreign minister, Per Stig Möller, belonged to the Conservatives (KF), who are less integrationist than the liberal party (V) of Prime Minister Fogh Rasmussen. Finally, the Finnish centre party (KESK) of Prime Minister Paavo Lipponen is less integration prone than the liberal social democratic party of Foreign Minister Erkki Tuomioja.

It goes without saying that all politicians listed in Table 5.2 are strong individual actors with personal opinions on and contributions to European treaty reforms. However, the reader should bear in mind that my dependent variable is the official

---

12. The exact wording of the question was: 'We would like to start this questionnaire with several broad questions about the positions of political parties *vis-à-vis* the EU. In the rows below you will find statements that describe various positions toward the EU. In the columns we have listed the names of the most important parties in [COUNTRY]. In each party column, please circle the number that corresponds to the statement that, in your mind, best describes the position toward the EU that the party's leadership has taken over the course of 1999. The overall orientation of the party leadership towards European Integration: Strongly opposed to European integration; Opposed to European integration; Somewhat opposed to European integration; Neutral towards European integration; Somewhat in favor of European integration; In favor of European integration; Strongly in favor of European integration'.

13. To preserve the two cases, I assume that the positions of Luxembourger parties were constant between 1996 and 2002. However, the results do not change once Luxembourg is excluded.

156 | european integration and its limits

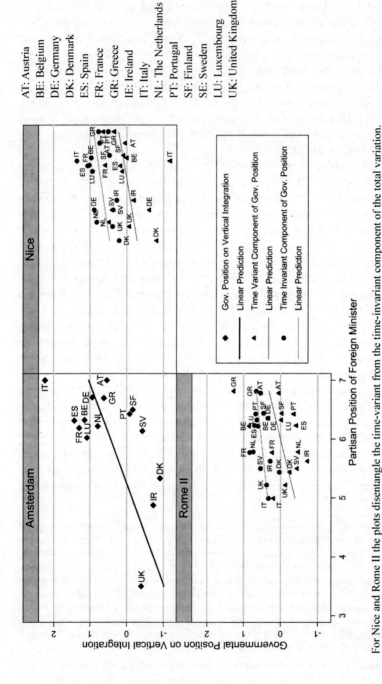

For Nice and Rome II the plots disentangle the time-variant from the time-invariant component of the total variation.
Source: Party position according to University of Chapel Hill expert surveys (Hooghe *et al.* 2008; Steenbergen and Marks 2007; see table 5.2).

Figure 5.7: Governmental positions plotted against the partisan position of the Foreign Minister

governmental position as perceived by experts right before the decisive stage of each IGC. Individuals are only relevant in so far as the interviewed experts factored them into their response when asked for the official position. Furthermore, even the discretion of the strongest political character is limited by certain institutional constraints such as their party, their staff or their electorate. In any case, in the context of the present book, I am more interested in how far these institutional factors support our understanding of European treaty reforms.

Given the fact that the interviews were scheduled before the decisive stage of the international negotiation, the expectation is that if parties matter, it should be those of the foreign minister rather than the head of government. The reason is that in almost all member states the foreign ministries led the process of domestic-preference formation until the prime ministers took over to negotiate the most conflictive parts of the deal. Figure 5.7 supports the overall argument that the partisan composition of the government matters (Hypothesis 2.4). Due to lack of space, I abstain from producing the same figure for the head of government, which, however, is very similar to the one for the foreign minister depicted in figure 5.7. Across all components of the observed variance, both the party of the head of government and the party of the foreign minister reveal a significant correlation to the official governmental position. For Amsterdam the radical anti-integrationist stance of the British Conservatives stands out. For Nice and Rome II, the figure separates the time-variant and invariant parts of observed governmental positions. As regards positional changes, I find Italy to be an outlier that exerts a strong leverage on the results. The reason is that the Italian position at Amsterdam was outstandingly integrationist and party politics can hardly explain its fallback into the normal range. Nevertheless, the figure illustrates that the partisan position of the foreign ministry and, to a slightly lesser extent, of the head of government can explain both the time-invariant component of as well as the observed changes in governmental position.

Furthermore, it was argued in Chapter 2 that when formulating their position, ministers are not only controlled by their own party, but rather by the parliament as an institution (Hypothesis 2.5). Parliamentary decisions in committee and plenum are usually taken by simple majority rule. Assuming that seats in committees are allocated proportionally, the decisive actor for controlling the government is the median MP. In twenty-nine of the forty-five cases, the party of the median MP equals the party of the head of government. Accordingly, all three variables reveal a very high correlation and I abstain from further visual analysis.

Finally, the theoretical discussion in Chapter 3 points toward the fact that parliamentary control differs from country to country (Hypothesis 2.6). According to this argument, the correspondence between the position of the government on the one hand and the position of the parliament depends on the mechanisms of parliamentary oversight. Empirical studies suggest that legislative institutions such as a strong committee system with proportional assignment of seats can have a significant impact on policy formulation (Müller and Strom 2000). Most of these studies highlight the argument that strong committees, in combination with a formal parliamentary scrutiny procedure, strengthen the opposition parties.[14] This type of parliamentary control is particularly effective if the opposition can play one coalition partner off the others. Viewed from this angle, the representatives from all major parties can successfully amend the proposal of the minister in charge before the international negotiations.

Across all EU member states, parliamentary involvement in preparation of IGCs covers a wide spectrum. However, institutional provisions are remarkably stable across time. In Greece, Italy, the Benelux countries as well as most central European member states, the parliamentary control rights comprise of hearings and a general right of information. By contrast, prior research suggests that in eight of the fifteen old member states, parliamentary committees were formally involved in the formation of the national position (Stoiber 2003: 277; König and Hug 2006[15]): Austria, Denmark, Finland, Germany, Ireland, Spain, Sweden and the UK. Furthermore, parliamentary scrutiny existed in the domestic position formation processes of Lithuania, Hungary and Estonia (Stoiber 2003: 277; König and Hug 2006). By formal parliamentary scrutiny, this means that parliaments held veto power over the formulation of the official national position. However, this does not imply that the governmental position revealed at the subsequent IGC represents the officially crafted positions one-to-one. Not only do governments enjoy certain discretion, but parliamentary committees rarely deal with every issue on the international agenda. Nevertheless, I suspect that the impact of parties on the national position is stronger in political systems that provide for mechanisms of formal parliamentary scrutiny. Both the party of the median MP and the party of the ministers benefit from formal involvement, which reinforces their powers to control the government.

Figure 5.8 provides ample support for this hypothesis. For the subgroup of countries without formal parliamentary scrutiny, the effect of parties on the time-invariant component of a governmental position becomes entirely insignificant. In this group the only remaining significant correlation is between positional changes and the partisan position of the median MP. The results for the group of countries that provide for parliamentary scrutiny are mirror-inverted. The correlation between the parties and governmental position is highly significant and strong. Finally, governments from countries with parliamentary scrutiny reveal a significantly less integrationist position. Given that the governing parties are on average more integrationist than opposition parties, these findings support Hypothesis 2.6 that parliamentary scrutiny is indeed an effective tool to limit governments' discretion when revealing their position at the international bargaining table.

---

14. By contrast, Martin and Vanberg (2005) suggest that formal parliamentary scrutiny reduces ministerial drift and, accordingly, is to the benefit of the governmental coalition as a whole.
15. For Rome II, see individual country chapters in König and Hug 2006.

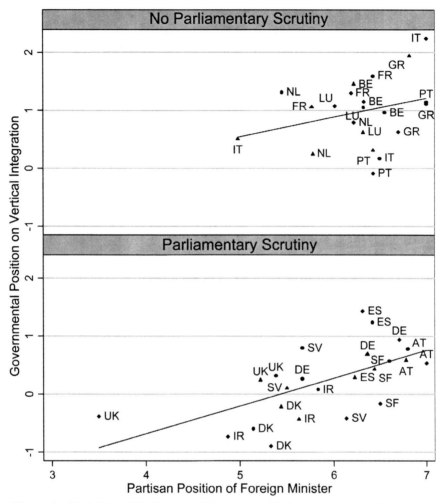

AT: Austria; BE: Belgium; DE: Germany; DK: Denmark; ES: Spain; FR: France; GR: Greece; IE: Ireland; IT: Italy; NL: The Netherlands; PT: Portugal; SF: Finland; SE: Sweden; LU: Luxembourg; UK: United Kingdom

Source: Party position according to University of Chapel Hill expert surveys (Hooghe *et al.* 2008; Steenbergen and Marks 2007; see Table 5.2)

Figure 5.8: Governmental positions plotted against the partisan position of the Foreign Minister by involvement of national parliament during the preference formation stage

Table 5.3: OLS Regressions to explain governmental positions on vertical integration (without lagged dependent variable)

(N=45)	Context	Economy	Median	Referendum	Trend	Party in Office	Median MP	Formal Scrutiny I	Formal Scrutiny II	First Order
α Amsterdam	0.33 (0.26)	0.33 (0.26)	0.14 (0.22)	-0.14 (0.22)	0.36 (0.27)	0.28 (0.22)	0.32 (0.25)	-0.03 (0.21)	0.31 (0.21)	0.09 (0.20)
α Nice	0.42 (0.26)	0.42 (0.26)	0.35 (0.22)	-0.02 (0.23)	0.44 (0.26)*	0.32 (0.22)	0.16 (0.24)	0.17 (0.21)	0.36 (0.20)*	0.03 (0.21)
α Rome II	0.34 (0.18)*	0.38 (0.19)**	0.44 (0.15)***	0.86 (0.19)***	0.35 (0.18)*	-2.96 (0.80)***	-1.92 (0.91)**	-0.11 (1.31)	-1.52 (1.58)	2.00 (1.42)
Balance of Trade (%GDP)	-2.43 (1.53)									
Net Transfers (% GDP; log)	-0.06 (0.14)									
Median Voter			0.39 (0.09)***							
Median Voter (w. Referendum)				0.38 (0.17)**						0.18 (0.18)
Referendum (w.o. Referendum)				0.41 (0.09)***						0.28 (0.10)**
Referendum				-0.72 (0.19)***						-0.61 (0.19)***
Trend in Public Opinion					1.61 (1.28)					

what explains governments' positions on european integration? | 161

(N=45)	Context	Economy	Median	Referendum	Trend	Party in Office	Median MP	Formal Scrutiny I	Formal Scrutiny II	First Order
Party of Foreign Minister						0.55 (0.13)***				
Party of Median MP							0.39 (0.16)**			
Party of Median MP (w. scrutiny)								0.42 (0.17)**		
Party of Median MP (w.o. scrutiny)								0.12 (0.21)		
Formal Scrutiny								−2.47 (1.69)	−1.26 (1.84)	−0.99 (1.73)
Party of Foreign Minister (w. scrutiny)									0.46 (0.14)***	0.29 (0.13)*
Party of Foreign Minister (w.o. scrutiny)									0.36 (0.25)	0.48 (0.22)*
adjusted R^2	0.02	0.04	0.29	0.43	0.03	0.30	0.14	0.32	0.40	0.55
F	0.45	1.30	6.94	7.52	1.04	7.29	3.22	5.47	6.93	7.65
prob > F	0.247	0.250	0.000	0.000	0.384	0.000	0.000	0.000	0.000	0.000
RMSE	0.72	0.71	0.60	0.54	0.72	0.60	0.67	0.58	0.55	0.48

DISCUSSION OF RESULTS

Before Maastricht, intergovernmental bargaining over European treaty reforms was determined by powerful producer interests. The single most important topic on the agenda was mutual market access with the ultimate goal of establishing a common market. At that time, the economies of member states were characterised by distinctive structural differences, namely a group of relatively rich industrialised states in the North and a group of states with a large agricultural sector in the South. Accordingly, the vast majority of voters silently supported and shared the producer interest in the common market, a fact Inglehart (1971) termed 'permissive consensus'.

However, for the post-Maastricht era, my empirical results indicate that this economic logic is no longer applicable. Governments of member states that either benefit from EU transfer payments or reveal a large, positive trade balance are not automatically supportive of further integration. Given the shift of agenda from establishing a common market toward political integration, this finding comes as no surprise. Instead, my results provide ample support for the relevance of the domestic arena. In short, the national position responds to the political dynamics of a heterogeneous public opinion as well as party politics. These findings deal a severe blow to all those who criticise the process of European integration for its elitist and undemocratic nature.

Table 5.3 summarises the results from a static, cross-sectional perspective. First, it illustrates that governmental positions do represent the preferences of their median voters. Or, more precisely, the variation among governmental positions can be explained by the variation among median voters. Previous research suggests that, if measured on the same scale, governments prefer substantially more integrationist reforms than the median voter (Hug and Schulz 2007). However, the results do not support my hypothesis that referenda create a better representation of median voters by their government. Instead, governments that tie their hands by announcing referenda appear on average less integration-prone. Or, governments that are less integrationist are more likely to announce referenda. The most notable exceptions to this general trend are the Luxembourger, French and Belgian governments, which announced referenda on the Constitutional Treaty, but revealed a relatively pro-integrationist position. An alternative explanation for this pattern is the strategic use of referenda at the international bargaining table. Governments may voluntarily limit their discretion by announcing ratification via referendum. This, however, is only a promising strategy for those governments that are relatively satisfied with the status quo of European integration (Finke and König 2009; König and Hug 2001).

In addition, the official governmental position can be explained by the party in office, in particular the party membership of the foreign minister who leads the domestic preparation of EU treaty reforms. The same is true with respect to the partisan position represented by the median MP, though the effect of the foreign minister is twice as strong. In brief, parties matter for European treaty reforms because they are important constraints that limit the discretion of the individual minister. Ultimately, he needs partisan support to achieve parliamentary approval and for his future political career, both within the party and in the general election. Yet for parties without sufficient information, partisan and parliamentary control would remain without effect. Therefore, one way to foster governmental accountability is to support the right of formal parliamentary scrutiny. As regards the static perspective, this notion is supported by the significant interaction effect in Table 5.3.

Among the most striking findings is the very weak correlation between the position of the party in office as well as the median MP. If anything, this finding indicates that, in total, EU politics are still of little relevance for domestic politics and national elections. Furthermore, it points toward the existing heterogeneity among domestic actors. The first-order model somewhat dilutes the effect of formal parliamentary scrutiny. Even more interesting, the significant effect of the median voter is now restricted to the non-referendum cases. Overall, the position of the median voters and the governing party explain roughly 56 per cent of the observed variation.

In the introduction to this chapter, it was argued that existing studies cannot analyse the political interaction between heterogeneous domestic interests because their empirical focus is limited to a single IGC. By contrast, a longitudinal research design can forego the unitary actor assumption. If the official governmental position is a result of conflicting domestic interests, its changes should correspond to changes in public opinion as well as the partisan composition of government and parliament. In order to analyse positional changes, in Table 5.4 I add a lagged depend variable. The baseline model includes context-level-effect plus the lagged depend variable. It explains approximately 30 per cent of observed variation among governmental positions revealed at Nice and Rome II.

First, the position of the median voter is irrelevant for our understanding of the observed changes in governmental positions. However, this does not mean that politicians turn their backs on public opinion when adjusting their position from one IGC to the next. In particular, when formulating the national position, governments' discretion is limited by the short-term trend in public opinion.

Second, governmental positions change in the preferred direction of the party in office as well as the party that provide the median MP. However, the role of formal parliamentary scrutiny is less evident. On the one hand, it seems to protract change in the preferred direction of the median MP. On the other hand, the existence of formal parliamentary scrutiny strengthens the explanatory power of the party in office. Whereas the second effect supports my overall argument, the first effect appears counterintuitive. Anyway, the limited sensitivity to changes in the partisan composition of parliament could be the flipside of effective parliamentary control at previous IGCs.

Finally, Table 5.4 lists the estimates of a first-order model, which includes the short-term trend in public opinion as well as the position of the party governing the foreign office. Both of the effects turn out to be significant, explaining roughly 57 per cent of the observed variation.

Bottom line, this chapter provides robust evidence that official governmental

Table 5.4: OLS Regressions to explain governmental positions on vertical integration (including lagged dependent variable)

(N=30)	Context	Economy	Median	Referendum	Trend	Party in Office	Median MP	Formal Scrutiny I	Formal Scrutiny II	First Order
α Nice	0.46 (0.18)**	0.45 (0.18)**	0.44 (0.19)**	0.25 (0.23)	0.50 (0.16)***	0.38 (0.17)**	0.42 (0.16)**	0.42 (0.15)**	0.39 (0.16)**	0.45 (0.14)***
α Rome II	0.07 (0.15)	0.11 (0.16)	0.14 (0.20)	0.38 (0.25)	0.08 (0.14)*	-2.11 (0.91)**	-2.37 (0.84)***	-2.34 (1.18)*	-1.18 (1.32)	-0.26 (1.27)
$Y_{i,t-1}$	0.35 (0.11)***	0.32 (0.12)**	0.28 (0.16)*	0.25 (0.16)	0.365 (0.10)***	0.25 (0.12)**	0.30 (0.10)***	0.22 (0.14)	0.11 (0.13)	0.14 (0.13)
Balance of Trade (% GDP)		-1.55 (1.27)								
Net Transfers (% GDP; log)		0.05 (0.13)								
Median Voter			0.08 (0.12)							
Median Voter (w. Referendum)				0.17 (0.21)						
Referendum (w.o. Referendum)				0.09 (0.13)						
Referendum				-0.32 (0.24)						
Trend in Public Opinion					3.15 (1.04)***					2.47 (1.02)**

(N=30)	Context	Economy	Median	Referendum	Trend	Party in Office	Median MP	Formal Scrutiny I	Formal Scrutiny II	First Order
Party of Foreign Minister						0.38 (0.16)**				
Party of Median MP							0.42 (0.14)***			
Party of Median MP (w. scrutiny)								0.28 (0.24)		
Party of Median MP (w.o. scrutiny)								0.46 (0.19)**		
Formal Scrutiny								-0.66 (2.00)	-1.18 (1.32)	-1.74 (1.71)
Party of Foreign Minister (w. scrutiny)									0.42 (0.22)*	0.37 (0.18)*
Party of Foreign Minister (w.o. scrutiny)									0.28 (0.21)	0.13 (0.20)
adjusted R^2	0.30	0.31	0.29	0.29	0.46	0.41	0.46	0.52	0.46	0.57
F	7.31	4.24	4.89	3.41	9.34	7.68	9.17	7.19	6.02	6.99
prob > F	0.001	0.009	0.007	0.018	0.000	0.000	0.000	0.001	0.001	0.000
RMSE	0.49	0.49	0.50	0.49	0.43	0.45	0.43	0.41	0.43	0.38

positions on vertical integration are the results of dynamic and competing domestic interests rather than structural economic differences. Only one-third of the observed variation can be explained by either time-invariant, country-specific difference or the context of a particular IGC. What are the consequences of this finding for European integration?

First of all, Chapter 4 provides evidence that governmental positions are a powerful indicator for explaining European treaty reforms. At Nice and Rome II, member states applied the standard procedure of IGCs. In the first step, a task force defined the agenda. Thereafter, the presidency settles the less conflictive issues via bilateral shuttle diplomacy. Finally, high-salience issues are resolved at a concluding summit. This procedure resulted in Pareto-superior and Pareto-efficient reforms for all participating governments. As a consequence, these reforms were compromises at the lowest common denominator. If, however, governmental positions respond to the dynamics of domestic politics, the win-set at the intergovernmental-level must be variable, too. Accordingly, the set of feasible outcomes depends on the short-term trends in public opinion and the constellation of partisan government in all EU member states.

Furthermore, the set of feasible reforms may change during the process of a single IGC. The likelihood for such changes increases with the duration of the negotiation process. As a consequence, governments' information over other states' reform positions can only be incomplete. Under this circumstance, bargaining theory predicts a high potential for inefficient outcomes. This is what happened at the Convention, which prolonged the negotiation process. Even worse, governments and Convention delegates were not only confronted by incomplete information over others' preferences, but left with imperfect information over the procedure itself. The ultimate consequence was a reform treaty located outside the intergovernmental win-set and, finally, ratification failure (see Chapter 4).

Furthermore, my results contribute to the ongoing debate over Europe's democratic deficit (Moravcsik 2004; Follesdal and Hix 2006). In particular, the intergovernmental procedure of treaty revision has been frequently criticised for its missing procedural legitimacy, i.e. low transparency and accountability (Risse and Kleine 2008). The empirical results suggest that the European integration project reveals a significant degree of electoral accountability after all. When formulating the national position, governments consider the opinions of their voters as well as the positions of their own political parties. The relevance of the latter depends on the involvement of the parliament in the domestic position-formation process.

This chapter analysed domestic-level explanations for governments' positions on vertical integration. However, my prior empirical and theoretical analysis of constitutional choice revealed that governments' evaluations of competing constitutional design depends on two parameters. The present chapter had a clear focus on actors' preferences over the level of integration (e). The next chapter deals with governmental positions on the decision-rule (k) and its relationship to the chosen level of vertical integration.

chapter six | the effect of nonseparable preferences in eu treaty negotiations

So far the analysis of the domestic origins of governmental positions has been restricted to vertical integration. In this chapter, the second, institutional conflict dimension is brought back in. In particular, the theoretical relevance of the conditionality of governmental preferences over the design of the decision-rule is discussed, in addition to their preferences for a particular level of vertical integration. First, the strict assumptions, that have been made in earlier chapters when considering governments' positions on vertical integration as separable from their positions on the reform of the decision rule, are revisited. Second, a set of hypotheses are proposed on the relevance of nonseparable preferences across member states and policy areas. Third, the statistical model, introduced in Chapter 3, is advanced such that it is capable of testing my hypotheses on the relationship between both conflict dimensions explicitly. Finally, the endogenous change of preferences implied by the concept of nonseparability are analysed along the sequence of decisions taken at Rome II, which illustrate the effect on the negotiation outcome.

THEORETICAL RELEVANCE

On first sight, the explanation for governmental positions on institutional reform appears straightforward. After all, any realistic reform of the decision-rule discussed at Amsterdam, Nice or Rome II involved an element of strengthening proportional representation. In particular, the redistribution of voting weights finally agreed at Nice and the double-majority rule[1] repeatedly discussed at all three IGCs implied a redistribution of relative voting power to the benefit of larger member states (Baldwin *et al*. 2001). Therefore, Hypothesis 3.1 expects large member states to be more favourable toward abandoning the principles of unanimity and consensus. The empirical results presented in Chapters 3 and 4 support this expectation. Furthermore, 'the crucial issue is not how decisions are taken, but what decisions are adopted'.[2] Therefore, the preferences over institutional reforms depend on how governments evaluate the heterogeneity costs implied by potentially unfavourable European policies. Hence, governments with outlier preferences will

---

1. The voting threshold agreed at Nice required a majority of member states, more than 62 per cent of the EU's population and about 74 per cent of the weighted votes. The voting weights ranged from twenty-nine (Germany, France, UK and Italy) to three (Malta). Under a double-majority scheme, the voting weights would be skipped. Accordingly, the remaining criteria for the voting threshold are a qualified majority of member states and a qualified majority of the population.
2. Summary of the Danish position available online: http://europa.eu.int/en/agenda/igc-home/ms-doc/state-dk/basisdk.htm, (accessed 12 October 2005).

prefer decision-rules that grant them high voting power. In the 1990s this most certainly was the perspective of many central European governments with relatively low wages, a large agricultural sector and low social as well as environmental standards (Hypothesis 3.2). Again, the empirical results presented in Chapter 3 find these countries generally less supportive of expanding majority voting and lowering the voting thresholds.

On closer inspection, governmental preferences over the decision-rule might not only depend on population size, but on the current state of vertical integration, which actors compare to their ideally preferred level of integration. On the other hand, governments might just as well condition their preference on vertical integration upon certain reforms of the decision rule. For example, during the Nice IGC, the Finnish government objected that, before any extension of EU competences, the functioning and decision-making efficiency of existing policy areas should be ensured. The Finnish delegation argued that this would demand a vast extension of QMV.[3] In Chapter 2, it was explained that if such conditionality over the choice of vertical integration on the one hand and the decision-rule on the other exists, governmental preferences must be considered nonseparable.

So far, my empirical analysis has been restricted to the assumption of separable preferences. Again, the separability assumption implies that actors' preferences over the level of integration are independent of the de facto design of the decision-rules (Enelow and Hinich 1984). Or, vice versa, their preferences over the design of EU decision-rules are independent from the competences delegated. However, with regard to constitutional politics in the EU, this assumption of separable or unconditional preferences appears to be unrealistic. For example, France might prefer deeper cooperation in justice and home affairs *only if* decision-making in this area will become more efficient by extending majority voting and lowering the voting thresholds. Ireland, on the other hand, might prefer deeper cooperation in the same area *only if* it retains its veto right. One important consequence of this bi-directional conditionality is that it may reduce the size of the win-set for potential reforms. Another, more general consequence of nonseparable preferences is that the sequence of decisions matters (Enelow and Hinich 1984; Lacy 2001). Actors will adjust their preferences on one issue dimension in response to the de facto or expected outcome on the other dimensions. Accordingly, conditional preferences grant additional powers to the agenda-setter.

In the remainder, a distinction is made between the directions of this interdependence (Enelow and Hinich 1984). The case where actors prefer more efficient decision-rules in reaction to higher de facto transfer of competences is called '*positive complementary*'. The case where actors prefer less efficient decision-rules in reaction to higher de facto transfer of competences is called '*negative complementary*'. In other words, the investigation centres on whether the preference of a particular member state is, in fact, nonseparable and (if so) in which direction.

For this purpose, it is important to recall the two-parametric model of consti-

---

3. Summary of the 'Report of the Finnish government, February 1996', published online: www.europarl.europa.eu/igc1996/pos-fi_en.htm#start, (accessed 12 December 2005).

tutional choice presented in Chapter 2. More specifically, governments evaluate different constitutional designs by comparing the heterogeneity or decision-costs (C) to efficiency gains implied by economics of scale and scope (D). Accordingly, the ideal constitutional design $\{K_i^*; E_i^*\}$ maximises D-C. However, both C and D are a function of the level of integration (E) and the decision rule (K). Both C and D are monotonically increasing in the level of integration (E), but with diminishing returns. Thus, the most preferred level of integration depends on the relative slope of C and D. As long as this slope depends exclusively on the level of integration (E) and not on the decision-rule (K), governments' preferences over K and E can be considered separable. If, however, their evaluation of E depends on the decision-rule K (or vice versa), preferences over the level of integration and the decision-rule are nonseparable.

If existent, this nonseparability can take on either of two directions. Some governments might be more willing to delegate additional competences to the EU under a majoritarian, efficient decision-rule (*positive complementarity*). These member states would stress that the total decision-costs depend on the decision-rule multiplied by the number of decisions taken under this rule. Others might reject additional EU competences unless they retain a high level of voting power; in some cases even veto power (*negative complementarity*). These member states would argue that the total heterogeneity costs depend on the decision-rule multiplied by the number of decisions taken under this rule. The question is: how can we explain such different directions of nonseparability?

One possible answer to this question focuses on the history of European integration. Member states began collectivisation by transferring those policy competences to the EU level, in which all of them expect high potential efficiency gains *(D)* and low heterogeneity costs (*C*). More specifically, this has been the case for the establishment of the common market. The more European integration progresses, the lower the marginal increase of benefits from any additional transfer of competences, but the higher the marginal increase of heterogeneity costs *(C)*. These costs materialize whenever a member state faces unfavourable EU policies that imply high costs of adaptation and, at least temporarily, competitive disadvantages (Treib 2005; König-Archibugi 2001).[4] Such unfavourable policies can be expected under two conditions: first, high preference asymmetry among member states, in particular a high conflict in the Council of Ministers; second, unfavourable policies prove that a member state has been too weak to either shift the result to its favour or veto a law proposal altogether. Following this line of reasoning, a switch from high voting thresholds toward lower thresholds would have two general consequences.[5] First, *ceteris paribus*, all member states are more likely to be outvoted. Second, the importance of voting power decreases relative to other

---

4. König-Archibugi (2001) refers to this as 'policy conformity' instead of homogeneity.
5. There exists a third, very popular effect of voting-rule reform: redistribution of voting power among member states. In the best of all worlds, a member state wants to ensure efficiency gains by reducing the veto power of others, and to increase his own voting power to avoid heterogeneity costs (e.g. Widgren 1999; König and Bräuninger 1998).

power resources such as agenda setting, and budgetary and informational power (Bailer 2006: 43). In Chapter 2, it was argued that it appears reasonable to assume that governments from large and rich member states possess more of these alternative power resources than poor member states. Hence, their relative power to avoid heterogeneity costs despite higher preference asymmetry increases when the voting threshold decreases. Therefore, the expectation is that rich member states' preferences over the transfer of competences and the decision-rule are nonseparable and positive complementary. By contrast, the preferences of governments from poor and small member states are nonseparable and negative complementary (Hypothesis 4.1).[6]

Moreover, there is also an expectation that the importance and direction of nonseparability not only varies across governments, but also across reform issues. Empirically, this variation depends on an issue's importance for the intergovernmental conflict space. In other words, an issue cannot reveal a high degree of nonseparability in either direction unless it is of significant relevance for the intergovernmental conflict space.

Moreover, the above logic makes little sense in policy areas without (or with a very low level of) preference asymmetry. Why should governments care about their relative power if all of them hold identical preferences anyway? According to Alesina *et al.* (2002), preferences should be rather similar in matters of international trade, common market, international relations and non-sectoral business relations. By contrast, the same authors find that the following areas are characterised by high preference asymmetry: education, research, environment, citizens' protection (AFSJ), social protection, taxation, agriculture, regional and, partly, monetary policy.[7] Hence, the expectations is that the effect of nonseparable preferences is stronger in policy areas with a higher degree of preference asymmetry.

In the next section, the statistical ideal point estimation is advanced such that it accounts for nonseparable preference. Subsequently, the empirical results are compared to my theoretical claims. I then test in how far the theory of nonseparable preferences provides an endogenous explanation for the observed change in governmental positions from one IGC to the next. Thereafter, the effect of sequential decisions on governments' conditional positions during the negotiation at Rome II is illustrated. For this purpose, I simulate governments' positions along the sequence of decisions taken by the IGC and compare the simulated values to governments' public reactions at decisive moments of the IGC. In doing so, I analyse in how far nonseparable preferences provide an endogenous explanation for positional changes that occur during a single IGC (Hypothesis 4.2). Moreover, the sequential analysis fosters our understanding of why some governments signed the Constitutional Treaty, although they should have preferred the Treaty of Nice.

---

6. This argument suggests that the nonseparability of governmental preferences is positively correlated to country size and therefore to governments' positions on the decision-rule itself. Please note that neither theory nor measurement preclude such a correlation.

7. For a discussion of the economic effects of the division of competences, consult Alesina *et al.* 2001, 2002; Wacziarg 1999; Collignon 2002.

ESTIMATING THE NONSEPARABILITY OF GOVERNMENTAL PREFERENCES

According to the Euclidean voting model, governments' evaluation of a reform outcome depends on the Euclidean distance between its ideal point x and the status quo sq, as compared to the distance between its ideal point x and the reform outcome o in a d-dimensional policy space. In Chapter 3, I find that the intergovernmental conflict over European treaty reforms has two dimensions, i.e. vertical integration and the decision rule. To account for the potential nonseparability between – as well as for – the different salience of the two dimensions, the Euclidean utility function is appended by a column vector a, which contains two elements capturing the nonseparability in government's utility calculation over both dimensions.[8] Equation 6.1 depicts the complete Euclidean utility function of actor i.

$$U_i(o, sq) = \sqrt{(x_i - sq) \, a_i(x_i - sq)} - \sqrt{(x_i - o) \, a_i(x_i - o)}$$

Equation 6.1

So far, my strategy for estimating governments' ideal positions on European treaty reforms follows the standard two-parametric-item response model (e.g. Clinton et al. 2004; Jackman 2001; Martin and Quinn 2002). In Chapter 3, it was explained how the existing statistical models correspond to the Euclidean voting model. Person parameters correspond to actors' ideal points, and item parameters allow for the interpretation of latent conflict space. However, all existing statistical models are built on the assumption of separable preferences, i.e. an actor's choice on one issue does not depend on the collective outcome of other issues (Enelow and Hinich 1984). Instead, they assume that both dimension are equally separable,

hence $a = \begin{bmatrix} 0 \\ 0 \end{bmatrix}$

Accordingly, the two-dimensional Euclidean voting model with nonseparable preferences transforms into the following statistical model:[9]

$$Y_{i,j}^* = U_i(sq_j) - U_i(o_j) = \sqrt{(x_i - sq)'a_i(x_i - sq)} + \eta_{i,j} - \sqrt{(x_i - o)'a_i(x_i - o)} + v_{i,j}$$

Equation 6.2

$$= -\alpha_j + \beta_{1j}x_{1i} + \beta_{2j}x_{2i} \quad \text{(see Equation 3.5)}$$

---

8. Here, I assume that both elements of the vector are identical, which intuitively means '*that the effect of the expected level of one policy on the marginal value of another is the same, regardless of which policy is fixed first. It is worth noting, that there is nothing inherent in the model that requires A to be symmetric*'. (Hinich and Munger 1999: 216).

9. In a d-dimensional space, the observed choices are modelled accordingly (suppressing indices over actors i and items j):

$$Y^* = -\alpha + \beta'x + \sum^d \sum^d q_{hk}a_{ik} + a_{hk}(\beta_h x_k + \beta_k x_h) + \varepsilon$$

$$-2a_i x_{1i}(o_1 - sq_1) + 2a_i x_{2i}(o_2 - sq_2) + 2a_i(o_1 o_2 - sq_1 sq_2) + \eta_{i,j} - v_{i,j}$$
Equation 6.3[10]

$$= -\alpha_j + \beta_{1j} x_{1i} + \beta_{2j} x_{2i} + q_j a_i + a_i(\beta_{1j} x_{2i} - \beta_{2j} x_{1i}) + \varepsilon_{i,j}$$
Equation 6.4[11]

where a_i indicates the sole element of the column vector. Once estimated, it tells us in how far actor i's preferences are nonseparable across dimensions 1 and 2. On the other hand, $q_j = (o_1 o_2 - sq_1 sq_2)$ gives information about the importance of item j for the latent construct of non-separability. All other parameters of the statistical model in Equation 6.4 are already discussed in Chapter 3.[12]

The challenge of this model is that non-separability conditions an actor's preferences on one dimension upon the outcome of other dimensions. In the two-dimensional example, the conditional ideal point on dimension 1, x_1^* can be calculated by the following equation (Enelow and Hinich 1984):

$$x_1^* \mid o_2^\sim = x_1 - \left(\frac{a}{s_1}\right)(o_2^\sim - x_2)$$
Equation 6.5

Where $o_2^\sim$ defines the observed outcome on the second dimension, s_1 is the relative salience the actor attaches to dimension 1 and a indicates the strength and direction of the non-separability between both dimensions. If preferences on both dimensions are separable, i.e., a approaches 0, the conditional position x_1^* equals the unconditional position x_1. On the one hand, Equation 6.5 is offered as a possible explanation for observed positional changes, which is endogenous to the negotiation process. On the other hand, it tremendously complicates the estimation because it makes identification of the statistical model impossible. In any case, I am interested in how far the concept of non-separability adds to the explanatory power of the standard model. Therefore, I suggest a two-stage estimator. The first stage estimates the standard two-parametric item response model. The results of this stage are extensively discussed in Chapters 3 and 4. The second stage constrains the item and the person parameters to the values resulting from stage 1, but estimates those parameters capturing the effects of non-separability (a_1, q_j), the item difficulty parameter and the cut-off points, if applicable.

---

10. For the first part of Equation 6.3 "$-\alpha_j + \beta_{1j} x_{1i} + \beta_{2j} x_{2i}$" please consult Chapter 3, Equations 3.1–3.5.

11. The two new terms bear the following intuition: $a_i(\beta_{1j} x_{2i} - \beta_{2j} x_{1i})$ estimates in how far an actor's agreement to a reform of item j depends on the interaction of his ideal point with the item parameter of the other dimension. The second new term, $q_j a_i$, corrects actor i's nonseparability for each issues j. In other words, if q_j is negative it indicates that an actor with positive (negative) complementary preferences is less (more) likely to agree on reform of issue j.

12. Here, x_i denotes the ideal point of actor i;. α_j captures the overall difficulty across all actors to agree to a reform proposal on issue j; β_j captures in how far issue j discriminates between the latent dimensions of a given proposal space.

This two-stage estimation process has one well-known drawback. The potential bias of the second-stage error-term must, in most cases, be considered interdependent to the error resulting from the first stage (e.g. Lewis and Linzer 2005). Fortunately, the Bayesian estimation framework presented in Chapter 3 provides a straightforward way to carry over the error term from the first to the second stage by simply drawing the item and person parameters from their posterior distribution. In Chapter 3, the estimation of the first stage was discussed. For estimating the second stage, i.e. the non-separability parameters, the distribution of the person and item parameters are fixed to the results of the first stage, i.e. to the posterior distributions. Accordingly, the error terms of these distributions carry over, causing larger uncertainty of the second-stage estimates. The second-stage results are based on 10,000 burn-in iterations and 15,000 draws from the posterior distribution. In order to check the convergence, the algorithm has been restarted several times with varying length of iterations.

Table 6.1 presents the estimates for all member states at each of the three IGCs. The 95 per cent confidence intervals turn out large in comparison to those for the governmental positions described in Chapter 2. But then this is not surprising, given that they are inflated by combining the errors of the first and the second stage of the estimation. Nevertheless, in more than half of the observed cases, the 95 per cent confidence interval does not include 0; in standard terminology, these cases are significant at the 5 per cent level. At Amsterdam, I find that only Germany, France, Spain and Italy reveal significantly positive complementary preferences. By contrast, the Belgian, Greek, Luxembourger, Portuguese and Swedish governments reveal significant and negative complementary preferences. At Nice, only Denmark and France reveal significant and positive complementary preferences; however, at the 10 per cent significance level, this group would be joined by Germany and the UK. By contrast, Belgium, Greece, Luxembourg, the Netherlands, Portugal and Sweden reveal significant and negative complementary preferences. At Rome II, the fifteen old member states experienced an average shift of about 0.5 points towards positive complementarity. At this conference, Austria, Belgium, Germany, France, Finland, Sweden and the UK would have accepted a higher level of integration if, at the same time, the reform of the decision-rule would have been more progressive than originally preferred by these countries. Note that among the old countries, only Ireland reveals the opposite, negative complementarity. As regards the new member states, the Irish are joined by the governments of Cyprus, Estonia, Malta and the Slovak Republic. By contrast, the Hungarian and Slovenian governments revealed significant and positive complementary preferences. Note that these two countries were, back in 2003, considered the two strongest economies in central Europe.

Overall, the results support Hypothesis 4.1. There is a tendency that large and economically strong countries would be more supportive of further integration if accompanied by progressive reforms of the decision-rule. The opposite is true for governments from small and economically weak countries. Table 6.2 reports the

Table 6.1: Estimated effect of governments' nonseparable preferences (a_i) in 95% confidence interval

Country	Amsterdam			Nice			Rome II		
	a_i_lo95	a_i	a_i_up95	a_i_lo95	a_i	a_i_up95	a_i_lo95	a_i	a_i_up95
AT	-1.218	-0.517	0.131	-0.657	0.020	0.939	**0.989**	**1.347**	**2.072**
BE	**-1.951**	**-0.942**	**-0.175**	**-1.660**	**-0.989**	**-0.367**	**0.279**	**0.885**	**1.515**
DE	**0.504**	**1.230**	**2.111**	-0.117	0.422	1.133	**0.059**	**0.327**	**0.642**
DK	-1.452	-0.542	0.170	**0.522**	**1.186**	**2.369**	-0.102	0.351	0.880
ES	**0.358**	**1.189**	**2.317**	-0.836	0.142	1.098	-0.302	0.000	0.300
FR	**0.628**	**1.396**	**2.369**	**0.138**	**1.092**	**2.167**	**0.031**	**0.456**	**0.868**
GR	**-1.798**	**-1.051**	**-0.367**	**-1.049**	**-0.523**	**-0.048**	-0.220	0.553	1.468
IE	-0.836	-0.140	0.422	-2.519	-0.187	2.540	**-1.151**	**-0.647**	**-0.187**
IT	**0.505**	**1.252**	**3.104**	-0.841	-0.281	0.148	-0.185	0.033	0.266
LU	**-1.351**	**-0.625**	**-0.023**	**-1.887**	**-1.199**	**-0.581**	-0.428	-0.074	0.295
NL	-0.622	0.088	0.419	**-2.207**	**-1.261**	**-0.465**	-0.326	0.035	0.410
PT	**-1.229**	**-0.552**	**-0.017**	**-1.319**	**-0.601**	**-0.007**	-0.252	0.037	0.341
SF	-0.857	-0.304	0.117	-0.695	0.110	0.860	**0.088**	**0.411**	**0.811**
SV	**-1.859**	**-0.848**	**-0.130**	**-1.556**	**-0.880**	**-0.289**	**0.305**	**0.884**	**1.640**
UK	-0.472	0.081	0.313	-0.211	0.596	1.491	**0.017**	**0.367**	**0.822**
mean	*-0.777*	*-0.019*	*0.717*	*-0.993*	*-0.157*	*0.733*	*-0.080*	*0.331*	*0.810*
stdv.	*0.904*	*0.867*	*1.135*	*0.873*	*0.771*	*1.064*	*0.457*	*0.479*	*0.624*
CY							**-2.068**	**-1.336**	**-0.746**
CZ							-0.102	0.250	0.728
EE							**-1.665**	**-1.034**	**-0.523**
HU							**0.048**	**0.584**	**1.179**
LT							-0.625	-0.222	0.175
LV							-0.223	0.256	0.727
MT							**-1.431**	**-0.847**	**-0.375**
PL							-0.467	-0.040	0.376
SI							**0.147**	**0.616**	**1.161**
SK							**-0.805**	**-0.399**	**-0.078**
mean							*-0.719*	*-0.217*	*0.262*
stdv.							*0.680*	*0.688*	*0.765*

decomposition of variance. It is restricted to fifteen old member states because we lack longitudinal data for the ten new member states. Most remarkably, Rome

II causes a level-shift toward positive complementarity ($\alpha_{Rome\ II}$). In other words, the average complementarity among old member states increased significantly by 0.52 points. Together with the lagged dependent variable (β), this context accounts for roughly 15 per cent of the observed variation (N=30). Moreover, from Nice to Rome II, the complementarity in governmental preferences did not shift in lockstep. Although, governments' nonseparability at Amsterdam was strongly correlated with their nonseparability at Nice (r =0.49), it is entirely uncorrelated with governments' nonseparability estimated for Rome II. On closer inspection, the reason for this finding is that only those national governments responded to the new context, which previously revealed negative complementary preferences, most noticeably Belgium, Greece, Luxembourg, the Netherlands and Sweden. On first sight, my statistical findings support the argument that 'enlargement, first appearing as an antithesis to effective decision-making, could in a dialectic manner become the decisive element that provokes institutional reform aimed at greater decision-making efficiency' (Devuyst 2002: 22). However, on closer inspection, the majority of governments from new member states appeared not only sceptical toward far-reaching reforms of the decision-rule, but also revealed negative complementary preferences.

Table 6.2: Analysis of the variance of the estimated nonseparability in governments' preferences

N=30	α_i	Analysis of Variance
α Nice (s.e.)	0.14 (0.165)	Time-variant. context level
α Rome II (s.e.)	0.52 (0.234)	Time-variant. context level
β (s.e.)	0.25 (0.144)	Time-invariant. country level
ε_{it} (1-R^2)	0.78	Time-variant. country level

Finally, I test my hypothesis explicitly. Following Hypothesis 4.1, the expectation is that governments will reveal negative complementary preferences if they lack alternative power resources and thus rely on voting power to avoid high heterogeneity costs. The prototype of such a member state is small, economically weak and dependent on EU transfer payments. To operationalise the size and power of a country's economy, the absolute GDP is used. As an alternative, a government's ideal position on the reform of the decision-rule is used, which, however, is highly correlated to the GDP (Pearson's r >0.7). In order to operationalise a country's dependence on EU transfer payments, I resort to the received EU transfers as percentage of GDP. In Table 6.3, all three variables reveal the expected effect and a first-order model, which includes time-level fixed effects for each IGC, the governmental position on the decision-rule and the saldo of EU transfers as percentage of GDP explains approximately 33 per cent of the observed variation. These findings support Hypothesis 4.1.

According to my theory, nonseparability can only be relevant if actors expect high heterogeneity costs (Hypothesis 4.2). Overall, seventy-seven issues in our data set can be attributed to a specific policy area; the remaining items refer to cross-cutting institutional issues or very broad political norms, e.g. human rights. Theory expects high heterogeneity costs in those policy areas characterised by

Table 6.3: OLS regression on the estimated nonseparability in governments' preferences

(N=45)	GDP	Position on Decision Rule	EU Transfers (% Contribution)	First Order
α Amsterdam	-0.17 (0.26)	-0.12 (0.21)	-0.17 (0.22)	0.07 (0.23)
α Nice	-0.32 (0.19)	-0.41 (0.25)*	-0.40 (0.22)*	-0.43 (0.20)**
α Rome II	0.22 (0.21)	0.19 (0.17)	0.20 (0.24)	0.41 (0.22)
GDP	0.06 (0.01)***			
Position on Decision Rule		0.43 (0.10)***		0.35 (0.10)***
EU Transfers (% contribution)			0.23 (0.07)***	0.15 (0.06)***
F	5.36	7.23	4.98	7.40
RMSE	0.66	0.63	0.67	0.59

high international preference asymmetry. According to Alesina *et al.* (2002), low preference asymmetry prevails in foreign, external trade and common market policy as well as sectoral business relations. By contrast, the authors argue that high preferences asymmetry should be expected in agricultural, regional, economic (except for sectoral business relations), tax, employment, social, environmental and education policy as well as in justice and home affairs.

I follow Alesina *et al* (2002) and assign each of these seventy-seven questions to either category (see Table 6.4). This assignment predicts nonseparability (q_j) to turn out significant in fifty-four of the seventy-seven issues. Indeed, we find a significant effect for thirty-one of these questions (57.4 per cent). By contrast, the assignment predicts q_j to be insignificant for the remaining twenty-three issues. This prediction is correct for twenty issues (90.0 per cent). In other words, the classification of policy areas suggested by theory correctly matches the statistical estimates in more than almost 67 per cent of the cases. Table 6.4 returns the largest estimates of q_j for economic, monetary, taxation as well as social and employment policy. However, the statistical model consistently misclassifies issues related to environment as well as issues related to justice and home affairs. Furthermore, the results are mixed for foreign policy, in which economic theory would expect low heterogeneity costs. These results indicate that heterogeneity costs may not be restricted to economic costs in the narrow sense, but may extend to political costs implied by unpopular decisions. Among the cross-cutting, institutional issues the design of the voting rules reveals outstandingly large and significant parameters for all three IGCs under investigation.

The empirical evidence presented so far proves that governmental positions over the decision-rule cannot be considered independent from the level of vertical integration and vice versa. Moreover, the observed variation across member states supports Hypothesis 4.1. Governments from large and economically powerful

Table 6.4: *Item-level effect of the nonseparability in governments' preferences*

Label	Issue	q_i_lo95	q_i	q_i_up95
A_1.1	Citizenship of the Union	-0.634	-0.117	0.361
A_1.3	Fundamental Rights (introduction)	-0.449	-0.086	0.251
A_1.4	Fundamental Rights (monitoring)	-0.322	0.222	0.760
A_1.5	Principle of Subsidiarity (introduction)	-0.071	0.276	0.671
A_1.6	Principle of Subsidiarity (monitoring)	-0.830	-0.260	0.306
A_1.7	Transparency of Council meetings	-0.874	-0.368	0.119
A_1.8	Legal Personality of the Union	-0.394	0.110	0.612
A_2.1	*CFSP (planning and preparation)*	-0.613	-0.181	0.192
A_2.2	*CFSP (application of QMV)*	-0.358	0.054	0.418
A_2.3	*CFSP (implementation and ext. representation)*	-0.402	0.019	0.428
A_2.4	*CFSP (financing)*	-0.864	-0.446	-0.043
A_2.5	*Common Defence Policy*	-0.200	0.380	0.955
A_2.6	*Relations with WEU*	-0.364	0.108	0.563
A_2.7	*Common Armament Policy*	-0.401	0.251	0.939
A_3.1	*JHA (EU competences)*	0.018	0.419	0.829
A_3.2	JHA (applicability of EC method)	-0.144	0.180	0.516
A_3.3	JHA (application of QMV)	-0.376	0.017	0.412
A_3.4	JHA (democratic control)	-0.623	-0.181	0.231
A_3.5	JHA (judicial control)	-0.241	0.155	0.526
A_4.1	EP (allocation of seats)	0.162	0.682	1.232
A_4.2	EP (introduction of uniform electoral procedures)	-0.271	0.297	0.896
A_4.3	QMV (extension)	-0.535	-0.171	0.184
A_4.4	QMV (threshold)	-0.723	-0.289	0.135
A_4.5	QMV (voting weights)	0.291	0.981	1.730
A_4.6	QMV (dual majority)	0.231	0.803	1.431

Label	Issue	q_{i_lo95}	q_i	q_{i_up95}
A_4.7	Commission (composition)	0.989	1.746	2.498
A_4.8	*Enhanced Cooperation (flexibility clause)*	0.191	0.739	1.296
A_4.9	*Enhanced Cooperation (conditions for flexibility: application of QMV)*	0.010	0.488	0.991
A_5.2	EP (application and reform of procedures)	-0.540	-0.064	0.406
A_5.3	EP (scope of Co-decision and assent)	-0.621	-0.206	0.174
A_5.4	Commission (role of EP in nomination)	-0.823	-0.244	0.331
A_5.5	EP (budgetary powers)	-0.407	0.195	0.801
A_5.6	National Parliaments (powers in legislative process)	-0.306	0.094	0.488
A_5.7	Commission (powers in legislative process)	-0.692	-0.211	0.220
A_5.8	ECJ (jurisdiction)	-0.520	0.054	0.636
A_5.9	Ctte. of Regions (areas of consultation and inst. autonomy)	-0.507	-0.059	0.360
A_5.10	ESC (areas of consultation and inst. autonomy)	-0.318	0.207	0.706
A_6.1	*Employment (chapter and objective)*	-0.618	-0.186	0.251
A_6.2	*Employment (monitoring committee)*	-1.574	-0.916	-0.328
A_6.3	*Environment (EU competences and role of EP)*	-0.452	-0.120	0.200
A_6.4	*Environment (exception from SEM)*	-0.343	-0.037	0.280
A_6.5	New Policy Areas (EU competences)	-0.662	-0.151	0.300
A_6.6	*External economic relations (EU competences)*	-0.883	-0.352	0.170
N_I1	Number of Commissioners	-0.264	0.008	0.290
N_I2.1	ECJ (composition)	-0.549	-0.157	0.221
N_I2.2	ECA (composition)	-0.326	0.077	0.491
N_I2.3	Ctte. of Regions (composition)	-0.478	0.070	0.582
N_I2.4	Economic and Social Committee (composition)	-0.480	0.067	0.588
N_I3	*European Public Prosecutor*	-1.362	-0.846	-0.356

Label	Issue	q_i_lo95	q_i	q_i_up95
N_II1	Commission (internal hierarchy/ organisation)	-0.265	0.040	0.340
N_II2	Commission (political accountability towards EP)	-0.232	0.067	0.357
N_II3	EP (allocation of seats)	-0.125	0.314	0.762
N_II4	QMV (voting weights)	-0.394	-0.057	0.297
N_II5	QMV (principle or case wise extension)	-0.921	-0.564	-0.224
N_II6	Co-decision (extension)	-0.828	-0.482	-0.150
N_II7	Closer cooperation	-0.577	-0.140	0.312
N_III1	*Level of competence and voting rule: defence*	-0.817	-0.425	-0.045
N_III2	*Level of competence and voting rule: environmental protection*	-0.268	0.017	0.293
N_III3	*Level of competence and voting rule: monetary*	-0.490	-0.178	0.120
N_III4	*Level of competence and voting rule: cooperation with developing countries*	-0.237	0.067	0.377
N_III5	*Level of competence and voting rule: health and social welfare*	-0.867	-0.465	-0.078
N_III6	Level of competence and voting rule: basic rules for media and press	-0.209	0.083	0.384
N_III7	*Level of competence and voting rule: workers' rights vis-a-vis their employers*	-0.388	0.044	0.442
N_III8	*Level of competence and voting rule: Immigration policy*	-0.252	0.130	0.515
N_III9	Level of competence and voting rule: Fundamental Human Rights	-0.846	-0.490	-0.135
N_III10	*Level of competence and voting rule: fight against unemployment*	-1.265	-0.745	-0.243
N_III11	*Level of competence and voting rule: agriculture and fishing*	-0.075	0.211	0.492
N_III12	*Level of competence and voting rule: support for economically depressed regions*	-0.111	0.161	0.450
N_III13	*Level of competence and voting rule: education*	-1.612	-1.038	-0.511

Label	Issue	q_{i_lo95}	q_i	q_{i_up95}
N_III14	Level of competence and voting rule: technological research	-0.225	0.134	0.505
N_III15	Level of competence and voting rule: value added tax rates	-0.011	0.289	0.586
N_III16	Level of competence and voting rule: foreign policy towards non-EU countries	-0.227	0.077	0.369
N_III17	Level of competence and voting rule: cultural policy	-1.511	-0.919	-0.386
N_III18	Level of competence and voting rule: political asylum	-0.147	0.242	0.651
N_III19	Level of competence and voting rule: fight against drugs	-0.426	-0.075	0.305
R_1	Charter of Fundamental Rights	-0.210	0.090	0.388
R_2	Subsidiarity	-0.346	-0.045	0.254
R_3	Religious reference	-0.521	-0.304	-0.102
R_4	Right to withdraw from the Union	0.222	0.489	0.763
R_5.A	Economic objectives : market economy	-0.735	-0.399	-0.081
R_5.B	**Economic objectives : employment**	0.055	0.235	0.425
R_5.C	Economic objectives : competitiveness	-0.602	-0.281	0.027
R_6	Presidency of the European Council (organisation)	-0.448	-0.233	-0.024
R_7	Presidency of the European Council (nomination)	-0.309	-0.020	0.274
R_8	QMV	-0.679	-0.399	-0.140
R_9	Number of commissioners	-0.287	0.016	0.312
R_10	Appointment of Commission President (role of Council. EP or nat. parliaments)	-0.227	0.056	0.344
R_11	Appointment of Commissioners (role of EP)	-0.018	0.271	0.575
R_12	*External representation*	-0.246	0.005	0.253
R_13.a	**Minister of Foreign Affairs (role of Commission in appointment)**	-0.149	0.159	0.478
R_13.b	*Minister of Foreign Affairs (role of EP in appointment)*	0.197	0.533	0.893
R_14	ECJ Jurisdiction	-0.683	-0.419	-0.185

the effect of nonseparable preferences in eu treaty negotiations | 181

Label	Issue	q_i_lo95	q_i	q_i_up95
R_15.B	Legislative initiative for European Parliament	-0.236	0.054	0.349
R_15.C	Legislative initiative for Council	-0.247	0.040	0.327
R_15.E	Legislative initiative for citizens	-0.296	0.006	0.295
R_16	Enhanced cooperation	-0.290	-0.039	0.200
R_17.1	*Level of competence for Agriculture*	0.218	0.452	0.714
R_17.2	*Level of competence for Structural and cohesion politics*	0.251	0.596	0.950
R_17.3	Level of competence for the Area of Freedom, Security and Justice	-0.103	0.127	0.371
R_17.4	*Level of competence for Foreign Policy*	-0.244	0.068	0.378
R_17.5	Level of competence for Economic Policy	-0.037	0.342	0.658
R_17.6	Level of competence for Tax harmonisation	-0.144	0.166	0.476
R_17.7	Level of competence for Employment Policy	-0.075	0.239	0.558
R_17.8	Level of competence for Social Policy	-0.176	0.139	0.464
R_17.9	*Level of competence for Health Policy*	0.258	0.574	0.917
R_17.10	Level of competence for Environment Policy	-0.101	0.197	0.512
R_17.11	Level of competence for Education Policy	-0.056	0.247	0.555
R_17.12	*Level of competence for research, technological development and space*	-0.004	0.318	0.652
R_18.A2	Voting rule (Council) for Structural and cohesion politics	-0.236	0.055	0.364
R_18.A3	Voting rule (Council) for Area of Freedom, Security and Justice	-0.376	-0.075	0.226
R_18.A5	*Voting rule (Council) for Tax harmonisation*	-1.047	-0.660	-0.278
R_18.A6	*Voting rule (Council) for Monetary Policy*	-1.247	-0.850	-0.487
R_18.A7	*Voting rule (Council) for Economic Policy*	-0.986	-0.609	-0.271
R_18.A8	Voting rule (Council) for Employment Policy	-0.541	-0.210	0.112

Label	Issue	q_i_lo95	q_i	q_i_up95
R_18.A9	*Voting rule (Council) for Social Policy*	-0.770	-0.434	-0.119
R_18.A10	*Voting rule (Council) for Social security rights*	-1.313	-0.890	-0.494
R_18.A11	Voting rule (Council) for Common Foreign Policy	-1.217	-0.793	-0.400
R_18.A12	*Voting rule (Council) for Defence Policy*	-0.823	-0.454	-0.102
R_18.B1	Decision rule (EP) for Agriculture	-0.227	0.076	0.386
R_18.B2	Decision rule (EP) for Structural and cohesion politics	-0.092	0.215	0.537
R_18.B3	Decision rule (EP) for Area of Freedom, Security and Justice	-0.259	0.028	0.309
R_18.B4	*Decision rule (EP) for Internal market*	-0.595	-0.282	0.015
R_18.B5	*Decision rule (EP) for Tax harmonisation*	-1.099	-0.704	-0.335
R_18.B6	*Decision rule (EP) for Monetary policy*	-1.522	-1.090	-0.673
R_18.B7	*Decision rule (EP) for Economic Policy*	-1.661	-1.212	-0.799
R_18.B8	*Decision rule (EP) for Employment Policy*	-0.906	-0.564	-0.250
R_18.B9	*Decision rule (EP) for Social Policy*	-0.692	-0.372	-0.065
R_18.B10	*Decision rule (EP) for Social security rights*	-1.200	-0.786	-0.408
R_18.B11	Decision rule (EP) for Common Foreign Policy	-0.672	-0.350	-0.038
R_18.B12	*Decision rule (EP) for Defence Policy*	-0.668	-0.352	-0.038
R_19	Rights of EP in the adoption of the budget	-0.085	0.167	0.434
R_20	SGP I (flexibility)	-0.090	0.197	0.495
R_21	SGP II (debt/ GDP criterion)	-0.026	0.314	0.621
R_22	*Defence Cooperation*	-0.507	-0.223	0.046
R_23	External borders (management)	-0.004	0.233	0.480
R_24	*Migration and Asylum*	-0.023	0.211	0.445

Note Mean of posterior distribution plus lower and upper bound of 95% confidence intervals. Issues which could be assigned to specific policy areas are printed in italics – bold where theory expects non-separability (q_i) to turn out significant.

states reveal a positive complementarity. Confronted with a higher level of integration than they had originally hoped for, they would adjust their position on the decision-rule toward majoritarianism. By contrast, small and economically weak states reveal negative complementary preferences. Confronted with a higher level of integration than they had originally hoped for, governments from these states would be eager to maintain the voting and veto power. Finally, the effect of nonseparable preferences is particularly relevant for policy areas in which economists expect a high preference asymmetry among governments.

SIMULATION OF ENDOGENOUS CHANGE

In Chapter 5, exogenous explanations for positional change were discussed. Governments' positions on European integration change in response to changes in the partisan composition of government and parliament and in reaction, the short-term trend in public opinion. The study of nonseparable preferences provides an alternative explanation for positional change (Lacy 2001), which is endogenous to EU-level negotiations. Generally speaking, the theory expects that actors will adjust their position on one issue dimension in response to the real or expected outcome on the other dimension (Enelow and Hinich 1984). In this section, the relevance of endogenous preference change for European treaty negotiation is illustrated. First, it is important to step back and examine how far the reforms agreed at any particular IGC predetermined a national governments' preferences at the subsequent IGC. Second, a sequential analysis of the Rome II IGC is provided, which sheds light on how governments could agree on a relatively progressive treaty reform. In particular, the focus is on two open questions: what explains the de facto agenda-setting power of the Convention? Why did some governments even sign the reform treaty although they preferred the status quo under the Treaty of Nice? For this purpose, the IGC is subdivided into three major stages, namely the presentation of the draft proposal by the president of the Convention (June 2003), the failed summit under the Italian presidency (December 2003) and the successful summit under the Irish presidency (June 2004).

In the two-dimensional intergovernmental conflict space, the conditional ideal point on dimension 1 (dimensions 2), $(x_1^* x_2^*)$ can be calculated by Equation 6.5 (Enelow and Hinich 1984). In other words, the theory of nonseparable preferences expects governments to adjust their ideal point on one dimension in response to the outcome of other dimensions. For example, at the Amsterdam IGC, the French government revealed positive complementary preferences between vertical integration and the design of the decision-rule. In Chapter 3, it was illustrated that the Treaty of Amsterdam provided for less integration than the French had hoped for. According to the theory of nonseparable preferences, the French position on the decision-rule should have moved leftward, i.e. toward unanimity. On the other hand, the Treaty of Amsterdam did not fulfill the French hopes for a substantial extension of QMV either. In response, the theory of nonseparable preferences predicts that the French should have adjusted their position on vertical integration downward, i.e. toward less integration.

Regarding the empirical evaluation of these theoretical claims, the decision must be made on whether or not the information in the data sets contains governments' unconditional positions. The assumption of truly unconditional preferences would imply that when formulating their positions, governments ignore the status quo; this assumption is highly unlikely. Instead, it is assumed that domestic-preference formation takes place against the background of the *status-quo*. In other words, my data contains governments' positions on European treaty reforms conditional upon the status quo.[13]

In Chapter 3, it was found that governmental position on vertical integration can be explained by preferences of the median voter, the short-term trend in public opinion, the position of the governing party and the existence of a formal parliamentary scrutiny procedure. By contrast, I argue that the position on the horizontal dimension corresponds to population size and economic power. On this dimension, domestic actors are less relevant and governmental positions reveal a higher degree of stability across time. In how far does the endogenous perspective on positional change add to the exogenous explanations discussed so far? In how far are governmental positions observed at Nice (Rome II) a reaction to the reforms agreed at Amsterdam (Nice)?

In order to answer these questions, I extend the linear decomposition of variance introduced in Chapter 5 by an additional term that estimates the effect of the predicted endogenous change (γ). First, I apply Equation 6.5 to calculate governments' positions conditional upon the Treaty of Amsterdam (Treaty of Nice). Second, I use these conditional positions as a predictor for the positions observed at Nice (Rome II). Presuming perfect measurement and the irrelevance of exogenous factors, my predictions should be perfectly correlated to the observed positions ($\gamma = 1$). Yet from Chapter 5, we already know that this is not the case.

Table 6.5 displays the linear decomposition of variance with and without this measure of endogenous positional change. As regards the vertical dimension, my endogenous predictor of change turns out with the correct sign, but insignificant (p>0.37). Once we control for any of the exogenous explanations, such as public opinion or partisan preferences, the effect turns entirely random, even producing a wrong sign. The interpretation of this finding is straightforward. First, positional change is primarily explained by domestic politics, as found in Chapter 5. Second, governments are not the only ones to react to the actual treaty reforms. In fact, parties and voters form their positions against the background of the status quo, too. Accordingly, these variables would cover any endogenous explanation for positional change.

As regards governments' positions on the decision-rule, the effect of endogenous change is much stronger. The time-invariant and context-level effects alone explain roughly 45 per cent of the observed variance. However, adding endogenous change increases the explanatory power to more than 50 per cent. Overall, my endogenous predictor of change is weakly significant and

---

13. To account for this assumption, I transfer governments' observed positions (x^*) to their unconditional, unobserved positions (x) by reorganising Equation 6.5 as follows:

(1) $x_1^* | sq_2 = x_1 - \left(\frac{a_{12}}{s_1}\right)(x_2 - sq_2)$ and $x_2^* | sq_1 = x_2 - \left(\frac{a_{12}}{s_1}\right)(x_1 - sq_1)$, where $s_2 = 1$ and $s_1 = 1$

(2) $x_1 = \dfrac{a_{12}x_2^* + a_{12}^2 sq_1 - a_{12}sq_2 - x_1^*}{(a_{12}^2 - 1)}$ and $x_2 = \dfrac{a_{12}x_1^* + a_{12}^2 sq_2 - a_{12}sq_1 - x_2^*}{(a_{12}^2 - 1)}$

Table 6.5: Analysis of the observed variance in governmental positions including an endogenous predictor for change

N=30	x vertical	x vertical	x dec.rule	x dec.rule	Analysis of Variance
α Nice (s.e.)	0.07 (0.16)	0.05 (0.16)	0.03 (0.25)	0.23 (0.25)	Time-variant. context level
α Rome II (s.e.)	-0.46 (0.18)	-0.48 (0.17)	0.45 (0.17)	0.34 (0.19)	Time-variant. context level
β (s.e.)	0.35 (0.12)	0.43 (0.13)	0.61 (0.13)	0.79 (0.15)	Time-invariant. country level
ε^{it} (1-R^2)	0.65	0.61	0.55	0.39	Time-variant. country level
γ (s.e.)		0.25 (0.19)	–	0.83 (0.42)	Time-invariant. endogenous

robustly correlated to the time-variant, country-level residual $\varepsilon_{i,t}$ (r = 0.31).

So far, my empirical analysis seems to support the theoretical relevance of governments' nonseparable preferences over the level of European integration and the design of the decision- rule.[14] Next, I illustrate the role of endogenous positional change during a single IGC. For this purpose, I select Rome II because it is the most current, very well documented and most challenging as regards the explanation of the final outcome. More precisely, I will evaluate governmental positions conditional upon three decisive steps along the negotiation process: the incomplete compromise reached under the Italian presidency in December 2003; the compromise reached ahead of the final summit under the Irish presidency in 2004; and the final compromise, i.e. the Constitutional Treaty. For this purpose, I first locate the intermediate results of the IGC within the two-dimensional space. Subsequently, I predict governments' positional shifts in response to the intermediate results. Next, I compare governments' public reactions to my predictions. Finally, I discuss the implications of these dynamics for our understanding of the international negotiations over European treaty reforms.

Table 6.6 documents the sequential character of the intergovernmental agreements. In particular, it sorts the sixty-five issues contained in the DOSEI data set according to their last appearance in official documents issued by either the Council presidency or the Presidium of the Convention, the assumption being that this is the date the issue was settled. Obviously, this is an *ex-post* judgment. Nevertheless, I consider the last appearance in official documents a good indicator for the expected outcome at the time of the IGC. Table 6.6 indicates that almost half of the issues had been settled during the Convention. Among them are many

---

14. According to Equation 6.5, a more precise evaluation of endogenous positional change should incorporate information on the relative salience actors attach to each dimension. Unfortunately, the data does not contain information on salience.

low-conflict issues such as the rejection of an extended right of initiative for EP and national parliaments, the extension of the codecision procedure to all areas except for regional policy, the definition of the EU's political objective, the general applicability of the subsidiarity principle, but also the definition of the Union's competences in the areas of foreign as well education policy. Apparently, the limited extension of QMV to economic, currency and employment areas was settled during the Convention, too. With only one exception, all of these issues are last mentioned in official documents issued between May 12 and June 12, 2003, just ahead of the concluding debate, which took place on June 13, 2003.

Following the theory of endogenous preference change, I expect governments to adjust their ideal position in reaction to the Convention proposal. The interesting question in this regard is *in how far* the Convention proposal altered governments' expectations over the outcome of the IGC. In technical terms, this is the quest for o^-, the expected outcome on which a government conditions its position. Given the public statements and bilateral negotiations before the start of the IGC, it appears reasonable to assume that governments had a fair idea which set of issues would be excluded from the intergovernmental bargaining table. Hence, the expected reform o^- was located somewhere between the Treaty of Nice (including the modification on the twenty-nine issues already settled by the Convention) and the far-reaching Convention proposal.

Figures 6.1 and 6.2 depict governments' positions conditioned upon either end of this spectrum.[15] In particular, Figure 6.1 shows the shift of governmental positions from being conditional upon the Treaty of Nice ('ToN') to being conditional upon the minimum reform as defined by the twenty-nine issues settled by the Convention in June 2003 ('Jun03'). The governments of Ireland, Italy, Latvia, Malta, Luxembourg, Estonia and the Slovak Republic shift their position in lockstep to the location of the minimal compromise. By contrast, their colleagues from Denmark, Sweden, Poland, the Czech Republic, Belgium, France and Greece move in the exact opposite direction. Moreover, all governments would have preferred the minimal compromise over the Treaty of Nice, with the Irish being more or less indifferent.

However, as described in Chapter 4, the Convention proposal was far more progressive, including hotly contested reforms on both dimensions. Figure 6.2 presents the shift of governmental positions from being conditional upon the minimum compromise ('Jun03') to being conditional on the Convention proposal ('Conv'). Most obviously, the French and German governments would have preferred the complete package. Hence, it comes as little surprise that Schröder

---

15. The governmental positions and nonseparability parameters used in this section are the results of a separate estimation that exclusively relies on the sixty-one contested issues of the DOSEI data set. The reason is that it was impossible to code the reforms agreed at Rome II for issues found in the Nice data set (for more information on the data please consult Chapter 3). However, the estimates are highly correlated to those from the joint estimation ($r > 0.87$). For more information please refer to Finke (2009).

Table 6.6: Sequence of intergovernmental decisions

Constitutional Issues (DOSEI- data collection)	Date of Agreement
Agreements until June 2004	
QMV	18.06.2004, CIG 82-85/04
Number of Commissioners	18.06.2004, CIG 82-85/04
Presidency of the European Council	18.06.2004, CIG 81/04
Voting rule (council) for Tax Harmonisation	18.06.2004, CIG 81/04
Voting rule (council) for Common Foreign Policy	18.06.2004, CIG 81/04
Rights of EP in the adoption of the budget	18.06.2004, CIG 81/04
Charter of Fundamental Rights	18.06.2004, CIG 82-85/04
Scope of ECJ Jurisdiction	18.06.2004, CIG 81/04
Level of competence for Structural and cohesion policies	18.06.2004, CIG 84-85/04
Level of competence for Freedom, Security and Justice	18.06.2004, CIG 81,83-85/04
Level of competence for Economic Policy	18.06.2004, CIG 82-85/04
Level of competence for Employment Policy	18.06.2004, CIG 82-85/04
Level of competence for Social Policy	18.06.2004, CIG 81/04
Voting rule (council) for Stability and Growth Pact	18.06.2004, CIG 82-85/04
Religious reference in the preamble	14.06.2004, CIG 80/04
Decision rule (EP) for Structural and cohesion policies	24.05.2004, CIG 79/04
Level of competence for Health Policy	24.05.2004, CIG 79/04
Appointment of Commissioners (role of EP)	17.05.2004, CIG 75/04
Voting rule (Council) for Area of Freedom, Security and Justice	17.05.2004, CIG 75/04
Voting rule (Council) for Social security rights	17.05.2004, CIG 75/04
Presidency of the European Council (nomination)	13.05.2004, CIG 76/03
Appointment of Commission President (role of Council, EP or nat. parliaments)	13.05.2004, CIG 76/03
Minister of Foreign Affairs (role of Commission in appointment)	13.05.2004, CIG 76/03
Voting rule (Council) for Structural and cohesion politics	13.05.2004, CIG 76/03
Voting rule (Council) for Defence Policy	13.05.2004, CIG 76/03
External representation	29.04.2004, CIG 73/04

Constitutional Issues (DOSEI- data collection)	Date of Agreement
Agreements until December 2003	
Enhanced cooperation	12.12.2003, CIG 60/1/03
Level of competence for Tax Harmonisation	12.12.2003, CIG 60/1/03
Voting rule (Council) for Social Policy	27.10.2003, CIG 38/03
Voting rule (Council) for Defence Policy	27.10.2003, CIG 38/03
Right to withdraw from the Union	27.10.2003, CIG 37/03
Level of competence for Agriculture	27.10.2003, CIG 37/03
Level of competence for Environment Policy	27.10.2003, CIG 37/03
Level of competence for research, technological development and space	27.10.2003, CIG 37/03
Migration and Asylum	27.10.2003, CIG 37/03
Agreement upon convention	
Legislative initiative for citizens	12.06.2003, CONV 797/1/03
Minister of Foreign Affairs (role of EP in appointment)	12.06.2003, CONV 797/1/03
Economic objectives: competitiveness	12.06.2003, CONV 797/1/03
Subsidiarity	30.05.2003, CONV 724/1/03
Legislative initiative for Council	30.05.2003, CONV 727/03
Voting rule (Council) for Monetary policy	30.05.2003, CONV 727/03
Voting rule (Council) for Economic Policy	30.05.2003, CONV 727/03
Decision rule (EP) for Area of Freedom, Security and Justice	30.05.2003, CONV 727/03
Decision rule (EP) for Tax Harmonisation	30.05.2003, CONV 727/03
Decision rule (EP) for Monetary policy	30.05.2003, CONV 727/03
Decision rule (EP) for Economic Policy	30.05.2003, CONV 727/03
Decision rule (EP) for Common Foreign Policy	30.05.2003, CONV 727/03
Decision rule (EP) for Defence Policy	30.05.2003, CONV 727/03
External borders (management)	30.05.2003, CONV 727/03
Economic objectives: market economy	30.05.2003, CONV 724/1/03
Economic objectives: employment	30.05.2003, CONV 724/1/03
Level of competence for Foreign Policy	15.05.2003, CONV 748/03
Voting rule (Council) for Agriculture	12.05.2003, CONV 729/03

Constitutional Issues (DOSEI- data collection)	Date of Agreement
Voting rule (Council) for Internal market	12.05.2003, CONV 729/03
Voting rule (Council) for Employment Policy	12.05.2003, CONV 729/03
Decision rule (EP) for Agriculture	12.05.2003, CONV 729/03
Decision rule (EP) for Internal market	12.05.2003, CONV 729/03
Decision rule (EP) for Employment Policy	12.05.2003, CONV 729/03
Decision rule (EP) for Social Policy	12.05.2003, CONV 729/03
Decision rule (EP) for Social security rights	12.05.2003, CONV 729/03
Legislative initiative Commission	24.04.2003, CONV 691/03
Legislative initiative for European Parliament	24.04.2003, CONV 691/03
Legislative initiative for National parliaments	24.04.2003, CONV 691/03
Level of competence for Education Policy	06.02.2003, CONV 528/03

Note: Date of Agreement defines the latest date an issue had appeared in an official document issued either by the Convention (CONV) or by the Council Presidency (CIG).

Source: Data collection of the DOSEI-Project and own research (König and Finke 2007).

('I could sign it as it is.'[16]) and Chirac ('It is the best possible synthesis.') were mutually outbidding each other in praise of the Convention's work. The same is true for the British Labour government ('A good balance which ought not to be rattled'[17]) which definitely preferred the complete proposal over the minimum compromise. Likewise, the Spanish prime minister, Aznar, and his Portuguese counterpart, Barroso, restricted their criticisms to the symbolic issues of adding a reference to Christianity in the preamble.[18] Supporting Figure 6.2 the Italian government, represented by Prime Minister Berlusconi, reacted to the Convention proposal by demanding a more radical extension of majority voting. 'We too would like to expand the qualified voting rule at the expense of unanimity. We will try to go into this direction, but we all must be pragmatic and realistic'.[19]

Many other member states reacted less enthusiastically to the presentation of the Convention proposal; in particular the governments of Austria, Latvia, Denmark, Sweden, Hungary, the Netherlands, Finland and, most prominently,

---

16. Source: Gelie, P. 'Union Europeene; Les vingt-cinq chefs d'Etat et de gouvernement ont adopté hier à Salonique le projet de Constitution comme "document de base"; Giscard réussit son "grand oral"', *Le Figaro*, 21 June 2003.

17. See fn 16 above.

18. Source: 'From the top: how the member states' leaders view the new draft constitution'. *The Times* (London), 21 June 2003.

19. Source: 'Giscard passe le témoin européen à l'Italie; Le président de la Convention européenne a remis vendredi à Rome le projet de Constitution pour l'Europe élargie au président en exercice de l'Union. Avec le conseil de ne pas le toucher', *Le Temps*, 19 July 2003.

190 | european integration and its limits

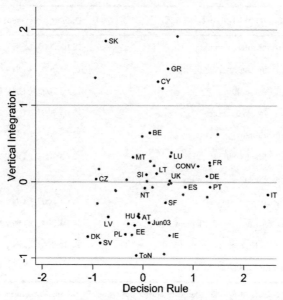

Unlabelled dots demarcate governmental positions conditional upon the Treaty of Nice

Figure 6.1: Governmental positions conditional upon the minimal compromise reached in June 2003

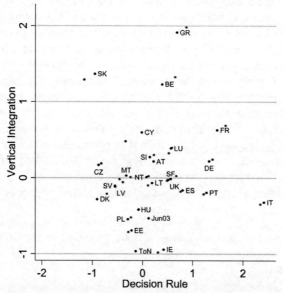

Unlabelled dots demarcate governmental positions conditional upon the minimal compromise reached in June 2003

Figure 6.2: Governmental positions conditional upon the Convention Draft

Poland moved away from the Convention proposal. For example, the Austrian chancellor, Schüssel, stated that his country had 'fundamental concerns' about several institutional reforms, in particular the planned office of a permanent Council president as well as the downsizing of the Commission.[20] The Austrian chancellor found support from the Hungarian government, which reiterated its preference to retain the 'one country, one Commissioner' principle, and rejected any plans to distinguish between voting and non-voting Commissioners. In a joint statement, both governments argued that the reform of the voting threshold proposed by the Convention, i.e., a simple majority of member states and 60 per cent of the enlarged EU's population, harms the interest of small countries.[21]

Acting for many of the smaller member states, the Dutch prime minister, Balkenende, formulated his government's concern that 'the European Council should not become the exclusive preserve of the large member states' and should not be turned into 'a new Legislative Council' acting 'as the pivot of the European legislative process'. Instead, his government favoured the current, decentralised organisation of the Council, not least because 'it is much better for European legislation to remain the responsibility of the existing Councils. It is the ministers in the various specialised areas who know best what impact European rules will have on citizens'.[22] Along the same lines, the Finnish president, Halonen, called for more balanced changes to the institutional elements of the constitution by setting limits on the powers of the European Council and its president. Furthermore, the Finnish government openly criticised the possibility for a smaller group of countries to form a 'core group' in defence policy.[23] The Irish government added to this list of deficiencies and announced that it would pursue 'a few important problems in the IGC'. In particular, the government opposed plans to harmonise criminal law or create a European public prosecutor and was willing to fight to maintain the national vetoes on taxation.[24] As regards the latter issue, it was strongly supported by the Estonian government.

According to Figure 6.2, the Danish and Swedish governments should have been the ones most radically opposed to the Convention proposal. They reveal the largest positional shift opposing any further integration under the proposed decision-rule. Even more so, they opposed any extension of majority voting, given

---

20. Source: Hauser, A., Konrad-Adenauer-Stiftung e.V. (Hrsg.), 'Das Gipfeltreffen von Thessaloniki – Eine neue Seite der Europäischen Geschichte wird aufgeschlagen', 30 Juni 2003. www.kas.de/proj/home/pub/9/1/year-2003/dokument_id-2130/index.html (accessed 3 December 2008).

21. Source: 'Hungary, Austria Exchange Views on EU Constitution', *Hungarian News Agency* (MTI), 16 July 2003.

22. Source: Speech by the prime minister, Dr. Jan Peter Balkenende, Eurocities Conference on European and Local Governance, The Hague, 23 June 2003 www.minaz.nl/Actueel/Toespraken/2003/06/ Speech_by_the_Prime_Minister_Dr_Jan_Peter_Balkenende_Eurocities_Conference_on_European_and_Local_Governance_The_Hague (accessed 20 December 2008).

23. Source: 'From the top: how the member states' leaders view the new draft constitution', *The Times* (London), 21 June, 2003

24. Source: 'From the top: how the member states' leaders view the new draft constitution'. *The Times* (London), 21 June 2003

the proposed level of integration. However, the public statements issued by both governments in response to the Convention do not support their position in Figure 6.2. The statements issued by the Danish prime minister, Anders Fogh Rasmussen, read rather diplomatically, calling the Convention proposal 'impressive and very ambitious' and a 'good foundation for negotiations'.[25] His Swedish colleague Göran Persson was also rather positive 'despite the fact that the Swedish representatives at the Convention had been very critical'.[26] However, during the IGC, both governments were pulling no punches in trying to stop the proposed reforms, as with Austria, Finland, the Netherlands and Poland.

One explanation for both governments' lack of open criticism is the increased pressure from their domestic opposition. As regards Denmark, the awareness of the upcoming referendum on the Constitutional Treaty may partly rationalise the reluctance to criticise the draft. Presenting the result of an uncomplicated IGC, which embraces the Convention's results, was considered an advantage for the advocates of the yes-vote, i.e. the government. A similar logic might apply to Sweden, where the governing Social Democratic Party was internally divided on many of the reform issues (Finke and König 2009). Likewise, the Finnish government came under increasing pressure from the domestic opposition. According to its critics, the Lipponen government had moved from the wrong assumption that the 'real' negotiations on the new Constitutional Treaty would have been conducted in the IGC. In response, opposition leaders publicly challenged the Finnish government to take a more active role in the IGC.[27]

Finally, the Polish government was the one most prominently criticising the Convention proposal, which President Kwasniewski perceived as a decisive step toward a federal European super state.[28] In contrast to Denmark and Sweden, the Polish government pursued an entirely different strategy. Instead of avoiding international conflict to be in a better marketing position domestically, they added fuel to the Euro-sceptic movements within Poland in order to gain domestic electoral support and to improve their international bargaining position. Considering Figure 6.2, it becomes clear that this was a credible strategy indeed. No other country's conditional position was located so close to the status quo. This perspective culminated in the infamous battle cry 'Nice or Death' by Jan Rokita, the leader of the conservative opposition.

Specifically, the government rejected any reforms that would have reduced the Polish veto power in any European decision-making body, most prominently in the Council of Ministers. All parliamentary parties supported a resolution asking the government to continue its efforts to maintain the institutional package

---

25. Sources: 'Le président de la Convention a remis le projet de Constitution européenne au sommet de Salonique; Le succès européen de Giscard', *Le Figaro*, 21 Juin 2003.

26. Source: Danmarks Radio P1, Copenhagen, in Danish 1400 GMT June 20, 2003, text of report by Danish radio on June 20.

27. Source: 'Country Report Sweden', *The Convention Watch*, available at: http://eucon.europa2004.it/ Watch2ed/Answer1-1.htm (accessed 11.01.2009).

28. Source: 'Poland will not accept "Federal" Europe', *The Baltic Times*, 10 July 2003.

agreed in Nice. In addition, the government strongly rejected any steps toward a European defence policy, which it thought would weaken the close collaboration within NATO.[29]

Bottom line, the Convention proposal induced endogenous positional changes, which polarised European governments. One group was eager to support the complete package, whereas another group wanted to reduce the list of reforms. In this sense, the starting point of the IGC was the text supplied by the Convention. In retrospect, a list of twenty-nine issues had been settled once and for all by the Convention. Figure 6.1 indicates that all governments would have preferred this minimal compromise ('Jun03') over the status quo ('ToN'). Subsequently, the governments' reactions to decisive steps during the IGC are discussed, namely the summit under the Italian presidency in December 2003 and the final summit under the Irish presidency in June 2004.

The Incomplete Italian Compromise
Under the leadership of Prime Minister Silvio Berlusconi, the Italian Council presidency had scheduled the decisive summit for December 12–13, 2003. At the beginning of the IGC, the presidency issued a document in which it recorded governments' agreement over nine additional issues (see Table 6.6). Governments had agreed to maintain the current division of competences in tax, social and agricultural policy as well as the voting rule over social and defence policies. However, they established the 'Permanent Structured Cooperation', which allows for Enhanced Cooperation in security and defence matters, but has to be agreed by unanimity in the European Council. Furthermore, governments agreed on far-reaching harmonisation of national policies in the areas of migration and asylum policy and they settled on minor extensions of the European education and research policy. Finally, they introduced a right to withdraw membership unilaterally. Nevertheless, on early Saturday morning, it became clear that the summit would not be able to resolve the remaining issues, which correspond to another twenty-three variables of the DOSEI data set. As a consequence, governments agreed to postpone the negotiations until the upcoming Irish presidency.

Figure 6.3 locates the incomplete compromise of December 2003 ('Dec03') in the intergovernmental conflict space. Furthermore, it depicts how governments should have adopted their positions according to my estimates of nonseparability. Overall, Figure 6.3 seems to resemble the trend observed in Figure 6.1. In particular, Denmark, Sweden Poland, Latvia, France, Greece and Belgium move downward, i.e. towards less integration.

How far do governments' public reactions correspond to Figure 6.3? The French and German governments made no secret of their disappointment. Both Schröder and Chirac observed that the adoption of a reform as progressive as the one presented by the Convention was primarily blocked by a number of smaller

---

29. Source: Hauser, A., Konrad-Adenauer-Stiftung e.V. (Hrsg.), 'Das Gipfeltreffen von Thessaloniki – Eine neue Seite der Europäischen Geschichte wird aufgeschlagen', 30 Juni 2003, www.kas.de/proj/home/pub/9/1/year-2003/dokument_id-2130/index.html (accessed 3.12.2008).

states (Denmark, Sweden, Austria, Estonia, Latvia, and Hungary) plus Poland, which turned out most outspoken in its opposition of the Convention draft. As a consequence, the two leaders deployed a twofold strategy. First, they re-awoke the idea of a core Europe, a 'pioneer group' of nations that could move forward with closer cooperation on areas such as the economy, justice and defence. Following Chirac, 'It will be the motor. It will set the example, allow Europe to go faster, better'.[30] Second, they publicly blamed the Polish government for its 'inflexibility' and its unwillingness to discuss any solution of the QMV reform based on the principle of a double majority.[31] The ultimate purpose of this double strategy was to raise the costs of continuous opposition or, as German chancellor Schröder had put it, to initiate a 'learning process' in Warsaw.[32]

The British Labour government found itself in a situation far more complex. On the one hand, it would have welcomed further reforms, in particular extended applicability and reform of the majority rule. On the other hand, it rejected any plans of a core Europe. One explanation for the latter is that it was widely believed that governments of the new member states would share the UK's reluctance to delegate sovereignty and, in many cases, its profound market liberalism. Hence, it comes as little surprise that Tony Blair welcomed the decision to postpone the negotiations, arguing that it is better 'to give it some time, for countries to have some time to find an accord'. Britain, he continued, would continue to work toward the successful creation of a constitution for the European Union, despite the collapse of talks in Brussels that weekend.[33] The reaction of the conservative Spanish government was very similar. On the one hand, Aznar rejected any responsibility for the failed summit by highlighting his 'constructive willingness to negotiate until the last moment'. On the other hand, he nourished the hopes that all twenty-five governments would find an agreement under the Irish presidency.[34]

Considering its position in Figure 6.3, it comes as little surprise that the Portuguese government turned out very unsatisfied with the failure of the summit, but hoped for a coherent proposal along the lines of the outcome of the Convention.[35] The Belgian foreign minister, Louis Michel, was more plainly vent-

---

30. Source: Ames, P. 'European Constitution Summit Collapses', *Associated Press Online*, 14 December 2003.
31. Source: Pries, K. 'Herz vor Verstand ; Auf der Suche nach den Schuldigen für das Brüsseler Debakel werden die Akteure überall fündig', *Frankfurter Rundschau*, 15 Dezember 2003.
32. Source: Berger, A. 'Der EU-Verfassungsgipfel ist geplatzt', *SonntagsZeitung*, 14 Dezember 2003.
33. Source: 'EU Summit Blair says leaders should take time find right constitution deal', *AFX.COM*, 13 December 2003.
34. Source: 'Les principales déclarations du sommet de Bruxelles', *Agence France Presse*, 14 Décembre 2003.
35. Source: 'Portuguese premier says no one country to blame for EU summit failure', BBC Monitoring Europe – Political, supplied by *BBC Worldwide Monitoring*, December 14, 2003; Source: RDP Antena 1 radio, Lisbon, in Portuguese, 1900 GMT December 13, 2003, text of a report by Portuguese radio on December 13.

ing his anger and, at least indirectly, blaming the new member states. 'Yes, I am disappointed and angry. This decision was the first that we had to take in the EU25. Some had preferred national interests over those of Europe'.[36]

As regards Austria, the Franco-German threat of a core Europe seemed to have hit the mark. Chancellor Schüssel emphasised Austria's commitment to being at the 'heart of a new Europe' ('It's in our interest to belong to the core group of Europe'.[37]). As before, the Danish and Swedish governments were rather cautious in their public statements. However, the Danish prime minister, Rasmussen, did not join the critics of the Italian presidency, but complimented them on the well-founded substantial preparation.[38] His evaluation matches with Figure 6.3, where Denmark would have been more or less indifferent between the compromise reached in December 2003 and the Treaty of Nice.

Unsurprisingly, the Polish government openly refused any responsibility for the failed summit. Furthermore, Prime Minister Leszek Miller threatened to permanently veto any reform of the voting rule, which would reduce Poland's relative voting power: 'We said: "Let us take all these good things from the constitutional treaty (the simplification of treaties, a joint foreign policy, greater power for the European Parliament) and this one fragment from the Nice Treaty, that is the division of votes". They did not agree, so as a punishment they have got all of Nice!'[39]

In sum, the Italian presidency pushed the compromise to the limit of what would have been acceptable to all governments – but not beyond. It was unable to reconcile the polarisation caused by the Convention proposal.

The Irish Presidency and the Constitutional Treaty
In January 2009 the Irish government took over the Council presidency. It scheduled the second summit to settle the intergovernmental dispute over the Constitution for June 17–18, 2004. Until this date, governments agreed upon eleven more issues, the majority of which had been settled during two meetings of the foreign ministers at the end of May 2004 (see Table 6.6). In particular, they agreed to maintain the current division of competences as regards health policy. Furthermore, governments finally rejected any extension of QMV to the area of social security rights. With regard to the appointment of Commissioners, the new wording carefully strengthened the role of the EP.[40] Furthermore, the compromise provided that the Commission president-elect would first select his Commissioners on the basis

---

36. Source: 'Synthèse Echec du sommet européen sur la Constitution Les intérêts nationaux ont prévalu sur celui de l'Europe', *SDA – Service de base français*, 13 Décembre 2003.
37. Source: 'EU Summit, Austria's Schuessel says committed to position at 'heart of Europe', *AFX. COM*, 13 December 2003.
38. Source: Klarskov, K. and H. Kaufholz, 'EU-Fiasko: Fogh: Trist Dag for Europa', *Politiken*, 14 December 2003.
39. Source: 'Premier says Poland made constructive proposals in Brussels', BBC Monitoring Europe – Political, supplied by *BBC Worldwide Monitoring*, December 16, 2003; Source: PAP news agency, Warsaw, in Polish 1947 GMT 16 December 2003.
40. According to the Constitution, the EP 'elects' instead of 'approves'.

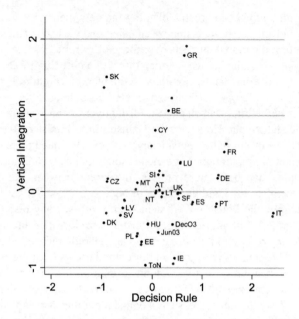

Unlabelled dots demarcate governmental positions conditional upon the minimal compromise reached in June 2003

Figure 6.3: Governmental positions conditional upon the compromise reached by the Italian presidency in December 2003

of suggestions made by the national governments and this body should then be approved by the EP. Governments agreed on an extended cooperation in criminal and justice proceedings and that a European Public Prosecutor could be introduced at a later date, but only if all member states and the EP agree. Furthermore, they enabled mutual defence commitments among subgroups of member states and established a European foreign minister to be accountable to and appointed by the Commission in cooperation with the Council president, but without further approval of the EP. Finally, only four days ahead of the summit, governments agreed on a preamble to include a religious reference, but not to Christianity.

Figure 6.4 depicts the location of this compromise in the two-dimensional conflict space ('Jun04'). In particular, the extension of QMV and the agreement over the Council presidency as well as the foreign minister caused a rightwards shift compared to the agreement reached in December 2003. In reaction to these developments, governments shifted their positions on vertical integration. In particular, the positions of the Slovak, Slovenian, Cypriot, Italian, Maltese, Irish, Estonian and Spanish governments moved upward, i.e. toward more integration. By contrast, the Danish, Swedish, Polish, Czech, Belgian, Greek, Finnish, Dutch, Lithuanian and Latvian governments moved downward, i.e. toward less integra-

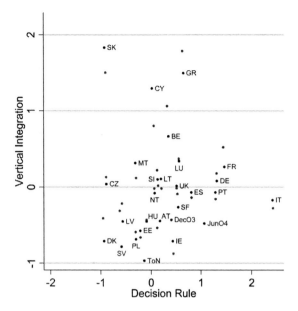

Unlabelled dots demarcate governmental positions conditional upon the compromise reached under the Italian presidency in December 2003

Figure 6.4: Governmental positions conditional upon the compromise reached shortly ahead of the final summit in June 2004

tion; as did the French, the German and the Portuguese governments, but for different reasons. Whereas the former group confronted more drastic reforms of the decision-rule than they had originally hoped for, the opposite was true for the latter three governments. Finally, the Irish government was about to formulate a reform package beyond a minimal compromise. In particular, the compromise which emerged just ahead of the final summit moved beyond what Denmark, Sweden, Estonia, Latvia and Poland would have preferred to the Treaty of Nice.

Ultimately, the Irish presidency provoked open resistance when launching its compromise proposal for the outstanding issues, in particular the reform of the QMV rules ahead of the final summit. A qualified majority was now defined as at least 55 per cent of the member states, comprising at least fifteen of them and representing at least 65 per cent of the EU's population. As compared to the provision under the Treaty of Nice, the new rules would have raised the population threshold, at least until the EU took in new members. Unsurprisingly, many of the smaller states felt passed over by the Irish presidency. The Finnish and Slovene prime ministers called the proposal 'unacceptable'. The Austrian chancellor seconded that this proposal was putting too much emphasis on population size and, in effect, strengthening the position of the larger member states.[41] Poland's prime minister, Marek Belka, demanded that any voting rule should be responsive to the opposition of at least 30 per cent of the EU's population or 40 per cent of member states. He demanded that an appropriate declaration should be added to the Treaty.[42] Besides the reform of QMV rules, the opposition concentrated on the proposed reform of the Commission. Here, the limit of what smaller member states were willing to tolerate was a declaration of intent to reassess the current size of the Commission in due time.

French President Chirac emerged as the spokesman of the larger countries. Referring to the compromise reached ahead of the concluding summit, he said: 'From now on limits exist which we cannot overstep. We will not accept any deviation from the proposals presented by the Irish presidency'. Naturally, this point of view was supported by the German and Italian governments.[43]

By and large, the final summit followed the presidency's proposal. In addition, the Constitutional Treaty provided for a smaller college of eighteen Commissioners by the year 2014. It strengthened the involvement of the EP in the annual budgeting procedure. Moreover, governments concurred that a team of three member states would preside over the Council for eighteen months. Each member of the team would hold the presidency for a period of six months, being assisted by the other two states on the basis of a common programme. The European Council would be chaired by a president appointed for two and a half years, appointed by unanimity of Council members, renewable once. Governments did not extent majority voting to foreign and tax policy, a decision particularly important to ensure the support of Ireland, Estonia and Poland. Likewise, governments did not extend the Union's competences in the areas of employment, social and economic policy (see Chapter 3).

Figure 6.5 located the final compromise, the Constitutional Treaty ('IGC'), in the two-dimensional conflict space. In reaction, I predict the positions of the Slovak, Irish, Cypriot, Maltese and Finnish governments to move up and rightwards, whereas the French, Greece, Belgian, Danish, Swedish and Latvian governments should have moved in the opposite direction. As a result, the Constitutional Treaty is located very close to Portugal, Germany, France and Spain. By contrast, governments of the following eight states would have preferred the Treaty of Nice: Denmark, Sweden, Poland, Latvia, Estonia, Ireland, and Austria and, though marginally, Hungary.

Against this background, it comes as little surprise that some governments hailed the Constitutional Treaty, in particular the German chancellor ('a his-

---

41. Source: Radio Slovenia, Ljubljana, June 18, 2004 (English summary).
42. Source: 'We need compromises, but we don't want a dog's dinner of a document', *The Irish Times*, 19 June 2004.
43. Source: Schnauder, A. 'Verfassung: Späte Einigung nach zähem Ringen', *Die Presse*, 19 June 2004.

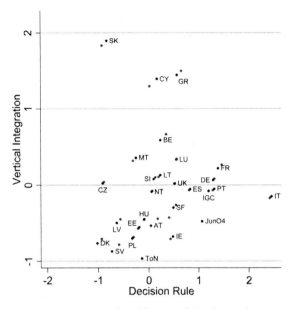

Unlabelled dots demarcate governmental positions conditional upon the compromise reached shortly ahead of the final summit in June 2004

Figure 6.5: Governmental positions conditional upon the Constitutional Treaty

toric decision which increases the Union's unity and governability'[44]) and the French president, Chirac, ('a good agreement for European a good agreement for France'[45]). At the same time, Chirac was careful enough to portray the result as a compromise: 'We, it's true, would have liked to have gone further still down the road of harmonization in social and fiscal areas, but of course we had to take everyone's opinions into account'.[46] The only government to evaluate the Treaty even more euphorically was the Portuguese, calling it 'splendid for Europe' because it enables European integration 'with many more member states' and 'splendid for Portugal, because the fundamental interests (…) have been fully enshrined in the European constitution'.[47] This assessment on the Constitutional Treaty matches with the Portuguese position in Figure 6.5.

---

44. Source: 'Staats- und Regierungschefs einigen sich auf Verfassung für Europa', *Agence France Presse* – German, 19 Juni 2004.
45. Source: 'Chirac: la Constitution'est bonne pour l'Europe et pour la France', *Agence France Presse*, 19 Juin 2004.
46. Source: Wielaard, R., 'EU leaders face a hard sell of constitution in parliaments and streets of Europe', *The Associated Press*, 19 June 2004, BC cycle.
47. Source: 'Portuguese premier hails agreement on EU constitution', BBC Monitoring Europe – Political, supplied by *BBC Worldwide Monitoring;* Source: RDP Antena 1 radio, Lisbon, in Portuguese 0700 GMT, 19 June 2004, text of a report by Portuguese radio on June 19.

Moreover, the statement of the British and Spanish governments were also very positive, with the Spanish prime minister, Zapatero, highlighting that the IGC had 'avoided a directorate in the EU'.[48] The Finnish government is located halfway between the Treaty of Nice and the Constitutional Treaty. Although it had to concede on many issues as, for example, the maintenance of Commissioners for every member state and a voting rule more favourable to smaller states, the government was overall satisfied with the compromise.[49]

The eight member states that, according to Figure 6.5, should have preferred the status quo can be subdivided in three groups. First, some member states found it hard to veto the final compromise because they had been favouring a rather integration-friendly position earlier on in the IGC (Figures 6.1–6.4) and committed themselves to the Convention proposal. In particular, this is true for Denmark, Sweden, Austria and Latvia. Accordingly, these countries found it hard to veto the Constitutional Treaty over reforms they supported earlier on in the process. Besides an unfavourable utility balance, such a veto would have created significant credibility and reputation costs. Accordingly, we observe cautiously positive evaluations from these governments, mostly emphasising the importance of an agreement as an end in itself as well as a proof of and 'guarantee for efficiency after enlargement' (Danish prime minister, Anders Fogh Rasmussen[50]).

Second, Ireland and Estonia have been appeased by a favourable solution to a single, but vital issue. As low-tax countries, both governments were united in their opposition against any attempt to harmonise European taxes or, even worse, the extension of QMV to this area (Gwiazda 2006; Finke 2006). It appears of little help to interpret the reactions of the Irish presidency, which, naturally, hailed the final compromise. However, the Estonian reactions to the final outcome were characterised by relief that the 'red line' of tax harmonisation had not been crossed. The government expressed 'satisfaction with the fact that an article on direct taxation was dropped from the Treaty text at the IGC and in the area of indirect taxation unanimity was preserved [...] Retaining unanimity voting in the area of taxation was one of the most important issues for Estonia at the IGC'.[51] Indeed, Table 6.6 reveals that the voting rule on taxation was among the last issue to be resolved. Accordingly, the Estonian foreign minister judged the final agreement to be 'no doubt a compromise, but favourable to Estonia'.[52]

Third, the consent of Hungary and Poland to the final outcome of the IGC remains difficult to explain. Certainly, reputation costs are an important factor in explaining the last-minute consent of the Polish government. The leader of the

---

48. Source: 'EU wakes up to new constitution battle', *Channel News Asia*, 19 June 2004.
49. Source: Convention Watch, No. 1, downloadable at: www.eu-consent.net/library/EU25Watch/EU-25_Watch-No1.pdf.
50. Source: Møller, P. S. 'Det Genforenede Europas Traktat', *Jyllands-Posten*, July 10, 2004.
51. Source: 'Convention Watch', No. 1, available at: www.eu-consent.net/library/EU25Watch/EU-25_Watch-No1.pdf (accessed 11.01.2009).
52. Source: 'European Council endorses EU Constitutional Treaty', *Baltic News Service*, 19 June 2004.

Polish Social Democrats stated that Poland had 'achieved a maximum on what was to be achieved. [...] Refusal to accept a compromise in a situation where 24 EU countries were ready to agree would have led to Poland's isolation from the rest of the union'.[53] Another explanation points to the effect of decision sequence, in particular the late Polish rise at a time all other governments had committed themselves to the compromise proposed by the Irish presidency. Furthermore, the Polish government had been well-aware that a veto would not have terminated the reform once and for all. This argument becomes clear when reading Prime Minister Marek Belka's justification of his final approval: 'But having derailed summits twice – and that's how it would have been interpreted by circles hostile to Poland – our position in negotiating the budget and the constitution (in another attempt) would have been very bad'.[54] In this comment he referred to the negotiations over the multi-annual financial framework 2007–2013. However, the reaction by the Law and Justice Party, which, already strong, indicated that the next president (Lech Kaczynski) and the next prime minister (Jaroslaw Kaczynski), would have potential ratification problems. In particular, the parliamentary leader of Law and Justice blamed the left government for a 'shameful capitulation' at the final summit.[55]

DISCUSSION OF THE RESULTS

In this chapter, the relation between governments' positions on vertical integration and their preferred decision rule is discussed. In particular, constitutional theories suggest that preferences over both dimensions were nonseparable. The choice of the decision-rule would have altered the legislative outcome and, accordingly, the distribution of gains and losses implied by vertical integration. Against this background, the present chapter makes three contributions.

First, I derive theoretical expectations about the importance and the direction of the potential nonseparability between the preferences over vertical integration and the decision-rule. In particular, I argue that governments of large and rich member states would prefer a majoritarian and efficient decision-rule when confronted with a higher level of vertical integration than they had originally hoped for (Hypothesis 4.1). The reason is that these governments possess alternative means of power and, accordingly, could compensate for a loss of veto and voting power. Therefore, rich member states are able to avoid the rising heterogeneity

---

53. Source: 'President says Poland "moral victor" in battle for EU Constitution', BBC Monitoring Europe – Political, supplied by *BBC Worldwide Monitoring*, June 21, 2004; Source: PAP news agency, Warsaw, in English 1434 GMT, June 21, 2004, text of report in English by Polish news agency PAP.

54. Source: 'Poland's prime minister says he accepted EU constitution to secure Polish influence', *Associated Press Worldstream*, 21 June 2004.

55. Source: 'Polish opposition leader attacks EU constitution "capitulation"', BBC Monitoring Europe – Political, supplied by *BBC Worldwide Monitoring*, June 19, 2004. Source: PAP news agency, Warsaw, in Polish 1330 GMT June 19, 2004, excerpt from report by Polish news agency PAP. Source: 'Europe Has Constitution, But Belka is in Trouble', Byline: mzjw, *Polish News Bulletin*, June 21, 2004. Source: 19–20 issue of *Rzeczpospolita*, p. A1; p. A3.

costs implied by a higher level of integration. However, this argument assumes preference asymmetry among member states. Therefore, I find that the average size of the nonseparability effect depends on the policy-specific degree of preference asymmetry (Hypothesis 4.2).

Second, I advance the statistical model of ideal-point estimation introduced in Chapter 3, such that it allows for an explicit estimation of nonseparability effects (Finke 2009c). The model uses patterns of ex ante survey responses to draw inferences about the conditionality of member states' preferences between two latent, orthogonal conflict dimensions. I then apply this statistical model to data on governmental positions revealed at the three post-Maastricht IGCs. The results confirm that richer member states tend to reveal a positive complementary preference between the decision-rule and the level of vertical integration. Furthermore, the results support the idea that this effect is stronger in policy areas characterised by a high level of preference asymmetry. Moreover, the results complement the exogenous explanations of positional change discussed in Chapter 5 with an endogenous explanation. In doing so, it reveals that European treaty reforms follow a path dependency, at least at the medium term. But whereas the endogenous explanation for positional change turns out robust and significant for the horizontal dimension, its effect on the vertical dimension is absorbed by domestic factors, such as partisan composition of government and public opinion toward European integration.

Third, I provide a stepwise analysis of the negotiations over the Constitutional Treaty. For this purpose, I simulate governments' positions as being conditional upon the Treaty of Nice, the Convention proposal, the minimal compromise reached under the Italian presidency (December 2003) and the compromise reached just ahead of the final summit in June 2004. If governments' positions are conditional upon the expected outcome, process and the sequence of decisions gain importance for our understanding of European treaty reforms. By and large, the predicted change of governmental positions matches with the public statements issued by governmental leaders at the time. Previous IGCs at Amsterdam (1997) and Nice (2000) had ended with reforms at the least common denominator. As a consequence, governments invoked the Convention on the Future of Europe. Unexpectedly, the Convention proposed a coherent and progressive reform treaty. Retrospective governments considered almost half of the reform issues to be settled before starting the IGC. However, governments haggled over the bindingness of the Convention proposal, which polarised the conflict among them. One group advocated the adoption of the complete reform package, whereas a second group reacted by opposing further reforms altogether. The failure of the summit headed by the Italian Council presidency offers proof of this conflict.

In comparison to the status quo under the Treaty of Nice, the decisions taken by December 2003 would have improved all twenty-five governments. Yet, in the end, the Irish presidency brokered a deal, which, in comparison to the status quo, eight countries should have rejected. My analysis reveals that the Austrian, Danish, Swedish and Latvian governments found it hard to revoke their commitment to vertical integration stipulated by the Convention proposal, even when confronted with unfavourable reforms of the decision-rule. As regards Ireland and

Estonia, the sequence of decisions matters in so far as both low-tax countries had a vital interest that matters of taxation would not be decided by QMV. This issue remained on the bargaining table until the final summit in June 2004. At the same time, the existence of vital issues reveals the limit of my statistical approach. Finally, my sequential analysis can hardly explain the Hungarian and Polish approval of the Constitutional Treaty. Following the public statements issues by both governments right after the concluding summit, they feared the negative reputational effect of vetoing the final compromise. Moreover, they expected adverse consequences for the upcoming negotiations over the EU budget.

In the end, the Constitutional Treaty was almost identical to the Convention proposal. Hence, it must be considered a landslide victory for the French and German as well as the Spanish and Portuguese governments. As regards the intergovernmental level, they eventually succeeded in overcoming the minimal compromises of earlier IGCs.

chapter seven | solving europe's constitutional quandary

STEERING THE FLEET THROUGH HEAVY WATERS

In February 1992 the heads of state and government signed the Treaty of Maastricht. Knowingly or not, this act constituted the beginning of a new era of Europe's integration project, an era of transition, enlargement, politicisation and incremental reform. At the end of the Cold War, political leaders found themselves under pressure from a growing queue of would-be new member states. Fifteen years later, the number of member states has more than doubled, from twelve in 1992 to twenty-seven in 2008. During the same period, Europe's political leaders struggled to attain three partly conflicting goals, which represent Europe's constitutional quandary.

First, economic scholars and many political leaders argued that the single market should be complemented and counterbalanced with political integration. Encouraged by economic theories of federalism, they demanded adding an external dimension by a common foreign, security, defence and energy policy. Others were eager to counterbalance the common market by strengthening coordination in social, environmental, fiscal as well as justice and home affairs. Fifteen years later, many of these issues remain on the agenda. However, this does not mean that integration did not proceed along this dimension – on the contrary: governments added an employment and a social chapter to the treaty framework, agreed on the Lisbon strategy, created permanent structured cooperation for defence policy, EU battle groups, an EU foreign minister, a stronger coordination of law enforcement via Europol and Eurojust, stronger coordination in migration and asylum policies, the inclusion of the Charter of Fundamental Rights, the Schengen information system, the Bologna process, the substantial reform of the common agricultural and regional policy – to name only the most important developments. Some of these developments have been initiated by passive or negative integration within the existing treaty framework (Heritier 2007), whereas most were attained as original treaty reforms.

Second, the increased law-making activities of the late 1980s and early 1990s led to a pledge to improve the EU's law-making capacity. A central means of this debate were reforms of the decision-making process, which ought to have lowered the threat of blockage and gridlock, in particular the extension of qualified majority voting and the lowering of the voting thresholds. Enlargement catalysed this debate in either of two directions. On the one hand, it increased the fear of standstill due to an increased number of states. On the other hand, it raised the fear of being outvoted by a hostile opposition. Fifteen years later, the EU moved from the principle of unanimity and consensus toward majoritarianism and proportionality.

Obviously, its decision-rules did not evolve into those used by sovereign nation states, let alone in Westminster-style, majoritarian systems, but compared to other international organisations, the degree of pooled sovereignty is extraordinarily high. In particular, governments agreed to lower the voting thresholds to 55 per cent of the member states and 65 per cent of the population, and they increased the applicability of QMV, excluding only highly salient areas such as taxation, social security, fiscal and foreign affairs. Furthermore, they designed the post of an elected president of the European Council, who ought to be the primary political leader of the Union. However, following the Irish 'no' on the Lisbon Treaty in June 2008, they revoked the decision to reduce the size of the Commission and they maintained the rotating presidencies for the Councils of Ministers.

Third, the Danish voters' 'no' on the Treaty of Maastricht and the razor-thin acceptance of the same Treaty in France (50.5 per cent 'yes' votes) marked the end of the 'permissive consensus'. Ultimately, European voters became increasingly aware of the integration process as its nature shifted from being a positive-sum, economic coordination game to a partly redistributive, mixed-motive game. At the level of secondary law, this shift is particularly evident when EU law is not created in the first instance, but existing EU law is to be reformed. Such reforms created winners and losers, which might provoke a powerful electoral response (Hix 2008). As a consequence, governments are eager to spare their voters the experience of negative EU policies. At the intergovernmental level, this constellation aggravated the conflict over individual member states' relative voting power. Moreover, the end of the permissive consensus started the debate over the EU's democratic deficit, fuelled by the political programme of Euro-sceptic opposition parties. To take the wind out of their sails, governments opted for an increased legitimisation, via empowerment of the voters at the EU level. In particular, they strengthened the EP by extending the codecision powers to more and more policy areas. Moreover, they empowered national parliaments in the EU decision-making process, created an EU-level popular initiative and created political posts such as the presidents of the European Council and the EU foreign minister, which was intended to personalise EU politics.

Yet this strategy contains two dangerous pitfalls. First, and inherent to the concept of a constitutional quandary, the empowerment of the EP counteracts the ambitions to increase decision-making efficiency (Schulz and König 2001; Golub 2008). Second, the reformers may very well overplay their hands and encourage a superficial, exclusively negative politicisation. At least during the transition from permissive consensus to a European 'demos', the EU might get stuck into a wave of Euro-scepticism. Instead of debating the contents of EU policies, voters might protest over their loss of national sovereignty and, counter-intuitively, take revenge by withdrawing their support for reforms intended to shift the power balance to their favour. Indeed, the negative referenda on the Constitutional Treaty in France and the Netherlands, as well as the first, negative Irish referenda on the Lisbon Treaty, indicate support for this argument. Even worse though, my empirical analysis proves that such a politicisation backlash might not be restricted to referenda. On the contrary, governmental positions correspond to domestic politics, in particular party positions and the short-term trend in public opinion, and therefore the backlash most likely affects all member states.

Against this background, the present book provides answers to the following three questions. First, what has been on the agenda of European treaty negotiations since Maastricht? And what were the most prevalent intergovernmental patterns of conflict during this period? Second, what are the mechanisms by which governments tried to solve Europe's constitutional quandary? How can we explain the reforms at Amsterdam and Nice as well those embedded in the Lisbon Treaty? Third, how can we explain the genesis and change of governmental reform positions? Subsequently, I summarise my findings before turning to the implications for the future of European integration.

To answer these questions the present book analyses government's revealed preferences at three post-Maastricht IGCs: Amsterdam (1996/7), Nice (2000) and Rome II (2003/4). Most importantly, it proves that the post-Maastricht intergovernmental conflict space is best understood along a classic, two-dimensional model of constitutional choice. On the one hand, governments struggled over the allocation of competences between the national and the EU levels. This dimension primarily corresponds to the objective of political integration. On the other hand, they fought over the distribution of power among each other. This dimension of conflict primarily relates to the goal of decision-making efficiency.

In the early days of European integration, both dimensions collapsed to a single *pro vs contra* integration dimension. At that time, European treaty reforms were almost exclusively dominated by economic coordination beneficial to all governments. Those with the largest economic benefits were eager to ensure the realisation of treaty changes via secondary law; hence they preferred far-reaching delegation of sovereignty and higher decision-making efficiency. This implies both strong and independent supranational organisation such as the Commission and the ECJ, in combination with a high passage probability of EU legislation achieved by the introduction and extension of QMV. To realise these gains, the beneficiaries were perfectly willing to pay financial side payments – if capable of doing so. In the end, a steady increase in European integration was observed, best explained by the distribution of producer interests and economic power at the time. This is the story of European integration from 'Messina to Maastricht' as masterfully told by Andrew Moravcsik's (1998) homonymous book.

However, with the Treaty of Maastricht, the project of economic coordination was more or less completed. At that point, European integration was increasingly dominated by a new agenda, including political integration, decision-making efficiency and democratic legitimacy. As a consequence, the intergovernmental conflict space of European treaty reforms turned truly two-dimensional. Since Maastricht, we observe governments that prefer political integration, while eager to retain control via unanimous, intergovernmental decision-making. At the same time, we observe governments that reject political integration, but are perfectly willing to lower the voting threshold, thereby forgoing their national veto power, in order to increase EU decision-making efficiency.

Obviously, this two-dimensional framework corresponds to two of the three goals that mark Europe's constitutional quandary, namely political integration and decision-making efficiency – but what about democratic legitimacy, the third and most prominently discussed goal of the post-Maastricht agenda? In general, democratic accountability can be achieved by either of three ways. First, democratic accountability is inversely related to the level of EU competences. A shift of policy competences back to the national-level would strengthen the link between voters and their elected representatives. On the other hand, such an auto limitation might reduce the output legitimacy of democratic government in the EU (Alesina et al. 2002). This would be the case if the positive effects of integration clearly improved the economic well-being and living standard of voters in all member states. Second, democratic accountability can be improved by empowerment of elected representatives at the EU level. In particular, this refers to extended powers of the EP and the national parliaments. At the level of intergovernmental conflict, both aspects of democratic legitimacy collapse with intergovernmental conflict over vertical integration. One likely reason for this collusion can be found in the fact that governmental positions correspond to their voters' opinions on European integration. Finally, democratic legitimacy has a procedural dimension, which presumes a European public sphere, i.e. a politicisation of European politics in the public debates of all member states. One way of achieving this goal is to increase the transparency of the EU decision-making procedures and the personalisation of European politics.

The empirical results on the dimensionality of the post-Maastricht intergovernmental conflict space are based on Item-Response model estimates, including governmental positions on more than 150 of the most important issues. By and large, the findings corroborate my theoretical expectations. The conflict dimension capturing the decision-rule refers to all those issues that touch upon the (in) equality of powers among member states, as there are the compositions of the European Commission; the design of the QMV rule; the applicability and rules for Enhanced Cooperation; the rotation and composition of the Council presidency; and the allocation of seats in the EP, the Committee of Regions and the ESC as well as the allocation of judges in the ECJ and the ECA. Other, less prominent issues refer to the internal hierarchy and organisation of the European Commission as well as the EP, the Committee of Regions, the ESC, the ECJ and the ECA.

The conflict over vertical integration centres on the transfer of legislative competences, most prominently in the areas of employment, environmental, fiscal, foreign and defence policy as well as justice and home affairs. Furthermore, vertical integration concerns the empowerment of domestic actors at the EU-level via the extension of the codecision procedure, a stronger role for national parliaments, the strengthening of the ECJ and the ECA as well as the up-valuation of the Committee of Regions and the Economic and Social Committee. As a precondition, governments negotiated the personalisation of European politics, such as an elected president of the European Council or an EU foreign minister.

Building upon this two-dimensional model of post-Maastricht European treaty negotiation, I explain the reforms agreed in the treaties of Amsterdam and Nice as well as in the Treaty Establishing a Constitution for Europe. I do so by analysing the negotiations at the European as well as the domestic levels. According to Moravcsik's (1998) analysis, treaty negotiations up to Maastricht are best explained as unconstrained intergovernmental bargaining games, with no role for procedural constraints, no role for supranational actors and a limited role for small states. In particular, the pre-Maastricht treaty reforms can be understood as a deal between Germany, the UK and France, who were willing and capable of ensuring smaller member states' consent by offering financial side-payments. In this perspective, domestic-producer interests are the only relevant domestic interests. They define the national economic interests that are supported by a vast majority of voters and political parties.

However, the developments since Maastricht have challenged the foundations of this perception. First, the European Community comprised a maximum of twelve member states since 1986, and even fewer before the first Northern and subsequent Southern enlargements. In 1991 when the Treaty of Maastricht was negotiated, the total GDP of Germany, France and the UK outweighed those of the remaining nine member states by a factor of 1.8; in terms of population size, this factor was 1.32. Hence, the three largest member states held an economic power almost twice as strong as the majority of all the other countries together. Today, the total economic power of the UK, Germany and France is roughly equal to those of the remaining twenty-four countries, and they account for only 201 of the 485 million inhabitants of the EU. Given this shift in the balance of economic power makes financial side-payments appear to be a less feasible strategy. In addition, the focus of the IGCs since Maastricht has shifted away from economic integration and coordination toward institutional reforms and political integration (Laffan 1997: 289).

And indeed, my empirical analysis supports the findings of earlier studies that governments of smaller member states are almost as important as the larger ones (e.g. König and Hug 2006; Slapin 2006). In particular, I find that the IGCs of Amsterdam and Nice agreed on the smallest common denominator located far beyond the positions of the core triumvirate of France, Germany and the UK. Instead, the history of post-Maastricht treaty reforms is best understood as a sequence of equilibrium and disequilibrium defined by the positions of all national governments.

Moreover, political leaders and academic observers found the reasons for these modest, sub-optimal reforms to be the standard procedure of intergovernmental negotiations. According to this procedure, the Council presidency had to settle the less conflictive issues via bilateral shuttle diplomacy, sparing the most hotly-contested issues for the final summit. Under this approach substantial agenda-setting and major logrolls could hardly be accomplished. Despite lengthy and costly bargaining processes, the outcomes reflect the least common denominator. In response, governments decided to increase the efficiency and effectiveness of intergovernmental bargaining by installing the Convention on the Future of Europe. As a matter of fact, the Convention has been strongly advocated by the larger and reformist member states such as France, Germany and Italy. In retrospect, the support of these states appears rather unsurprising.

Within the Convention, the president in the person of Valery Giscard D'Estaing proved to be a powerful, pro-integrationist agenda-setter. He played 'every trick in the book' to get his most preferred draft Constitutional Treaty (Tsebelis and Proksch 2007). However, his agenda-setting power suffered from a limited anticipation of the intergovernmental win-set and the ratification stage. In the end, his anticipation turned out overly optimistic, whereby D'Estaing underestimated the power of small and new member states, the latter being rather inactive in the Convention, which had been convened before the official accession date. At the subsequent IGC, governments considered almost half of the reform issues to be settled and, accordingly, that they should stay off the intergovernmental agenda. This subset contained exclusively issues of importance for vertical integration, in particular the extension of the codecision procedure, the empowerment of national parliaments and the future objectives of the EU. With regard to the remaining issues, governments haggled over the bindingness of the Convention proposal, which polarised the conflict among them. One group of member states advocated the adoption of the complete reform package, whereas a second group reacted by opposing further reforms altogether. The failure of the summit headed by the Italian Council presidency in December 2003 is a result of this polarised conflict.

The agreement reached by the Italian Council presidency in December 2003 would have improved all twenty-five governments over the Treaty of Nice. But in contrast to earlier IGCs, those governments that preferred more progressive reforms did not agree to such a minimal compromise. Instead, they pointed to the Convention proposal, which, in their perspective, implied a commitment by all governments to leap ahead. In the end, the Irish presidency brokered a deal that, in comparison to the status quo under the Treaty of Nice, some countries should have rejected. On closer inspection, the Austrian, Danish, Swedish and Latvian governments found it hard to revoke their commitments to integration stipulated by the Convention proposal, even when confronted with unfavourable reforms of the decision-rule. As regards Ireland and Estonia, the sequence of decisions matters in so far as both low-tax countries had a vital interest that matters of taxation would not be decided by QMV. This issue remained on the bargaining table until the final summit in June 2004. Moreover, the Polish government expected adverse consequences for the upcoming negotiations over the EU budget. In other words, financial side payments continue to exist, but they are less important for our understanding of the negotiation outcome than before Maastricht.

In the end, the Constitutional Treaty was almost identical to the Convention proposal and governments eventually overcame the minimal compromises of earlier IGCs. But at the same time, the procedural innovation prolonged the reform process and the uncertainties along the way. One obstacle unforeseen by Giscard D'Estaing was the record number of ten governments announcing referenda. Considering the subsequent failure to ratify the Constitutional Treaty and the unfinished ratification of the Lisbon Treaty, it remains an open question whether the intergovernmental success will carry over to the domestic arena.

Moreover, I find that governments' preferences over vertical integration and the decision-rule are nonseparable. In particular, economically powerful states lean toward lower voting hurdles once confronted with more EU competences than they had originally hoped for. On the contrary, small and economically weak states would prefer higher veto power once confronted with more EU competences than they had originally hoped for. The former group of states possesses alternative means to influence European policies, specifically the power of the purse. For that reason, they are unafraid of being overruled at the EU level, but rather fear the higher decision-making costs that would result from extending the current voting rules to additional policy areas. The opposite is true for the economically weak states, which possess limited alternative means of power. In Chapter 6, it was illustrated how such conditional preferences increase the importance of sequence for the bargaining outcome. The decentralisation of the agenda-setting process into three phases, namely the Convention, the Italian and the Irish presidencies, is essential for our understanding of the final outcome, i.e. the Constitutional Treaty.

Finally, I connect my longitudinal analysis of the negotiations at the EU-level to the domestic-preference formation processes. Previous research found that the variation of national positions across member states corresponds to structural socio-economic differences. Regarding the post-Maastricht era, most of these studies are restricted to single IGCs and therefore incapable of exploring the dynamic correspondence between governments and their domestic principals. Yet, from a normative perspective, the role of domestic actors – in particular voters and their elected representatives – is of utmost importance. Therefore, my analysis contributes to the ongoing discussion about the democratic legitimacy of European integration in general (e.g. Follesdal and Hix 2006) and European treaty revisions in particular (e.g. Risse and Kleine 2008).

Applying a longitudinal empirical research design, I argue that member states' economic characteristics, most of which are relatively stable across time, define a corridor for governmental positions. The position a government reveals at any particular IGC is determined by the political dynamics of the domestic-preference formation process. Specifically, from a cross-sectional perspective, the governmental positions revealed at each IGC correspond to those of the median voter and the partisan composition of government. Both effects are mediated by the institutional constraints of the domestic-position formation process. In particular, the effect of partisan composition of parliament and government turns out significantly stronger in countries that provide formal scrutiny powers to the national parliament.

The longitudinal perspective is even more interesting for identifying the short- and medium-term dynamics governing European integration at the domestic level. The changes in the revealed positions on European integration correspond to changes in the partisan composition of government and parliament. However, changes in governmental positions do not reflect the positions of the voters. At first glance, this seems to support those who assert that European integration is undemocratic. On closer inspection, governments are strongly aware of short-term trends in voters' opinions when formulating their position for the next IGC. If support for integration is increasing, the government changes its position in the same direction. The opposite is true as well; if support for integration is decreasing, the government becomes more cautious about taking a pro-European position.

It is well-documented that governmental leaders are usually more integrationist than their electorate (Schmitt and Thomassen 2000). However, they are not entirely out of touch, but carefully evaluate their domestic discretion when formulating their international bargaining position. This discretion is defined by the position of their party, their national parliament and their electorate, in each case mediated by applicable institutional constraints such as referenda or parliamentary scrutiny procedures. Hence, it comes as little surprise that the average governmental position is far more integrationist where unhampered by such institutional constraints.

Finally, governmental positions on the reform of the decision-rule appear relatively stable across all three post-Maastricht IGCs. A notable exception is Rome II. In reaction to Eastern enlargement, all governments were afraid of grid-lock and therefore willing to give up individual veto and voting power. Overall, governments' positions on the decision-rule corresponded to population size, as any realistic reform of the decision-rule contained an element of proportional representation. On closer inspection, this structural explanation must be complemented by an endogenous perspective, which reveals a distinct, medium-term path-dependency in EU treaty reforms. The theory of nonseparable preferences expects that actors adjust their ideal position on one dimension in response to outcomes on the other dimension. Applied to European treaty reforms, this implies that governmental positions reforming the decision-rule might be a reaction to the current split of competences between the EU and the domestic level, i.e. a reaction to previous treaty reforms. The empirical results support this endogenous explanation of positional change with regard to governments' positions over the decision rule. As regards vertical integration, this effect is absorbed by the exogenous factors such as partisan composition of government and parliament as well as public opinion on European integration.

Compared to its early history, European integration since Maastricht has become increasingly complex. The present analysis tries to accommodate this complexity. European treaty reforms involve contestation over more issues and among more actors at both the domestic and the European levels. Moreover, contestation takes place in a global environment characterised by economic, environmental and political challenges. Although the (Franco-German) engine of European integration is still pounding, its relative power can hardly be heard as the fleet of EU member states increases and the sea gets stormy. However, this does not mean that the fleet circles guideless and uncoordinated on the open sea. Captains just need more time to master their own ships, agree on a formation and a common direction before turning on the engines. Ultimately, the captains must listen to the crew, who may threaten to withdraw their support if unsatisfied about the direction of the voyage.

EUROPEAN INTEGRATION AND ITS LIMITS

Above all, any theoretical explanation must account for the increasing intricacy of European treaty reforms since Maastricht. This intricacy has its origins in Europe's constitutional quandary, defined by the conflicting goals of democratic legitimacy, decision-making efficiency and political integration. The empirical analysis of this quandary uncovers two limits to European integration: one being procedural and the other political in nature.

First, the classic approach of major IGCs prepared by expert groups, orchestrated by the Council presidency and finalised by powerful senior members – most prominently the Franco-German engine – appears out of date. This procedural limitation to integration has been particularly eminent with regard to institutional reforms, most notably after the failure of Nice. It has been partly substituted by two alternatives that, however, apply to different subsets of institutional rules. Often ignored, though very important, are those institutional changes that occur on a daily basis, for example the EP's right of investing individual Commissioners (Heritier 2007). But then, these incremental and informal changes can only work if actors share a common policy objective and interact in the shadow of the future. Regarding more hotly-contested issues that affect actors at different levels of government and involve a high degree of uncertainty over future lines of conflict, governments may want to ensure mutual commitment via primary law guarded by the supranational institutions, most notably the Commission and the ECJ.

The second, more prominently discussed alternative to reform the existing European treaty framework is the Convention method. On first sight, the results of this procedural innovation may appear unsatisfying and unfinished. A major problem of this approach is the procedural uncertainties along the way caused by the delegation of powers to a more or less independent, committee-like decision-making body. But then the installation of an agenda-setting decision-making body such as the Convention has been the very idea behind this novel procedure intended to overcome the mediocre results of earlier IGCs. And, despite all criticism, the Convention method has proven successful – at least at the intergovernmental level. Subsequently, there follows a description as to how the Lisbon Treaty, the most recent outcome of this reform effort, came about and how it differs from the Constitutional Treaty.

After the "no" results of the Dutch and French referenda in 2005, governments agreed on a so-called reflection period. In June 2007 the German Council presidency declared this period to be over and negotiated a compromise, which, in October 2007, was signed in Lisbon,[1] hence the Lisbon Treaty. It includes primarily cosmetic changes to the Constitutional Treaty, intended to appease integration-sceptical domestic actors and to reduce the number of necessary referenda significantly. The subsequent paragraphs list the most prominent changes:

---

1. Poland negotiated a few last-minute changes at the final summit. In particular, these changes included a slightly stronger wording for the revived Ioannina Compromise and the nomination of a permanent 'Polish' Advocate General, formally permitted by an increase in the number of Advocates General from 8 to 11.

- The Constitutional Treaty abandons the voting weights and sets the threshold at 55 per cent of the member states (comprising at least fifteen of them) representing at least 65 per cent of the EU's population. In the Lisbon Treaty governments agree to delay this reform until 2014 and added a transition period until 2017, during which a single member state can ask to proceed according to the Nice system (Presidency Conclusion, Doc. 11177/07: 17).
- The Constitutional Treaty strengthens the common instruments in the areas of the former second and third pillars, introduces a general right of initiative for the European Commission, mutual recognition in the area of civil and criminal law, further development of Europol and the common European border patrol (Piris 2006: 86). However, in the Lisbon Treaty, governments agree that single member states can ignore these developments and opt in at a later stage (Presidency Conclusion, Doc. 11177/07: 21).
- The Constitutional Treaty includes the Charter of Fundamental Rights, which was elaborated and agreed upon by the First European Convention in 2003. In the Lisbon Treaty, governments agree not to include the Charter in the Treaty text itself, but as a reference to ensure its legal bindingness. Moreover, the Lisbon Treaty enables opt-outs for single member states such as the UK and Ireland (Presidency Conclusion, Doc. 11177/07: 17).
- The Constitutional Treaty foresees a 'subsidiarity early warning system', which makes national parliaments responsible for monitoring the division of competences in the EU. The Lisbon Treaty strengthens the role of national parliaments. First, it grants the national parliaments a longer period to consider Commission proposals, second, a simple majority of national parliaments can force the Commission to withdraw its proposal (Presidency Conclusion, Doc. 11177/07: 17; Enc. 1, Title II).
- Moreover, in the Lisbon Treaty, governments agree to replace the title 'Minister of Foreign Affairs', which would have been introduced by the Constitutional Treaty, with 'High Representative of the Union's Foreign and Security Politics' (Presidency Conclusion, Doc. 11177/07: 16).
- Finally, governments abolished any terminology usually reserved for the political systems of sovereign nation states. As a consequence, the Lisbon Treaty is not a single, constitutional text. In contrast to the Constitutional Treaty, it does not contain an explicit mentioning of a flag, anthem or motto. EU legal acts will continue to be called directives, decisions and regulations, instead of European laws and framework laws, as foreseen in the Constitutional Treaty.

At the time of writing (October 2009), the Lisbon Treaty has been politically ratified in all twenty-seven member states. On October 7, 2009 a significant majority of Irish voters (67 per cent) adopted the Treaty on second attempt. A preliminary interpretation of this vote suggests that the change in public opinion can be explained by three factors. First, a more intensive campaign on behalf of the Lisbon supporters was witnessed. Second, Irish voters were appeased by the concession on such vital issues as tax and abortion policy. Moreover, governments refrained from reducing the number of Commissioners. Third, the financial crisis of 2007 caused a widespread fear of becoming economically isolated and clarified the economic benefits of Ireland being an EU member state. Currently, only the integration-sceptic Czech (Mr. Klaus) president threatens to hold back deposition and demand some minor changes with respect to the legal bindingness of the Charter of Fundamental Rights. In other words, the nucleus of the rather progressive reforms agreed by the Convention in June 2003 will in all likelihood become European treaty law in 2010. Considering the invocation of the Convention by the Laeken summit in December 2001 as its starting point and the ratification by the Irish voters in October 2009 as its end point, the entire reform phase[2] lasted for more than seven years. Compared to the duration of earlier reforms, this time-span gives proof to the complexity of the process and the imponderabilities along the way.

Considering the prominent talk about the EU's democratic deficit (Moravcsik 2004; Follesdal and Hix 2006), the second, political limit to integration is almost comforting: the political will of European voters. In the literature, the standard procedure of treaty revision has been frequently criticised for its missing procedural legitimacy, especially for its low transparency and accountability (Risse and Kleine 2008). The European Convention had been introduced as a method to increase transparency and enable participation beyond the political elite. In retrospect, the novel preparatory method might have increased the heterogeneity among delegates, but it hardly increased the transparency for a wider audience (Moravcsik 2004; Follesdal and Hix 2006; Tsebelis and Proksch 2007) – a reality described by the Luxembourgian prime minister, Jean-Claude Juncker, as 'the darkest of all dark chambers'.

Nevertheless, my empirical findings suggest that the domestic mechanisms of preference formation constitute an alternative toolbox for enhancing the legitimacy of EU treaty reforms. Still, there will be no wider audience admitted at the international bargaining table. However, governmental delegates must justify their official positions as well as the bargaining results toward the MPs from their own parties and the opposition parties. Overall, my results suggest that the mechanisms of legislative control work surprisingly well. A more direct democratic representation emerges wherever governments plan to ratify by means of referenda. But then, the negative popular votes in France, the Netherlands and, most recently, Ireland have forcefully illustrated the risks implied by this strategy.

Overall, the European integration project reveals a significant degree of electoral accountability after all. Its importance depends on the involvement of the parliament in the domestic-position formation process and, in particular, on the choice of the ratification instrument. If it is accepted that governmental positions are crucial for our understanding of European treaty reforms, these results indicate that the window for treaty reforms strongly depends on short-term trends in public

---

2. In technical, narrow terms, the process comprises two IGCs. Rome II, which officially began in September 2003 and ended in 2004, and the Lisbon IGC, which official began in July 2007 and ended in December 2007.

opinion. In brief, the Treaty of Maastricht ended the permissive consensus. Ever since, an increasing politicisation has been observed, and as a consequence, governmental discretion is increasingly limited by the domestic principals, including voters, parties and parliaments.

However, voters' opinions on European integration are not carved in stone, but are rather driven by their evaluation of how well their purpose is being served by the EU as compared to other levels of government (Luetgert 2007; Marks and Hooghe 2004). The competitive and mobile workforce is grateful for the extension of the job market, those subject to the Irish economy tattered by the 2008 financial crisis appreciate the safe harbor of the EMU, and EU support is usually higher where voters have little trust in their own political institutions (Sanchez-Cuenca 2000). Yet, public opinion and, even more so, voting behaviour does not entirely follow such a simple cost-benefit calculation. Often, voters are incapable of specifying their costs and benefits of future integration. Their capability to evaluate alternative levels of integration may, however, vary across policy areas. 'Economic theories work best when economic consequences are perceived with some accuracy, are large enough to matter, and when the choice a person makes actually affects the outcome' (Hooghe and Marks 2004: 2; Luetgert 2007). Alternatively, voters will follow ideologies and group identities often reinforced by opinion leaders and campaigns.

The failed referenda in France and the Netherlands (2004) as well as in Ireland (2008) produced a discussion over motives underlying electoral behaviour. A central question is how far it can be explained by voters' evaluations of the proposal ('issue-voting'), or whether it is subject to domestic party competition ('second order-voting') (i.e. Franklin et al. 1995; Binzer Hobolt 2006; Crum 2007). Because issue- and second order-voting are not exclusive, the process of opinion formation is central in these studies, in particular the role of political parties and elites in campaigning (Lupia 1994; Bowler and Donovan 1998, Gallagher 1988, Steenbergen et al. 2007). Garry et al. (2005) find that issue-voting (unlike second order-voting) increases with the intensity of the campaign. While the superior procedural legitimacy of referenda is without doubt, it may reduce the output legitimacy whenever voters get trapped between punishing (supporting) (un)popular national governments or supporting (opposing) European integration (Schneider and Weitsman 1996).

How can governments overcome this trap? First, the logic of second order-voting suggests that it becomes less likely the more often voters are granted the opportunity for direct participation. Hence, a rather unrealistic strategy to overcome the punishment trap would be an increased usage of direct democratic instruments throughout Europe. Second, procedural legitimacy could be fostered by other means, in particular by a stronger role for national parliaments. Following my empirical findings in Chapter 5, formal parliamentary scrutiny power improves the link between parliament and government. As a consequence, a powerful parliament limits the discretion governments enjoy when formulating their reform positions in preparation of IGCs.

However, parliamentary scrutiny rights will only improve democratic representation if European integration and, ultimately, European politics are relevant issues in the domestic arena of political contestation. Although recent research indicates an increasing importance of European politics in the media and in party manifestos (Peters 2005; Zürn 2006), it remains underrepresented if compared to its de facto political importance (Hix 2008).

Another frequently highlighted limit to integration is the trade-off between widening and deepening. Interestingly, Eastern enlargement had little direct impact on the logic underlying European treaty reforms. Enlargement did not alter the shape of the core. Moreover, those governments that should have preferred the Treaty of Nice over the Constitutional Treaty came from both old and new member states. Certainly, most central European governments rejected lower voting thresholds, the extension of QMV and a reduction in the size of the Commission as well as in any other supranational institution. However, in this regard they did not differ much from governments of equally-sized old member states. As regards vertical integration, their positions cover the entire range of possible reforms, with governments of Poland and Hungary being most integration-sceptic and their colleagues from the Slovak Republic, Cyprus and Slovenia being very integration-friendly.

More importantly, enlargement may have an indirect effect on treaty reforms by altering the positions of the old member states. Notably, enlargement caused a systematic change in old member states' positions on reforming the decision-rule. Given the threat of inefficiency potentially caused by Eastern enlargement, the governments of smaller member states appeared more favourable with regard to proportional decision-rules and lower voting thresholds. According to constitutional theory, enlargement may also cause a higher risk of individual governments being outvoted by a hostile coalition or grid-lock meaning the maintenance of the *status-quo* where old members could have agreed on a Pareto-improving reform (Pahre 2008; Steunenberg 2001). In the long run, such a decrease in the quality of EU policies could cause a decline in public support for European integration, a rise of Euro-sceptic parties and, ultimately, less integrationist governmental positions. However, enlargement may just as well have the opposite effect, leading to larger and faster economic growth, higher stability at Europe's borders and a more powerful bargaining position of EU member states toward third countries. Voters may just as well appreciate these developments, with support for political integration increasing. In brief, the effect of enlargement on European treaty reforms remains utterly uncertain. Even worse, we will never know how EU-12 or EU-15 would have evolved. Therefore, future empirical research can hardly isolate the effect of enlargement on European integration.

This book traces and explains European treaty reforms from Maastricht to Lisbon. In the beginning, it draws the picture of Europe's constitutional quandary and illustrates how governments struggled over the conflicting goals of political integration, decision-making efficiency and democratic legitimacy with Eastern enlargement approaching. The Lisbon Treaty is an important step toward each of these goals, but it is not the end of the road. Specifically, security, defence, energy and fiscal policies remain areas with a potentially high demand for closer cooperation, if not integration. Furthermore, the enlargement process is not yet over. Croatia, Macedonia and, most significantly, Turkey are on the list of candidate countries. Others, on the Western Balkans (Serbia, Albania, Kosovo, Bosnia and Montenegro) and the eastern periphery, most notably the Ukraine, keep knocking on Europe's doors. Finally, the institutional design of the EU appears to be settled with the reforms agreed in Lisbon. Sooner or later, the size of the Commission will pop up again. Moreover, future political integration may demand creative institutional solutions, along the logic of Enhanced Cooperation. Whenever the next IGC is convened and whatever its precise agenda looks like, the logic of treaty negotiations and domestic-position formation described in this book remains in place. Hopefully, when formulating their positions, governments will be even more responsive to their domestic principals.

references

Achen, C. (2006) 'Evaluating Political Decision Models', in C. Achen, T. König, R. Thomson and F. Stokman (eds), *The European Union Decides*, Cambridge: Cambridge University Press.
Akaike, H. (1973) 'Information theory and an extension of the maximum likelihood principle', in B. N. Petrov and P. Czaki (eds), *2nd International Symposium on Information Theory*, Budapest: Akademiai Kiado.
Alesina, A., Angeloni, I. and Etro, F. (2001) 'The Political Economy of International Unions', *NBER Working Papers 3117*, National Bureau of Economic Research, Inc., Cambridge.
– (2002) 'What does the European Union Do?', *European University Institute Working Papers*, 61, European University Institute, Florence.
Alesina, A. and Wacziarg, R. (1999) 'Is Europe Going Too Far?', *National Bureau of Economic Research Working Papers*, 6883, National Bureau of Economic Research, Inc., Cambridge.
Algieri, F. (2001) 'Die Europäische Sicherheits- und Verteidigungspolitik – erweiterte Handlungsspielräume für die GASP', in W. Weidenfeld (ed.), *Nizza in der Analyse – Strategien für Europa*, Gütersloh: Verlag Bertelsmann.
– (2005) 'Von der Macht der Zeitumstande und der Fortfuhrung eines integrationspolitischen Projekts: Die Gemeinsame Aussen- und Sicherheitspolitik im Verfassungsvertrag', in W. Weidenfeld (ed.), *Die Europäische Verfassung in der Analyse*, Gütersloh: Verlag Bertelsmann.
Algieri, F. and Bauer, T. (2005) 'Eine Frage der Macht: Die Europaische Union auf dem Weg zum sicherheits- und verteidigungspolitischen Akteur mit globaler Reichweite', in W. Weidenfeld (ed.), *Die Europäische Verfassung in der Analyse*, Gütersloh: Verlag Bertelsmann.
Alter, K. (1998) 'Who are the Masters of the Treaty?' *International Organization*, 52 (1): 121–47.
Antola, E. (2006) 'Finland: We have to live with this result', in F. Laursen (ed.), *The Treaty of Nice: Actor Preferences, Bargaining and Institutional Choice*, Brill Academic Publisher.
Aspinwall, M. (2007) 'Government preferences on European integration: An empirical test of five theories', *British Journal of Political Science*, 37: 89–114.
Bailer, S. (2005) *Nationale Interessen in der Europäischen Union. Macht und Verhandlungserfolg im Ministerrat*, Frankfurt a. M.: Campus Verlag.
– (2004) 'Bargaining Success in the European Union: The Impact of Exogenous and Endogenous Power Resources', *European Union Politics*, 5(1): 99–123.
Bailey, M. A. (2007) 'Comparable Preference Estimates Across Time and Institutions for the Court, Congress and Presidency', *American Journal of Political Science*, 51 (3): 433–58.
Baldwin, R., Berglöf, E., Giavazzi, F. and Widgren, M. (2001) *Nice Try: Should the Treaty of Nice be Ratified?*, Centre for Economic Policy Research, London.
Baliga, S. and Serrano, R. (1995) 'Multilateral Bargaining with Imperfect Information', *Journal of Economic Theory*, 67 (2): 578–89.
Banks, J. S. and Duggan, J. (2000) 'A Bargaining Model of Collective Choice', *American Political Science Review*, 94 (1): 73–88.
Beach, D. (2003) 'Towards a New Method of Constitutional Bargaining? The Role and Impact of EU Institutions in the IGC and Convention Methods of Treaty Reform', *Federal Trust Online Essay*, 13 (3), Online Available at: www.fedtrust.co.uk/uploads/constitution/13_03.pdf, (accessed in July 2007).
– (2006) 'Oiling the Wheels of Compromise. The Role and Impact of the Council Secretariat in EU Intergovernmental Negotiations', Paper presented at the annual meeting of the International Studies Association, San Diego, California, USA, 22 March 2006.
Benedetto, G. (2006) 'The United Kingdom and the Constitution for Europe' in S. Hug and T. König (eds), *Preference Formation and European Constitution-building. A Comparative Study in Member States and Accession Countries*, London: Routledge.
Benoit, K. and Laver, M. (2006) *Party Policy in Modern Democracies*, London: Routledge.

Binzer-Hobolt, S. (2006) 'Direct Democracy and European Integration', *Journal of European Public Policy*, 13: 153–66.
Black, D. (1958) *The Theory of Committees and Elections*, New York University Press.
Blair, T. (2000) '*IGC: Reform for Enlargement: The British Approach to the European Union Intergovernmental Conference 2000*', Report Presented to Parliament by the Secretary of State for Foreign and Commonwealth Affairs by Command of Her Majesty, February 2000, on line available at: www.fco.gov.uk/Files/kfile/CM7174_Reform_Treaty.pdf, (accessed 7 July 2007).
Blanck, K. (2006) 'Austria: Between Size and Sanctions', in F. Laursen (ed.), *The Treaty of Nice: Actor Preferences, Bargaining and Institutional Choice*, Brill Academic Publisher.
Blavoukos, S. and Pagoulatos, G. (2006) 'Portugal: in Quest for a New Role', in S. Hug and T. König (eds), *Preference Formation and European Constitution-building. A Comparative Study in Member States and Accession Countries*, London: Routledge.
Börzel, T. A. (2001) 'Non-compliance in the European Union: pathology or statistical artefact?', *Journal of European Public Policy*, 8: 803–24.
Bowler, S. and Donovan, T. (1998) *Demanding Choices: Opinion, Voting and Direct Democracy*, Ann Arbor: University of Michigan Press
Box, G. E. P. (1976) 'Science and Statistics', *Journal of the American Statistical Association*, 71: 791–99.
Bräuninger, T., Cornelius, T., König, T. and Schuster, T. (2001). 'The Dynamics of European Integration. A Constitutional Analysis of the Amsterdam Intergovernmental Conference' in M. D. Aspinwall and G. Schneider (eds), *The Rules of Integration. Institutionalist Approaches to the Study of Europe*, Manchester: Manchester University Press.
Brinegar, A. P. and Jolly, S. K. (2005) 'Location, Location, Location: National Contextual Factors and Public Support for European Integration', *European Union Politics*, 6 (2): 155–80.
Buchanan, J. M. and Tullock, G. (1962) *The Calculus of Consent: Logical Foundations of Constitutional Democracy*, Ann Arbor: University of Michigan Press.
Caporaso, J. (2007) 'The Promises and Possibilities of an Endogenous Theory of Institutional Change', *West European Politics*, 30(2): 392–404.
Carruba, Clifford J., Matthew Gabel and Charles Hankla. 2008. "Judicial Behavior under Politcial Constraints." unpublished working paper (Washington University in St. Louis).
Chae, S. and Yang, J.-A. (1994) 'A N-Person Pure Bargaining Game', *Journal of Economic Theory*, 62:86–102.
Chari, R. and Egea de Haro, A. (2006) 'Preference Formation and European Constitution-Building: The Spanish Perspective' in S. Hug and T. König (eds), *Preference Formation and European Constitution-building. A Comparative Study in Member States and Accession Countries*, London: Routledge.
Clinton, J., Jackman, S. and Rivers, D. (2004) 'The Statistical Analysis of Roll Call Data', *American Political Science Review*, 98 (02): 355–70.
Cohen, M. D., March, J. G. and Olsen, J. P. (1972) 'A garbage can model of organizational choice', *Administrative Science Quarterly*, 17 (1): 1–25.
Coleman, J. S. (1971) 'Control of Collectivities and the Power of a Collectivity to Act' in B. Lieberman (ed.), *Social Choice*, New York: Gordon and Breach.
Collignon, S. (2002) *The European Republic*, The Federal Trust, London.
Cox, G. W. and McCubbins, M. D. (1993) *Legislative Leviathan: Party. Government in the House*, Berkeley, CA: University of California Press.
Crombez, C. (1996) 'Legislative Procedures in the European Community', *British Journal of Political Science*, 26 (2): 199–218.
– (2000) 'Institutional Reform and Codecision in the European Union', *Constitutional Political Economy*, 11(1): 1043–4062
– (2002) 'Information, Lobbying and the Legislative Process in the European Union', *European Union Politics*, 3: 7–32.
– (2003) 'The Democratic Deficit in the European Union. Much Ado about Nothing?', *European Union Politics*, 4 (1): 101–20.
Cross, John G., *The Economics of Bargaining*, Basic Books, New York, NY, 1969.
Crum, B. (2007) 'Party Stances in the Referendums on the EU Constitution: Causes and Consequences of Competition and Collusion', *European Union Politics*, 8 (1): 61–82.
Day, S. and Shaw, J. (2003) 'The Evolution of Europe's Transnational Political Parties in the

Era of European Citizenship' in T. Borzel and R. Cichowski (eds), *The State of the European Union VI: Law, Politics, and Society*, Oxford: Oxford University Press.

de Boeck, P. and Wilson, M. (eds) (2004) *Explanatory Item Response Models: a Generalized Linear and Nonlinear approach*, New York/Berlin/Heidelberg: Springer.

de Schoutheete, P. (1997) 'Flexibility after Amsterdam: comparative analysis and prospective impact.' in J. Monar and W. Wessels. (eds) *The European Union after the Treaty of Amsterdam*, Continuum International Publishing Group, London

de Vries, C. E. (2007) 'Sleeping Giant: Fact or Fairytale?: How European Integration Affects National Elections', *European Union Politics*, 8 (3): 363–85.

Devuyst, Y. (2003) *The European Union at the Crossroads: The EU's Evolution from the Schuman Plan to the European Convention*, Brussels: PIE Lang.

Diermeier, D. and Krehbiel, K. (2003) 'Institutionalism as Methodology', *Journal of Theoretical Politics* 15 (2): 123–44.

Dinan, D. (2004) 'Governance and Institutions: The Convention and the Intergovernmental Conference', *Journal of Common Market Studies (Annual Review 2003/2004)* 42: 27–42.

Dixit, A. K. (1996) *The Making of Economic Policy: A Transaction-Cost Politics Perspective*, Cambridge: The MIT Press.

Dobbins, M., Drüner, D. and Schneider, G. (2004) 'Kopenhagener Konsequenzen: Gesetzgebung in der EU vor und nach der Erweiterung', *Zeitschrift für Parlamentsfragen* 35 (1): 51–68.

Dorussen, H., Lenz, H. and Blavoukos, S. (2005) 'Assessing the Reliability and Validity of Expert Interviews', *European Union Politics* 6(3): 315–37.

Downs, A. (1957) *An Economic Theory of Democracy*, New York: Harper.

Elgström, O. (2002) 'Evaluating the Swedish Presidency', *Cooperation and Conflict*, 37(2):183–189.

Enelow, J. M., and Hinich, M. J. (1984) *The Spatial Theory of Voting: an introduction*, Cambridge: Cambridge University Press.

Engel, C. (2006) 'Germany: A Story of Saving Face', in F. Laursen (ed.), *The Treaty of Nice: Actor Preferences, Bargaining and Institutional Choice*, Brill Academic Publisher.

Epstein, D. and O'Halloran, S. (1994) 'Administrative Procedures, Information and Agency Discretion', *American Journal of Political Science*, 38: 697–722.

– (1999) *Delegating Powers: A Transaction Cost Politics Approach to Policy Making Under Separate Powers*, New York: Cambridge University Press.

Eriksen, E. O., Fossum, J. E. and Menéndez, A. J. (2004) *Developing a Constitution for Europe*, London: Routledge.

Feus, K. (2001) 'Substantive Amendments – The Treaty of Nice explained', in M. Bond and K. Feus (eds), *The Treaty of Nice Explained*, London: The Federal Trust.

Finke, D. (2006) 'Estonia' in T. König and S. Hug (eds), *Policy-making Processes and the European Constitution: A Comparative Study in Member States and Accession Countries*, London/New York: Routledge.

– (2009a) 'Challenges to Intergovernmentalism: An Empirical Analysis of EU Treaty Negotiations since Maastricht', *West European Politics*, 32(3): 466–95.

– (2009b) 'Domestic Politics and European Treaty Reform: Analysing the Dynamics of Governmental Reform Positions', *European Union Politics*, 10 (3), Forthcoming.

– (2009c) 'Estimating the Effect of Non-Separable Preferences in EU Treaty Negotiations', *Journal of Theoretical Politics*, 21(4), Forthcoming.

Finke, D. and König, T. (2006) 'Finland: Centralized Consensus on EU Constitution Building' in T. König and S. Hug (eds), *Preference Formation and European Constitution Building; A Comparative Study in Member States and Accession Countries*, London: Routledge.

– (2009) 'Why Risk Popular Ratification Failure? A Comparative Analysis of the Choice of the Ratification Instrument in the 25 Member States of the EU', *Constitutional Political Economy*, Forthcoming.

Fiorina, M. (1977) *Congress-Keystone of the Washington Establishment*, New Haven: Yale University Press.

Follesdal, A. and Hix. S. (2006) 'Why There is a Democratic Deficit in the EU: A Response to Majone and Moravcsik', *Journal of Common Market Studies*, 44 (3): 533–62.

Franchino, F. (2005) 'A Formal Model of Delegation in the European Union', *Journal of Theoretical Politics*, 17: 217–47.

Franklin, M. N. (2006) 'Reaction for Notre Europe to Andrew Moravcsik's article: "What Can We Learn from the Collapse of the European Constitutional Project?", online available at: www.notre-europe.eu/en/speakers-corner/contributions/publication/reaction-of-markn-franklin-to-andrew-moravcsiks-article/ (accessed in July 2007).
Franklin, M. N., van der Eijk, C. and Marsh, M. (1995) 'Referendum Outcomes and Trust in Government: Public Support for Europe in the Wake of Maastricht', *West European Politics*, 18(3) 101–17.
Franklin, M. N., van der Eijk, C. and Oppenhuis, E. (1996) 'The Institutional Context: Turnout', in C. van der Eijk and M. N. Franklin (eds), *Choosing Europe? The European Electorate and National Politics in the face of Union*, Ann Arbor: University of Michigan Press.
Franklin, M. N. and Wlezien, C. (1997) 'The Responsive Public: Issue Salience, Policy Change, and Preferences for European Unification', *Journal of Theoretical Politics*, 9 (3): 347–63.
Friderich, H. B. (2002) 'A European Economic and Financial Constitution', *Convention Spotlight No. 5*, Bertelsmann Foundation, Gütersloh.
Gabel, M. (1998) 'Public Support for European Integration: An Empirical Test of Five Theories', *The Journal of Politics*, 60: 333–54.
Gabel, M. and Hix, S. (2002) 'Defining the EU Political Space: An Empirical Study of the European Elections Manifestos, 1979–1999', *Comparative Political Studies*, 35: 934–64.
Gallagher M. and Marsh, M. (1988) *Candidate Selection in Comparative Perspective: The secret garden of politics*, Sage: London.
Gallagher, M., Laver, M. and Mair, P. (2001) *Representative Government in Modern Europe*, New York: McGraw-Hill.
Garrett, G., Keleman, D. and Schultz, H. (1998) 'The ECJ, Governments, and legal Integration', *International Organization*, 52 (1): 149–176.
Garrett, G. and Tsebelis, G. (1996) 'An Institutional Critique of Intergovernmentalism', *International Organization*, 50 (2): 269–99.
Garry, J., Marsh, M. and Sinnott, R. (2005) '"Second-order" versus "Issue-voting" Effects in EU Referendums: Evidence from the Irish Nice Treaty Referendum', *European Union Politics*, 6 (2): 201–21.
Giering, C. (2001) 'Die Institutionellen Reformen von Nizza – Anforderungen, Ergebnisse, Konsequenzen' in W. Weidenfeld (ed.), *Nizza in der Analyse*, Gütersloh: Bertelsmann.
– (2003) 'Mutige Einschnitte und verzagte Kompromisse – das institutionelle Reformpaket des EU-Konvents', in C. Giering (ed.), *Der EU Reform-Konvent: Analyse und Dokumentation*, Gütersloh: Bertelsmann.
Golub, J. (1999) 'In the Shadow of the Vote? Decision Making in the European Community', *International Organization*, 53: 733–64.
– (2008) 'The Study of Decision-Making Speed in the European Union: Methods, Data and Theory', *European Union Politics*, 9 (1): 167–179.
Göler, D. and Marhold, H. (2003) 'Die Konventsmethode', *Integration*, 26 (4): 317–30.
Gwiazda, A. (2006) 'Poland: The Struggle for Nice', in S. Hug and T. König (eds), *Policy-making Processes and the European Constitution: A Comparative Study in Member States and Accession Countries*, London/New York: Routledge.
Hagedorn, F. (2005) 'Auf dem Weg zu einer europaischen Innenpolitik: Fortschritte durch den Verfassungsvertrag?' in W. Weidenfeld (ed.), *Die Europäische Verfassung in der Analyse*, Gütersloh: Verlag Bertelsmann.
Han, J.-H. (2007) 'Analysing Roll Calls of the European Parliament: A Bayesian Application', *European Union Politics*, 8 (4): 479–507.
Hayes-Renshaw, F., Van Aken, W. and Wallace, H. (2006) 'When and Why the Council of Ministers of the EU Votes Explicitly', *Journal of Common Market Studies*, 44(1): 161–94.
Heinemann, F. (2003) 'The Political Economy of EU Enlargement and the Treaty of Nice', in F. Praussello (ed.), *The Economics of EU Enlargement*, Milano: Franco Angeli.
Heritier, A. (2007) *Explaining Institutional Change in Europe*, OUP: Oxford.
Hinich, M. J. and Munger, M. C. (1997) *Analytical Politics*, Cambridge: Cambridge University Press.
Hinich, M. J. and Pollard, W. (1981) 'A New Approach to the Spatial Theory of Electoral Competition', *American Journal of Political Science*, 25: 323–41.

Hirschman, A. O. (1970) *'Exit, Voice, and Loyalty: Responses to Decline in Firms, Organizations, and States,* Harvard University Press.
Hix, S. (1999) 'Dimensions and Alignments in European Union Politics: Cognitive Constraints and Partisan Responses', *European Journal of Political Research* 35: 69–106.
– (2002) 'Parliamentary Behaviour with Two Principals: Preferences, Parties, and Voting in the European Parliament', *American Journal of Political Science*, 46: 688–98.
– (2004) 'Electoral Institutions and Legislative Behaviour: Explaining Voting-Defection in the European Parliament', *World Politics* 56 (1): 194–223.
– (2005) *The Political System of the European Union*, Houndmills: Macmillan.
– (2008) *What's Wrong with the Europe Union and How to Fix It*, 1st ed. Wiley & Sons.
Hix, S. and Crombez. C. (2005) 'Extracting Ideal Point Estimates from Actors' Preferences in the EU Constitutional Negotiations', *European Union Politics* 6: 353–76.
Hix, S. and Lord, C. (1997) *Political Parties in the European Union*. London: Macmillan.
Hix, S., Noury, A. and Roland, G. (2002) *How MEPS Vote*, Brussels: Weber Shandwick-Adamson, Brussels.
Hix, S., Noury, A. and Roland, G. (2006) 'Dimensions of Politics in the European Parliament', *American Journal of Political Science*, 50 (2): 494–511.
Hix, S., Noury, A. and Roland, G. (2007) *Democratic Politics in the European Parliament*, Cambridge: CUP.
Hooghe, L., Bakker, R., Brigevich, A. *et al.* (2008) 'Reliability and Validity of Measuring Party Positions: The Chapel Hill Expert Surveys of 2002 and 2006', unpublished ms.
Hooghe, L. and Marks, G. (2004) 'Does Identity or Economic Rationality Drive Public Opinion on European Integration?' *PSOnline: Political Science and Politics*, 37 (3): 415–20.
– (2005) 'Calculation, Community and Cues. Public Opinion on European Integration', *European Union Politics*, 6 (4): 419–43.
Hooghe, L., Marks, G. and Wilson, C. J. (2002) 'Does Left/Right Structure Party Positions on European Integration?', *Comparative Political Studies*, 35 (8): 965–89.
Hotelling, H. (1929) 'Stability in Competition' *The Economic Journal*, Vol. 39, No. 153. , pp. 41–57.
Hoyland, B. and Hageman, S. (2008) 'Parties in the Council', *Journal of European Public Policy*, 15(8): 1205–21.
Hug, S. and König, T. (2002) 'In View of Ratification. Governmental Preferences and Domestic Constraints at the Amsterdam Intergovernmental Conference', *International Organization*, 56 (2): 447–76.
Hug, S. and Schulz, T. (2007) 'Referendums in the EU's constitution building process', *Review of International Organizations*, 2: 177–218.
Iida, K. (1993) 'When and How Do Domestic Constraints Matter? Two-Level Games with Uncertainty', *Journal of Conflict Resolution*, 37: 403–26.
Iida, K. (1996) 'Involuntary defection in two-level games', *Public Choice*, 89: 283–303.
Inglehart, R. (1971) 'Value priorities and European integration', *Journal of Common Market Studies*, 10: 1–36.
Jackman, S. (2001) 'Multidimensional Analysis of Roll Call Data via Bayesian Simulation: Identification, Estimation, Inference and Model Checking', *Political Analysis*, 9 (3): 227–41.
Janning, J. (2001) 'Zweiter Anlauf – Die "verstarkte Zusammenarbeit" im Vertrag von Nizza', W. Weidenfeld (ed.), *Nizza in der Analyse*, Gütersloh: Bertelsmann.
Joergensen, K. E. (1997) *Reflective Approaches to European Governance*, London: Macmillan.
Johnson, V. E. and Albert, J. H. (1999) *Ordinal Data Modeling*, New York: Springer.
Jupille, J., Checkel, J. T. and Caporaso, J. (2003) 'Integrating Institutions: Rationalism, Constructivism and the Study of the European Union – Introduction', *Comparative Political Studies*, 36: 16–47.
Kassim, H. and Dimitrakopoulos, D. G. (2004) 'Deciding the Future of the European Union:Preference Formation and Treaty Reform', *Comparative European Politics*, 2 (3): 241–60.
Kenan, P. B. (1969) 'The Optimum Currency Area: An Electic View' in R. Mundell and A. K. Swoboda (eds), *Monetary Problems of the International Economy*, Princeton: Princeton University Press.
Kerremans, B. (2006) 'Belgium: More Catholic than the Pope?', in F. Laursen (ed.), In *The Treaty of Nice: Actor Preferences, Bargaining and Institutional Choice*, Leiden:

Martinus Nijhoff Publishers.
Kiewiet, D. R., and McCubbins, M. D. (1991) *The Logic of Delegation*, Chicago: University Press of Chicago.
Kim, S. Y. and Russett, B. (1996) 'The New Politics of Voting Alignments in the United Nations General Assembly', *International Organization*, 50(4): 629–52.
Klingemann, Hans-Dieter *et al.* 2006. *Mapping Policy Preferences II: Estimates for Parties, Electors and Governments in Central and Eastern Europe, European Union and OECD 1990–2003*. Oxford: Oxford University Press.
Koenig-Archibugi, M. (2004) 'Explaining Government Preferences for Institutional Change in EU Foreign and Security Policy', *International Organization*, 58: 137–74.
Kohler-Koch, B. and Rittberger, B. (2007) *Debating the Democratic Legitimacy of the European Union*, Rowman & Littlefield.
König, T. (2005) 'Measuring and Analysing Positions on European Constitution-building', *European Union Politics*, 6(3): 259–67.
– (2008) 'Why do member states empower the European Parliament?', *Journal of European Public Policy*, 15(2): 167–96.
– (2007) 'Vom Vertrag zur Verfassung und zurück zum Vertrag: Der EU-Reformprozess zwischen "Giscardisierung" und "Wolkisierung"', University of Mannheim, unpublished manuscript.
König, T. and Bräuninger, T. (1998) 'The Inclusiveness of European Decision Rules', *Journal of Theoretical Politics*, 10(1): 125–41.
– (2000) 'Governing the Enlarged European Union: Accession Scenarios and Institutional Reform', *Central European Political Science Review*, 1: 42–62.
– (2001) 'Decisiveness and Inclusiveness: Two Aspects of the Intergovernmental Choice of European Voting Rules', *Homo Oeconomicus*, XVII: 273–90.
– (2004) 'Accession and Reform of the European Union. A Game theoretical Analysis of Eastern Enlargement and the Constitutional Reform', *European Union Politics*, 5 (4): 419–39.
König, T., Daimer, S. and Finke, D. (2008) 'The Treaty Reform of the EU: Constitutional Agenda-Setting, Intergovernmental Bargains and the Presidency's Crisis Management of Ratification Failure', *Journal of Common Market Studies*, 46 (2): 337–63.
König, T. and Finke, D. (2007a) 'Reforming the equilibrium? Veto players and policy change in the European constitution-building process', *The Review of International Organizations 2* (2): 153–76.
– (2007b) 'Agents and Loyalty. Analyzing Delegates' Discretion in the Negotiations over a Constitution for Europe', Typescript, University of Mannheim. Earlier version of this paper presented at the 3rd ECPR General Conference, Budapest, 8–10 September 2005.
König, T. and Hug, S. (2000) 'Ratifying Maastricht. Parliamentary Votes on International Treaties and Theoretical Solution Concepts', *European Union Politics*, 1 (1): 93–124.
– (eds), (2006) *Preference Formation and European Constitution-building. A Comparative Study in Member States and Accession Countries*, London: Routledge.
König, T. and Junge, D. (2008) 'Veto Player Theory and Consensus Behaviour' in D. Naurin, and H. Wallace (eds) *Unveiling the Council of the European Union. Games Governments Play in Brussels*, Palgrave Studies in European Union Politics, Basingstoke: Palgrave Macmillan.
König, T. and Luetgert, B. (2003) 'The Treaty of Nice. Intergovernmental Conferences, Domestic Constraints and the Reform of European Institutions', paper presented at the First ECPR General Conference, Marburg, July 2003.
König, T., Luetgert, B. and Dannwolf, T. (2007) 'Quantifying European Legislative Research. Using CELEX and PRELEX in EU Legislative Studies', *European Union Politics*, 7: 553–74.
König, T. and Pöter, M. (2001) 'Examining the EU Legislative Process. The Relative Importance of Agenda and Veto Power', *European Union Politics*, 2 (3): 329–51.
König, T. and Slapin, J. (2006) 'From Unanimity to Consensus: An Analysis of the Negotiations at the EU's Constitutional Convention', *World Politics*, 58 (3): 413–45.
König, T., Warntjen, A. and Burkhart, S. (2006) 'The European Convention: Consensus without unity?' in T. König and S. Hug (eds) *Policy-making Processes and the European Constitution: A Comparative Study in Member States and Accession Countries*, Routledge: London.

Koremenos, B., Lipson, C. and Snidal, D. (2001) 'The Rational Design of International Institutions', *International Organization* 55 (4): 761–800.
Krasner, Stephen D. *Sovereignty. Organized Hypocrisy*, Princeton University Press, Princeton 1999.
Kratochwil, F. and Ruggie, J. (1986) 'International Organization: The State of the Art on the Art of the State', *International Organization*, 40(4): 753–75.
Krehbiel, K. (1991) *Information and Legislative Organization*, Ann Arbor: University of Michigan Press.
Kreppel, A. and Tsebelis, G. (1999) 'Coalition formation in the European Parliament', *Comparative Political Studies*, 32: 933–66.
Krishna, V. and Serrano, R. (1996) 'Multilateral Bargaining', *The Review of Economic Studies*, 63 (1): 61–80.
Lacy, D. (2001) 'A Theory of Nonseparable Preferences in Survey Responses', *American Journal of Political Science*, 45 (2): 239–58.
Laffan, B. (1997) 'The IGC and Institutional Reform of the Union', in A. Pijpers and G. Edwards (eds), *The Politics of European Treaty Reform*, London: Pinter.
Lamers, K. J. and Schäuble, W. (1994) 'Schäuble-Öamers-Papier-1', online available at www.wolfgang-schaueble.de, (accessed in June 2006).
Laursen, F. (2002) *The Amsterdam Treaty: National Preference Formation, Interstate Bargaining and Outcome*, Odense University Studies in History and Social Sciences, No. 245, Odense.
– (2005) *The Treaty of Nice. Actor Preferences, Bargaining and Institutional Choice*, Leiden: Brill.
– (2006) *The Treaty of Nice: Actor Preferences, Bargaining and Institutional Choice*, Leiden: Martinus Nijhoff Publishers.
Laver, M. and Shepsle, K. (1996) *Making and Breaking Governments. Cabinets and Legislatures in Parliamentary Democracy*, Cambridge: Cambridge University Press.
Lenz, H. and Dorussen, H. (2006) *Policy-making Processes and the European Constitution: A Comparative Study in Member States and Accession Countries*, London/New York: Routledge.
Lenz, H., Dorussen, H. and Ward, H. (2007) 'Public commitment strategies in intergovernmental negotiations on the EU Constitutional Treaty', *Review of International Organizations* 2: 131–52.
Lewis, J. and Linzer, D. A. (2005) 'Estimating Regression Models in Which the Dependent Variable Is Based on Estimates', *Political Analysis*, 13(4): 345–64.
Lijphart, A. (1999) *Patterns of Democracy*, New Haven: Yale University Press.
Lodge, J. (1994) 'Transparency and Democratic Legitimacy', *Journal of Common Market Studies*, 32 (3): 343–68.
Luetgert, B. (2007) 'Disentangling the Roots of Public Support for European Integration: Exploring the Effect of EU Policy', Dissertation manuscript in preparation for publication.
Luetgert, B. and Dannwolf, T. 'Mixing Methods: A Nested Analysis of EU Member State Transposition Patterns', *European Union Politics*, 10 (3) forthcoming.
Lupia, A. (1994) 'The effect of information on voting behaviour and electoral outcomes: An experimental study of directed legislation', *Public Choice*, 78(1):65–86.
Mackel, N. (2006) 'Luxembourg: Balancing EU and National Interests', in F. Laursen (ed.), *The Treaty of Nice: Actor Preferences, Bargaining and Institutional Choice*, Brill Academic Publisher.
Magnette, P. (2001) 'Appointing and Censuring the European Commission: The Adaptation of Parliamentary Institutions to the Community Context', *European Law Journal*, 7: 292–310.
– (2004) 'Deliberation or negotiation? Forging a Constitutional Consensus in the Convention on the Future of Europe' in E. O. Eriksen, J. E. Fossum and A. Menendez (eds), *Developing a Constitution for Europe*, London: Routledge.
Mahncke, D. (1997) 'Reform of the CFSP: from Maastricht to Amsterdam', in J. Monar and W. Wessels (eds), *The European Union after the Treaty of Amsterdam*, Continuum International Publishing Group.
Majone, G. (1996) *Regulating Europe*, London: Routledge.
– (1997) 'The New European Agency: Regulating by Information', *Journal of European*

Public Policy, 4 (2): 262–75.
- (1998) 'Europe's "Democratic Deficit": The Question of Standards', *European Law Journal,* 4 (1): 5–28.
- (2002) 'Delegation of Regulatory Powers in a Mixed Polity', *European Law Journal,* 8: 319–39.
- (2006) 'Reaction for Notre Europe to Andrew Moravcsik's article: "What Can We Learn from the Collapse of the European Constitutional Project?"', available online at www.notre-europe.eu/en/speakers-corner/contributions/publication/reaction-ofgiandomenico-majone-to-andrew-moravcsiks-article/, (accessed in July 2007).

Marks, G. and Hooghe, L. (2006) 'The Neofunctionalists Were (Almost) Right: Politicization and European Integration', in C. Crouch and W. Streeck (eds) *The Diversity of Democracy: A Tribute to Philippe C. Schmitter,* Edgar Elgar, Northampton.

Marks, G. and Steenbergen, M. (2002) 'Understanding Political Contestation in the European Union', *Comparative Political Studies,* 35:879–92
- (2004) *European Integration and Political Conflict,* Cambridge: Cambridge University Press.

Marks, G., Steenbergen, M. R., Hooghe, L. and Baker, R. (2007) 'Cross-Validating Data on Party Positioning on European Integration', *Electoral Studies,* 26(1): 23–38.

Martin, A. D. and Quinn, K. M. (2002) 'Dynamic Ideal Point Estimation via Markov Chain Monte Carlo for the U.S. Supreme Court, 1953–1999', *Political Analysis,* 10 (2): 134–53.

Martin, L. W. and Vanberg, G. (2004) 'Policing the Bargain: Coalition Government and Parliamentary Scrutiny', *American Journal of Political Science,* 48 (1): 13–27.
- (2005) 'Coalition Policymaking and Legislative Review', *American Political Science Review,* 99 (01): 93–106.

Mattila, M. and Lane, J.-E. (2001) 'Voting in the EU Council of Ministers: Will Enlargement Change the Unanimity Pattern?' *European Union Politics,* 2: 31–52.

Mattila, M. and Raunio, T. (2006) 'Cautious Voters – Supportive Parties. Opinion Congruence between Voters and Parties on the EU Dimension', *European Union Politics,* 7 (4): 427–49.

Maurer, A. (2003) 'The Legislative Powers and Impact of the European Parliament', *Journal of Common Market Studies,* 41(2): 245–247.
- (2007) 'Das Europaische Parlament in der Vertragsreform', *WeltTrends- Papiere,* 2: 35–52.

Maurer, A. and Wessels, W. (2003) *Das Europäische Parlament nach Amsterdam und Nizza: Akteur, Arena oder Alibi?,* Baden-Baden: Nomos.

McCarty, N. and Meirowitz, A. (2007) *Political Game Theory: An Introduction,* 1st ed. Cambridge University Press.

McCubbins, M. D, Noll, R. G. and Weingast, B. R. (1987) 'Administrative Procedures as Instruments of Political Control', *Journal of Law, Economics and Organization,* 3(2): 243–77.

McCubbins, M. D. and Page, T. (1987) 'A Theory of Congressional Delegation', in M. D. McCubbins and T. Sullivan (eds), *Congress: Structure and Policy,* New York: Cambridge University Press.

McKelvey, R. D. (1976) 'Intransitivities in Multidimensional Voting Models and Some Implications for Agenda Control', *Journal of Economic Theory,* 12: 472–82.

Merlo, A. and Wilson, C. A. (1995) 'A Stochastic Model of Sequential Bargaining with Complete Information', *Econometrica,* 63(2): 371–99.

Miller, V. (2004) 'The Extension of Qualified Majority Voting from the Treaty of Rome to the European Constitution', UK House of Common Research Paper 94/54, online available: www.parliament.uk/commons/lib/research/rp2004/rp04-054.pdf, (accessed in June 2007).

Milner, H. V. (1997) *Interests, Institutions, and Information : Domestic Politics and International Relations,* Princeton: Princeton University Press.

Milton, G., Keller-Noellet, J. and Bartol-Saurel, A. (2005)*The European Constitution: Its Origins, Negotiation and Meaning,* London: John Harper Publishing.

Moberg, A. (2002) 'The Nice Treaty and the Voting Rules in the Council', *Journal of Common Market Studies,* 40(2): 259–82.

Monar, J. (2001) 'Justice and Home Affairs', *Journal of Common Market Studies (Annual Review),* 42: 117–33.

- (2006) 'Justice and Home Affairs', *Journal of Common Market Studies*, 44 (1): 101–17.
- (2008) 'Justice and Home Affairs', *Journal of Common Market Studies*, 46 (1): 109–26.
Monar, J. and Wessels, W. (2001) *The European Union after the Treaty of Amsterdam*, New York: Continuum.
Moravcsik, A. (1998) *The Choice for Europe: Social Purpose and State Power from Messina to Maastricht*, Ithaca: Cornell University Press.
- (1999) 'Is Something Rotten in the State of Denmark? Constructivism and European Integration', *Journal of European Public Policy* 6: 669–81.
- (2002) 'In defence of the "Democratic Deficit": Reassessing Legitimacy of the European Union', *Journal of Common Market Studies*, 40: 603–24.
- (2004) 'Is there a "Democratic Deficit" in World Politics? A Framework for Analysis', *Government and Opposition*, 39: 336–63.
- (2006) 'What Can We Learn from the Collapse of the European Constitutional Project?', *Politische Vierteljahresschrift*, 47: 219–41.
Moravcsik, A. and Nicolaïdis, K. (1999) 'Explaining the Treaty of Amsterdam: Interest, Institutions and Influence', *Journal of Common Market Studies*, 37(1): 59–85.
Moser, P. (1996) 'The European Parliament as a Conditional Agenda Setter – What are the Conditions? A Critique to George Tseblis', *American Political Science Review*, 90 (4): 834–8.
Müller, W. C. and Strom, K. (ed.) (2000) *Coalition Governments in Western Europe*, Oxford: Oxford University Press.
Mundell, R. (1961) 'A Theory of Optimal Currency Areas', *American Economic Review*, 51: 657–65.
Muthoo, A. (2002) *Bargaining Theory with Applications*, Cambridge: Cambridge University Press.
Nentwich, M. and Falkner, G. (1997) 'The Treaty of Amsterdam: Towards a New Institutional Balance', *European Integration online Papers, (EioP)* 1(15): available online: http://eiop.or.at/eiop/texte/1997-015a.htm, (accessed in June 2007).
Niemann, A. (2007) *Explaining Decisions in the European Union*, Cambridge: Cambridge University Press.
Norman, P. (2003) *The Accidental Constitution; The Story of the European Convention*, Brussels: EuroComment.
Oates, W. E. (1972) *Fiscal Federalism*, New York: Harcourt Brace Jovanovich.
Oates, W. E. (1999) 'An Essay on Fiscal Federalism', *The Journal of Economic Literature*, XXXVII: 1120–49.
Olson, M. (1969) 'The principle of fiscal equivalence. The devision of responsibles among different levels of government', *American Economic Review*, 59: 479–98.
Ordeshook, P. C. (1976) 'The Spatial Theory of Elections: A Review and a Critique', in I. Budge, I. Crewe and D. Farlie (eds) *Party Identification and Beyond*, New York: Wiley.
Ostrom, E. (1990) *Governing the Commons: The Evolution of Institutions for Collective Action*, Cambridge: Cambridge University Press.
Padoan, P. C. (1997) 'The reforms in major policy areas. EU employment and social policy after Amsterdam: too little or too much?' in J. Monar and W. Wessels (eds), *The European Union after the Treaty of Amsterdam*, Continuum International Publishing Group.
Pahre, R. (1997) 'Endogenous Domestic Institutions in Two-Level Games and Parliamentary Oversight', *Journal of Conflict Resolution* 41: 147–74.
- (2007) *Politics and Trade Cooperation in the Nineteenth Century: The 'Agreeable Customs' of 1815–1914*, 1st ed., Cambridge: Cambridge University Press.
Pennings, P. (2002) 'The Dimensionality of the EU Policy Space', *European Union Politics*, 3: 59–80.
Peters, B., Brüggemann, M., Kleinen-von Königslöw, K. *et al.* (2005) in S. Leibfried and M. Zürn (eds) 'National and transnational public spheres: the case of the EU', *Transformations of the State?*, Cambridge: Cambridge University Press.
Pijpers, A. and Edwards, G. (eds) (1997)*The Politics of European Treaty Reform*, London: Pinter.
Piris, J.-C. (2006) *The Constitution for Europe. A Legal Analysis*, Cambridge: Cambridge University Press.
Plumper, T. and Schneider, C. J. (2007) 'Discriminatory European Union Membership and the

Redistribution of Enlargement Gains', *Journal of Conflict Resolution*, 51(4): 568–87.
Pollack, M. A. (2003) 'Learning from the Americanists (Again): Theory and Method in the Study of Delegation', *West European Politics*, 25 (1): 200–19.
Poole, K. T. and Rosenthal, H. (2000) *Congress: A Political-Economic History of Roll Call Voting*, Oxford: Oxford University Press.
Rabkin, J. A. (2006) 'Reaction for Notre Europe to Andrew Moravcsik's article: "What can We learn from the Collapse of the European Constitutional Project?"', www.notre-europe. eu/uploads/tx_publication/Moravcsik-ReponseRabkin-en_01.pdf, (accessed in July 2007).
Raunio, T. (1999) 'Facing the European Challenge', *West European Politics*, 22: 138–59.
Ray, L. (2003) 'Reconsidering the Link between Incumbent Support and Pro-EU Opinion', *European Union Politics*, 4: 259–79.
Riker, W. D. (1980) 'Implications of the Disequilibrium in of Majority Rule for the Study of Institutions', *American Political Science Review*, 74 (2): 432–46.
Risse, T. and Kleine, M. (2008) 'Assessing the Legitimacy of the EU's Treaty Revision Method', *Journal of Common Market Studies*, 45(1): 69–80.
Rittberger, B. (2005) *Building Europe's Parliament. Democratic Representation beyond the Nation-State*, Oxford: Oxford University Press.
– (2006) 'No Integration without Representation! European Integration, Parliamentary Democracy, and two forgotten Communities', *Journal of European Public Policy*, 13 (8): 1211–29.
Rittberger, B. and Schimmelfennig, F. (2006) 'Introduction: Theorizing the Constitutionalization of the European Union', *Journal of European Public Policy*, 13(8): 1148–67.
Rivers, D. (2003) 'Identification of Multidimensional Spatial Voting Models', online available at: http://jackman.stanford.edu/ideal/MeasurementConference/abstracts/river03.pdf. (accessed June 2007).
Romer, T. and Rosenthal, H. (1978) 'Political Resource Allocation, Controlled Agendas, and the Status Quo', *Public Choice*, 33: 27–45.
Rynning, S. (2006) 'European Security and Defence Policy: Coming of Age?' in F. Laursen (ed.), *The Treaty of Nice: Actor Preferences, Bargaining and Institutional Choice*, Brill Academic Publisher.
Sanchez-Cuenca, I. (2000) 'The political basis of support for European integration', *European Union Politics*, 1 (2): 147–71.
Sandholtz, W. (1996) 'Membership Matters: Limits of the Functional Approach to European Institutions', *Journal of Common Market Studies*, 34: 403–29.
Sapir, A., Aghion, P., Bertola, G. *et. al* (2003) 'An Agenda for a Growing Europe. Making the EU Economic System Deliver', Report to the European Commission.
Schelling, T. C. (1960) *The Strategy of Conflict*, Cambridge, MA: Harvard University Press.
Schimmelfennig, F. (2001) 'The Community Trap: Liberal Norms, Rhetorical Action and the Eastern Enlargement of the European Union', *International Organization*, 55: 47–80.
Schmitt, H. and Thomassen, J. (1999) *Political Representation and Legitimacy in the European Union*, Oxford: Oxford University Press.
– (2000) 'Dynamic Representation: The Case of European Integration', *European Union Politics*, 1 (3): 318–39.
Schneider, G. and Weitsman, P. A. (1996) 'The Punishment Trap: Integration Referendums as Popularity Contests', *Comparative Political Studies*, 28 (4): 582–607.
Schneider, G., Finke, D. and Bailer, S. (2009) 'Bargaining Power in the European Union: An Evaluation of Competing Game-Theoretic Models', *Political Studies*, 57(3) forthcoming.
Schofield, N. (2004) 'Equilibrium in the Spatial "Valence" Model of Politics', *Journal of Theoretical Politics*, 16 (4): 447–81.
Schofield, N. and McKelvey, R. (1986) 'Structural Instability of the Core', *Journal of Mathematical Economics*, 15: 179–88.
Scully, R. M. (1997) 'The European Parliament and the Co-decision Procedure: A Reassessment', *Journal of Legislative Studies*, 3: 58–73.
Schulz, H. and König, T. (2000) 'Institutional Reform and Decision-Making. Efficiency in the European Union', *American Journal of Political Science*, 44 (4): 653–66.
Schulz, T. (2006) 'France: The President takes all', in T. Konig and S. Hug (eds), *Preference Formation and European Constitution-building; A Comparative Study in Member States and Accession Countries*, London: Routledge.

Schulz, T. and Chabreckova, M. (2006) 'Slovakia: Avoiding Conflict to Secure Stability', in T. Konig and S. Hug (eds), *Preference Formation and European Constitution-building; A Comparative Study in Member States and Accession Countries*, London: Routledge.
Selck, T. (2004) 'On the Dimensionality of European Union Legislative Decision-Making', *Journal of Theoretical Politics*, 16: 203–23.
Shapley, L. S. and Shubik, M. (1954) 'A Method for Evaluating the Distribution of Power in a Committee System', *The American Political Science Review*, 48(3):787–92.
Shepsle, K. A. (1979) 'Institutional Arrangements and Equilibrium in Multidimensional Voting Models', *American Journal of Political Science*, 23 (1): 27–59.
Slapin, J. (2006) 'Bargaining Power at Europe's Intergovernmental Conferences: Testing Institutional and Intergovernmental Theories', *International Organization* 62: 131–62.
Steenbergen, M. and Marks, G. (2007) 'Evaluating Expert Surveys', *European Journal of Political Research*, 46(3): 347–366.
Steenbergen, M. R., Edwards, E. E. and de Vries, C. E. (2007) 'Who's Cueing Whom? Mass-Elite Linkages and the Future of European Integration', *European Union Politics*, 8 (1): 13–35.
Stehn, J. (2002) 'Towards a European Constitution: Fiscal Federation and the Allocation of Economic Competences', *Kiel Working Paper 1125*, Kiel: Kiel Institute for World Economics.
Steunenberg, B. (1994) 'Decision Making Under Different Institutional Arrangements: Legislation by the European Community', *Journal of Institutional and Theoretical Economics*, 150: 642–69.
– (2001) 'Enlargement and institutional reform in the European Union: Separate or connected issues?' *Constitutional Political Economy*, 12: 349–68.
Stoiber, M. (2003) *Die nationale Vorbereitung auf EU Regierungskonferenzen: interministerielle Koordination und kollektive Entscheidung*, Frankfurt a. M.: Campus-Verlag.
Stokman, F. N. and Van Oosten, R. (1994) 'The Exchange of Voting Positions: An Object-Oriented Model of Policy Networks' in B. Bueno de Mesquita and F. N. Stokman (eds), *European Community Decision Making: Models, Applications, and Comparisons*, New Haven: Yale University Press.
Stubb, A. (2002) *Negotiating Flexibility in the European Union: Amsterdam, Nice and Beyond*, Basingstoke: Macmillan-Palgrave.
Thomassen, J. and Schmitt, H. (1999) *Political Representation and Legitimacy in the European Union*, Oxford: Oxford University Press.
Thomson, R., Achen, C., König, T. and Stokman, F. (eds) (2006) *The European Union Decides*, Cambridge: Cambridge University Press.
Thomson, R., Boerefijn, J. and Stokman, F. (2004) 'Actor alignments in the European Uniondecision making', *European Journal of Political Research*, 43: 237–61.
Thurner, P. W., Kroneberg, C. and Stoiber, M. (2003) 'Strategisches Signalisieren bei internationalen Verhandlungen. Eine quantitative Analyse am Beispiel der Regierungskonferenz 1996', *Zeitschrift für Internationale Beziehungen*, 10 (2): 287–320.
Thurner, P. W. and Pappi, F. U. (2006) 'Domestic and International Politics during EU Intergovernmental Conferences. Bridging the Gap between Negotiation Theory and Practice', *Negotiation Journal*, 22 (2): 167–85.
Thurner, P. W., Pappi, F. U. and Stoiber, M. (2002) 'EU Intergovernmental Conferences: A Quantitative Analytical Reconstruction and Data-Handbook of Domestic Preference Formation, Transnational Networks and Dynamics of Compromise during the Amsterdam Treaty Negotiations', *Arbeitspapiere Mannheimer Zentrum für Europäische Sozialforschung Nr. 60*, online available: www.mzes.uni-mannheim.de/publications/wp/ wp-60.pdf, (accessed in August 2007).
Treib, O. (2005) 'Party Politics, National Interests and the Constitutional Treaty: Cleavage Structures in the Negotiations on the Future of EU Social Policy', Paper presented at the 3rd ECPR General Conference, Budapest, Hungary, 8–10 September 2005.
Tsebelis, G. (1994) 'The Power of the European Parliament as a Conditional Agenda Setter', *American Political Science Review*, 88: 128–42.
– (2002) *Veto Players: How Political Institutions Work*, Princeton: Princeton University Press.
– (2006) 'The European Convention and the Rome and Brussels IGCs: A veto players

analysis', in S. Hug and T. König (eds), *Policy-making Processes and the European Constitution: A Comparative Study of Member States and Accession Countries*, London/New York: Routledge.
– (2008) 'Thinking about the Recent Past and the Future of the EU', *Journal of Common Market Studies*, 46 (2): 265–92.
Tsebelis, G. and Garrett, G. (1998) 'An Institutional Critique of Intergovernmentalism', *International Organization* 50 (2): 269–99.
– (2000) 'Legislative Politics in the European Union', *European Union Politics*, 1(1): 9–36.
Tsebelis, G. and Proksch, S. O. (2007) 'The Art of Political Manipulation in the European Convention', *Journal of Common Market Studies*, 45*(1):* 157–186.
Tucker, J., Pacek, A. and Berinsky, A. (2002) 'Transitional Winners and Losers: Attitudes Toward EU Membership in Post-Communist Countries', *American Journal of Political Science*, 46(3): 557–71
Uebersax, J. (1991) *Latent class agreement analysis with ordered rating categories*, Rand Cooperation.
Vaubel, R. (2006) 'Principal-agent problems in international organizations', *The Review of International Organizations* 1 (2): 125–38.
Veebel V. and Ehin, P. (2003) 'Positions of 10 Central and Eastern European Countries on EU Institutional Reforms: Analytical Survey in the framework of the CEEC-DEBATE project', Université Catholique de Louvain, C. Franck and D. Pyszna-Nigge (eds), Louvain-la-Neuve/Brussels, June 2003.
Voeten, E. (2005) 'The Political Origins of the Legitimacy of the United Nations Security Council', *International Organization* 59(3): 527–57
Volkens, A. (2005) 'Programmatische Stellungnahmen nationaler Parteien zur Europäischen Union', in J. Alber and W. Merkel (eds), *Europas Osterweiterung: Das Ende der Vertiefung? (WZB-Jahrbuch 2005)*, Berlin: Edition sigma.
Volkens, A., McDonald, M., and Klingemann, H.-D. (2006). *Mapping Policy Preferences II: Estimates for Parties, Electors and Governments in Central and Eastern Europe, European Union and OECD 1990–2003*, Oxford: Oxford University Press.
Wallace, W. and Smith, J. (1995) 'Democracy or Technocracy? European Integration and the Problem of Popular Consent', *West European Politics*, 18 (3): 137–57.
Warntjen, A. (2007) 'Steering the Union. The Impact of the EU Presidency on Legislative Activity in the Council', *Journal of Common Market Studies*, 45(5): 1137–55.
Weidenfeld, W. (1998) *Amsterdam in der Analyse*, Gütersloh: Verlag Bertelsmann.
– (2001) *Nizza in der Analyse*, Gütersloh: Verlag Bertelsmann.
– (2005) *Die Europäische Verfassung in der Analyse*, Gütersloh: Verlag Bertelsmann Stiftung.
Wessels, W. and Maurer, A. (2003) *'Fifteen into One?: The European Union and Its Member States'*, Manchester: Manchester University Press.
Widgren, M. and Baldwin, R. (2003) 'The Draft Constitutional Treaty's Voting Reform Dilemma', *CEPS Policy Brief* No. 44, November 2003.
Wiener, A. (ed.) (2007) 'Contested Meanings of Norms: The Challenge of Democratic Governance beyond the State', *Comparative European Politics*, 5(1) (Special Issue).
Wüst, A. and Schmitt, H. (2007) 'Comparing the views of parties and voters in the 1999 election to the European Parliament', in *Elections & Domestic Politics. Lessons from the past and scenarios for the future*, Notre Dame.
Yataganas, X. A. (2001) 'The Treaty of Nice: The Sharing of Power and the Institutional Balance in the European Union- A Continental Perspective', *Jean Monnet Working Paper 1/01*, Jean Monnet Center for International and Regional Economic Law at the NYU Law School.
Zeitlin, J. (2005) 'Introduction: The Open Method of Coordination in Question', in J. Zeitlin and P. Pochet (eds), *The Open Method of Coordination in Action: The European Employment and Social Inclusion Strategies*, P.I.E.-Peter Lang.
Zimmer, C., Dobbins, M. and Schneider, G. (2004) 'The Contested Council: The Conflict Dimensions of an Intergovernmental EU Institution', *Political Studies*, 53 (2): 403–22.
Zürn, M. (2006) 'Zur Politisierung der Europäischen Union', *Politische Vierteljahresschrift*, 47: 242–51.

appendix | bridgers

Bridgers enable unambiguous comparison of questions or case of different data sets. They are necessary to render the resulting person and item parameters comparable across time. The following bridgers have been available to connect each combination of data sets:

1. Nice – Amsterdam:
    * N_I.1 / A_121-123 (composition of the Commission)
    * N_II.3 / A_4.1 / A_82 (allocation of seats in the EP)
    * N_II.5 / A_114; A_4.3 (application of QMV)
    * N_II.7 / A_4.8 (Enhanced Cooperation)
    * N_III.2 / A_61 (QMV for environmental issues)
    * *N_II.3 / A_82 (allocation of seats in the EP)*
    * *and at the level of cases the Treaty of Amsterdam*

2. Constitutional IGC – Amsterdam:
    * *R_18A.3 / A_36 (QMV extension to AFSJ)*
    * R_5.b / A_45 (objective: high level of employment)
    * R_18A.8 / A_55 (QMV extension to employment)
    * R_T1 / A_187 (EU legislative competencies for tourism)
    * R_17.6 / A_194 (EU legislative competencies for taxation)
    * R_18A.11 / A_204 (QMV extension to CFSP)
    * R_9 / A_121-123 (composition of the Commission)
    * R_15.b / A_5.1 (right of initiative for EP)

3. Constitutional IGC – Nice:
    * R_18A.6 / N_III.3 (QMV extension to monetary policy; partly[1]!)
    * R_18A.9 / N_III.5 (QMV extension to social policy; partly!)
    * R_18A.11 / N_III.16 (QMV extension to foreign policy; partly!)
    * R_18A.12 / N_III.1 (QMV extension to defence policy; partly!)
    * R_9 / N_I.1 (composition of the Commission)
    * *and at the level of cases the Treaty of Nice*

---

1. The DOSEI questionnaire provides the choice between 'EU QMV' and 'EU Unanimity', while the Nice questionnaire provides the choice between 'domestic competence', 'EU unanimity' and 'EU QMV'. If actor had chosen 'domestic competence' the corresponding value on the DOSEI question has been coded 'missing'.

Legend (for a detailed key please see Annex 1):

R_'x' = (either: DOSEI questionnaire, question number 'x'; or: EP Task Force Report, issue number 'x')

N_'x' = (Nice questionnaire, question number 'x')

A_'x' = (either: Amsterdam questionnaire, question number 'x'; or: EP Task Force Report, issue number 'x')

index

A

Achen, C. 59
AFX.COM 195 n.33, 195 n. 37
Agence France Presse 194 n.34, 199 n.44, n.45
agricultural policy 38 n.5, 45, *90, 92*, 108, 119, *179, 181, 188, 189,* 203
  see also Common Agricultural Policy (CAP)
Ahern, B. 154, 155
Akaike, H. 81 n.16
Akaike's Information Criterion (AIC) 81
Albania 218
Albert, J. H. 79 n.10, 81 n.15
Alesina, A. 11, 44, 45, 46, 170, 176, 208
Algieri, F. 107, 117
Alter, K. 41
Amato, G. 154
Amsterdam
  IGC 1996/7 6, 8, 10, 15, 18, 19, 20, 21, 30, 49, 52, 55, 57, 65, 74–5, 96, 97–106, 202, 207
    national positions 81, 82, *83*, 105, *136*
    reform issues *31–7*, 39, 61, 69
  Treaty of (ToA) 8, 9–10, 11, 20, 62, 67, 80, 97–106, 131, 183
Antola, E. 111
Area of Freedom, Security and Justice (AFSJ) 98, 117–18, 119, 126, 168
  IGC reforms and *31, 32, 33, 34, 35, 36, 94,* 108, 121, 122, *181, 187, 188*
Aristotle 73
Aspinwall, M. 54, 55, 56, 81 n.16, 82 n.19, 134, 138, 143
Associated Press 194 n.30, 199 n.46, 201 n.54
Austria
  EU integration 6, 19
  EU policy and 60, 82, 98, 99, 100, 191, 192, 195, 197–8, 200, 202, 210
  political parties and 154
Aznar, J. M. 154, 189, 194

B

Bailer, S. 13, 29, 38, 62, 170
Bailey, M. A. 20, 79
Balazs, P. 127, 130
Baldwin, R. 9, 38, 61, 111, 167
Baliga, S. 68
Balkenende, J. P. 154, 191
Baltic News Service 200 n.52
Baltic Times, The 192 n.28
Banks, J. S. 68 n.38
Barroso, M. 154, 189
Bauer, T. 117
Bayesian models 78
BBC 115
BBC Worldwide Monitoring 194 n.35, 195 n.39, 199 n.47, 201 n.53, n.55
Beach, D. 51, 63, 64
Belgium
  EU policy preferences 52, 82, 99, 194–5
  political parties and 154
  referenda 58, 160
Belka, M. 196, 201
Benedetto, G. 60, 121
Benoit, K. 21, 51
Berger, A. 194 n.32
Berlin Summit (1999) 109
Berlin Wall, fall of 5
Berlusconi, S. 82, 84, 154, 189, 193
Binzer-Hobolt, S. 69, 216
Black, D. 73
Blair, T. 41, 115, 149, 154, 194
Blanck, K. 107 n.26, 111
Blavoukos, S. 127
Bond, M. 37
Börzel, T. A. 42
Bosnia 218
Bowler, S. 216
Box, G. E. P. 74
Bräuninger, T. 11, 38, 39, 47, 52, 55, 57,

139, 169 n.5
Brinegar, A. P. 57, 143
Buchanan, J. M. 12, 23, 24, 27, 30, 43, 44–5, 58
Bulgaria 76 n.6

C

Calculus of Consent, The 23
Caporaso, J. 15
Cardiff Summit (1998) 106
Chabreckova, M. 123
Chae, S. 68
Channel News Asia 198 n.48
Chari, R. 120
Charter of Fundamental Rights 109, 119, 126, 132, 205, 214, 215
Chirac, J. 122, 154, 155, 189, 193, 194, 198, 199
Christophersen, H. 127
citizenship (EU) 86, *87*, 101, *177*, *181*
Clinton, J. 20, 78, 169
Cohen, M. D. 49 n.23
Coleman, J. S. 38
Collignon, S. 11, 45, 121, 170 n.7
Committee of Regions 9, 13, *14*, 41, 42, 76, 84, *88*, *90*, 102, 103, 111, 112, 127 n.59, *178*, 208
Common Agricultural Policy (CAP) 6, 52, 53
  EU budget and 56 n.30, 139
Common Armament Policy *89*, *177*
Common Foreign and Security Policy (CFSP) 10, 77
  Enhanced Cooperation and 117
  IGC reforms 10, *31*, *32*, *33*, *34*, *35*, *36*, 86, *87*, *88*, 97, 99–100, 104, 108, 112, 116, 119, *121*, 122, *177*, *187*, *188*
  WEU integration and 107
  see also foreign and security policy
Comparative Manifestos Project 155
Conference of Community and European Affairs Committees of Parliaments of the European Union (COSAC) 101–2, 119
constitutions 23
constitutional choice, model of 46, 51, 54, 60–1, 168–9, 207
constitutional design and reform 1, 11–12, 17, 23, 53

decision rules and 23–9, 169
constitutional theory 43, 217
Constitutional Treaty 11, 15, 16, 17, 19, 23, 47, *48*, 63, 80, 82, 118–26, 170, 185, 192–203, 210–11, 213–14
  human rights provisions 119
  national positions *136*, 195–203
  preparation of 68–9
  referenda on 145, 162, 206
  reform issues *31–7*, 120–6, 192–202, 213–14
  role of President in 68–9, 122, 195–9, 202, 210
  see also Rome II
Convention on the Future of Europe *see* European Convention
Cox, G. W. 43
Council of Europe *see* European Council
Council of Ministers 18
  control of 42
  intergovernmental conflict in 51
  qualified majority voting in (QMV) 7, 9, 30, 38
  reform of 30
  rotating presidency 206
  Treaty of Amsterdam and 100, 104
  Treaty of Nice and 9, 10
  see also European Council
Croatia 218
Crombez, C. 11, 18, 39, 40 n.9, 42, 51, 52, 63, 101
Crum, B. 57, 216
Czechoslovakia
  EU policy preferences 50, 82
  referenda 58 n.32, 215
Cyprus 130, 217

D

D'Alema, M. 82, 84, 115, 154
Dannwolf, T. 40
Day, S. 23 n.1, 42
de Boeck, P. 20
D'Estaing, V. G. 16, 68, 126, 127, 130, 132, 210
de Fries, G. 127
de Gaulle, C. 17
de Schoutheete, P. 8
de Villepin, D. 69
de Vries, C. E. 57

Decision Making in the European Union (DEU) 30–1, 38
defence policy *see* foreign and security policy
democratic legitimacy 6–7, 11, 12, 13, 42–3, 44, 47, 53–4, 70, 208, 211, 212
Denmark
 EU policy preferences 50, 60, 62, 82, 191–2, 194, 200, 202, 210
 integration and 81, 82
 political parties and 154, 155
 Rome II 123
 referenda 58 n.32
  Maastricht Treaty, rejection of (1992) 7, 206
  Nice, Treaty of and 167 n.2
  Rome II and 21
Devuyst, Y. 41, 103, 122, 175
Die Presse 198 n.43
Diermeier, D. 29
Dimitrakopoulos, D. G. 63
Dinan, D. 50, 116
direct democracy 32, 42, 216
Dixit, A. K. 43 n.12
Dobbins, M. 38
Domestic Structures and European Integration (DOSEI) 77–8, 117, 128, 130 n.64, 185, 186 n.15, *189*, 193
Donovan, T. 216
Dorussen, H. 18, 118
Downs, A. 73
Duggan, J. 68 n.38

E

Economic and Social Committee (ESC) 9–10, 13, *14*, 40, 76, 111, 127 n.59
 IGC reform 37, 41, 42, 43, 84, *88*, *90*, 102, 103, 111, 112, *178*, 208
Economic Theory of Democracy, An 73
Edinburgh Agreement 7
Edwards, G. 50, 97
Egea de Haro, A. 120
Ehin, P. 122 n.54
Elgström, O. 16, 68
employment policy 33, *36*, 38 n.5, 56, 79, 86, *87*, *88*, *89*, *93*, 99, 101, 104, 108, 113 n.42, 122, *178*, *181*, *187*, *188*, *189*, 205
 law 5, 8, 13, 20

rights 32, 33, *179*
Enelow, J. M. 27, 62, 168, 171, 172, 183
Engel, C. 110 n.33, 115
Enhanced Cooperation 86, 103–4, 107, 108, 112, 113, 116, 123, *177*, *188*, 193, 208, 218
 QMV and 121, *177*
environment protection 8, 33, *34*, 56, 100–1, 176
 reforms *90*, *93*, *178*, *181*, *188*
Epstein, D. 43, 44
Eriksen, E. O. 50
Estonia 82, 128, 198, 200, 203, 210
EUobserver 118
Eurobarometer Surveys 21, 56, 143, 144
Eurojust 118, 205
European Aeronautic Defence and Space Company (EADS) 107
European Armament Agency 24
European Charter of Fundamental Rights 101
European Commission 9, 13, 16, 39–40, 63, 77, 214
 accountability of 75, 76, *178*
 Budget Report (2004) 139
 democratic legitimacy and 6–7
 Enhanced Cooperation and 86, 103–4
 IGC reform issues 9, *31*, *36*, 37, 39, 89, *91*, 104, 109–10, 113, 119, 120, *178*, *187*, 191, 198, 206, 213
 decision-rule and 102, 104, 109, 120
 President of 9, 12, *14*, 37, 40, 101, 120, *180*
 transparency in 42
European Convention 1, 2, 8, 11, 12, 16–17, 18, 38, 45, 55, 68–9, 77, 97, 116, 126–30, 132, 185–6, *188–9*, *190*, 192–3, 202, 209–10, 213, 215
 see also Laeken European Council, Declaration; Rome II
European Council 9, 13, *14*, 19
 Corfu meeting (1994) 97–8
 decision-making in 42, 54–5, 75
 IGC reforms *31*, *36*, 37, *87*, *95*, 121, 191, 198
 Laeken meeting 115–16
 Madrid meeting (1995) 98
 president, role of 2, 68–9, 77, *96*,

121–2, 189
    presidential election reform *31,* 41,
        43, 84, 86, *95,* 103, 116, 131,
        180, 187, 206, 208
    see also Council of Ministers
European Court of Auditors (ECA) 13, *14,*
    40, 76
    IGC reform of *32, 37,* 42, 43, 84, *90,*
        112, 208
European Court of Human Rights 126
European Court of Justice (ECJ) 13, *14,*
    40, 76, 207
    IGC reform issues *31, 32, 37,* 41, 42,
        84, 90, *90, 92,* 109, 112, 113,
        178, 180, 187, 208, 213
'European Governance' 39
European Monetary Union (EMU) 5, 8, 10,
    19, 112, 216
    IGC reform issues *34,* 46
European Parliament (EP) 9, 12, 17, 38–9,
    63, 64, 76, 77
    Committee on Constitutional Affairs
        117
    elections in 42, 69, 75
    empowerment of 13, *14,* 39, 43, 49
        n.24, 57, 84, 86, 101, 104, 122,
        206, 208
    IGC reform issues 9, *31–4, 36, 37,*
        38–9, 75, 84, *87, 88, 89, 91, 92,*
        93, 94, 95, 101, 103, 119, 120,
        121, *177, 178, 179, 180, 182,*
        185, *187, 189,* 195, 198, 206,
        208
    intergovernmental conflict in 51
    MEPs role in 39
    Task Force Report 75, 78, 80 n.13
European Policy Institutes Networks
    (EPIN) 117
European Public Prosecutor 76, *92,* 98,
    178, 191, 196
European Social Chapter (1997) 99
European Union
    accountability in 42, 44, 86, 119–20,
        165, 208, 215
    budget 139
    decision-making in 30–1, 38, 44, 46,
        61–2, 63, 70, 205, 207–8, 211
        International Relations Model 51
        codecision procedure 104, 186,
            208

democratic representation in 42, 45,
    53–4, 166, 208, 216–17
Gross National Income 56, 64, 139,
    209
enlargement of 6, 15, 19, 131, 133,
    205, 217
    Eastern 2004/5) 49 n.24, 64, 66,
        70, 97, 107, 113, 123, 137,
        212, 217
    economic power and 15, 64
    Northern (1995) 64, 131, 209
    Southern 64, 131, 209
national sovereignty and 23, 43, 53,
    104, 109, 206, 214
    Enhanced Cooperation and 50,
        84, 86, *88*
    parliamentary position and 60–1
    patterns of conflict 47–50, 52, 54
    policy-making competences and
        44–5, 168
    revealed preferences and 47, 50
        n.25, 63
    see also member states (EU)
origins of 5, 7
political integration and 134, 140,
    162–4, 165, 205, 207
    limits of 212–18
    see also member states (EU)
power distribution and 23–4, 64–5,
    67, 207
transparency in 42, 44, 102, 208, 215
trade among members 138–40, *141*
voter preference studies of 57–60
Europol 118, 205, 214

F

Falkner G. 102. 103 n.19
federalism 53–4
    economic theories of 44, 45
Feus, K. 37, 108
Finke, D. 49, 52, 55, 57, 60 n.34, 63, 64,
    69, 79, 125, 143, 162, 186 n.15, 192,
    200, 202
Finland 60 n.34, 149
    EU integration 6, 19
    EU policy and 29, 60, 99 n.7, 191,
        192, 197, 200
        party affiliation and 154, 155
        QMV and 168

Fiorina, M. 43
Fischer, J. 69, 127
Follesdal, A. 11, 42, 53, 56, 166, 211, 215
foreign and security policy 5, 8, 100–1,
    117, *182*, 186, *188*, 193, 196, 205
    European Minister of Foreign Affairs
        and 43, 122, 214
    Rome II 117–18
    Treaty of Amsterdam and 8, 100–1,
        104, 177
    Treaty of Nice and 107, *180*
    see also Common Foreign and
        Security Policy (CFSP)
Fortuyn, L. P. 154
France 149
    EU enlargement and 15, 16
    EU integration 6, 19
    EU policy and 10, 18, 21, 61 n.37,
        99, 149, 209
        Constitutional Treaty 198, 199,
            203, 206
        Empty Chair Crisis (1966) 53
        preferences and 50, 52, 54, 62,
            64, 67, 69, 83, 84, 99, 168,
            183, 186, 193
        party affiliation and 154, 155
    referenda 58, 69, 132, 162, 206, 213,
        215, 216
        Maastricht Treaty (1992) 7, 206
    Secrétariat Général du Comité
        Interministériel (SGCI) 149
    semi-presidentialism in 60
Frankfurter Rundschau 194 n.31
Franchino, F. 40
Franklin, M. N. 11, 42, 57, 143 n.6, 216
Friderich, H. B. 45

G

Gabel, M. 51, 57, 143
Gallagher, M. 59, 216
Garrett, G. 40, 41, 51, 64
Garry, J. 216
Gelie, P. 187 n.16–17
General Affairs Council 122
Germany 15, 61 n.37
    Bundestag 97
    EU policy 26, 131, 209
        Constitutional Treaty 198–9, 203
        defence policy 118
        enlargement debate and 15, 16,
            97, 115
        party affiliation and 154
        policy preferences 48, 49, 50,
            52, 54, 64, 67, 69, 84, 98,
            99, 100, 115, 186, 193,
            198–9
    referenda 58
    Social Democrats 154
Giering, C. 109, 115, 116
Göler, D. 68, 125
Golub, J. 30, 39, 206
Governing the Commons 24
Greece
    EMU and 112
    EU policy and 10, 21, 60, 82, 99
    referendum (2005) 11
    Turkey, relationship with 99 n.8
Gwiazda, A. 200

H

Hagedorn, F. 117, 118
Hageman, S. 78
Haider, J. 154
Hain, P. 128, 130
Halonen, T. 191
Han, J.-H. 78
Hauser, A. 191 n.20, 193 n.29
Hayes-Renshaw, F. 51
Heinemann, F. 37, 96
Heritier, A. 204, 213
Hinich, M. J. 27, 62, 73, 74, 168, 171, 172,
    183
Hirschmann, A. O. 45 n.16
Hix, S. 11, 18, 29, 39, 42, 51, 52, 53, 56,
    63, 78, 166, 206, 211, 215, 217
Hololei, H. 127
Hooghe, L. 21, 51, 56, 57, 58, 143, *153*,
    155, *156*, *159*, 216
Hotelling, H. 73
Hoyland, B. 78
Hübner, D. 127
Hug, S. 15, 18, 21, 37, 49, 52, 57, 58 n.32,
    59, 60, 64, 75, 77, 78, 96, 106, 117,
    134, 145, 149, 162, 209
human rights 13, *32*, 84, *90*, *92*, 113, 119,
    175, *179*, *180*, *187*
Hungarian News Agency 189 n.21
Hungary 82, 117, 171, 191, 200, 203, 217

I

Iida, K. 64, 69
immigration/migration 34, 91, 98, 117, 118, *179, 182, 188,* 193
Inglehart, R. 7, 134, 160
Intergovernmental Conferences (IGCs) 1, 6, 16, 55
  bargaining, intergovernmental and 67–70, 162, 207, 209
  post-Maastricht 12–13, 15, 16, 162, 207, 209, 211, 213
  referenda and 59–61
  reform agendas 64
    decision-rule, design of and 167, 168, 176, 201, 212
    democratic legitimacy *31–3,* 70, 166, 211
    political integration *33–7,* 64, 70, 209
  sequence of *187–9*
  stages of 7–8, 54–5
  see also Amsterdam; member states (EU); Nice; Rome II
International Relations Model 51
Ireland
  EU policy and 18, 21, 26, 60, 82, 98, 99, 125 n.57, 186, 191, 197, 198, 202, 210
  political parties and 154, 155
  Fianna Fail 154
  Fine Gael 154, 155
  integration and 82, 171
    policy preferences 54, 200
  referendum (2008) 11, 58, 132, 145, 206, 214–15
Irish Times, The 198 n.42
Italy
  EU policy 21, 26, 61 n.37, 115, 209
    political parties and 154
    preferences 50, 52, 81–2, 83, 84, 165 n.1, 196
  referenda 58

J

Jäätteenmäki, A. 154
Jackman, S. 20, 74 n.1, 78, 171
Janning, J. 8, 112
Joergensen, K. E. 49

Johnson, V. E. 79 n.10, 81 n.15
Jolly, S. K. 57, 143
Jospin, L. 154, 155
Juncker, J.-C. 125, 213
Junge, D. 38, 51
Jupille, J. 49
justice and home affairs (JHA) 5, *88, 89,* 176, 205
  Treaty of Amsterdam and 8, 104
Jyllands-Posten 200 n.50

K

Kaczynski, J. 201
Kaczynski, L. 201
Kallas, S. 127
  Kalniete, S. 127
Kassim, H. 63
Kaufholz, H. 195 n.38
Kenan, P. B. 44
Kerremans, B. 111, 154
Kiewiet, D. R. 43
Kim, S. Y. 78
Klaus, V. 215
Klarskov, K. 195 n.38
Kleine, M. 166, 211, 215
Klingemann, H.-D. 155
Koenig-Archibugi, M. 46, 55, 56, 169
Kohl, H. 49, 82, 115, 131
Kohler-Koch, B. 6
Kok, W. 155
König, T. 6, 11, 15, 18, 19, 21, 30, 37, 38, 39, 49, 51, 52, 54, 55, 57, 75, 76, 77, 78, 96, 106, 116, 117, 125, 126, 128, 132, 134, 139, 149, 162, 169 n.5, 192, 206, 209
Koremenos, B. 40
Kosovo 218
Kratochwil, F. 49
Krehbiel, K. 29, 44 n.13
Kreppel, A. 63
Krishna, V. 68
Kwasniewski, A. 192

L

Lacy, D. 18, 27, 168, 183
Laeken European Council 115–16, 127, 213
  Declaration 17, 55, 64, 67, 69, 116 n.44

Laffan, B. 8, 64, 209
Lamers, K. 97
Lane, J.-E. 51
Latvia 200, 202, 210
Laude, Y. 189 n.17
Laursen, F. 37, 46, 57, 96, 98 n.3, 104, 106, 107, 108, 111, 115, 154
Laver, M. 21, 51, 59
Le Figaro 189 n.16, 193 n.25
Le Monde 56
Le Temps 189 n.19
Lenz, H. 55, 118
Lewis, J. 173
liberal inter-governmentalism 63, 64, 67, 106, 131
Lijphart, A. 12, 52
Linzer, D. A. 173
Lipponen, P. 154, 155, 192
Lisbon Treaty (LT) 8, 9, 10, 11, 82, 132, 205, 206, 208, 210, 213–15, 217
 see also Constitutional Treaty
Lodge, J. 42
Lopes, E. 128
Lord, C. 51 n.26
Luetgert, B. 18, 37, 40, 58, 76, 143, 216
Lupia, A. 216
Luxembourg 149
 EU policy preferences 52, 82, 155 n.13
 European Convention and 125
 referenda 58 n.32, 162

M

Maastrict Treaty (ToM) 5, 6, 7, 53, 64, 67, 80, 97, 106, 133, 134, 205, 206, 207, 209, 216
 economic coordination and 53, 207
 IGC studies 52
 ratification of (1993) 19
 reform agenda 1, 26
McCarty, N. 47 n.20
McCubbins, M. D. 43, 44 n.14
Macedonia 218
Mackel, N. 110 n.34
McKelvey, R. D. 16, 68, 73
Magnette, P. 42, 50
Mahncke, D. 37, 56, 99, 100
Majone, G. 11, 12, 42, 43 n.12, 44, 53, 99
majoritarianism 13, 17, 61, 62, 82–3, 115, 123, 130, 137, 205, 206
Malta 61 n.37, 76 n.6
Marhold, H. 70, 125
Marks, G. 51, 56, 57, 58, 143, *153,* 155, *156, 159,* 216
Marsh, M.
Martin, A. D. 30, 78, 80, 171
Martin, L. W. 59, 60
Mattila, M. 53, 59, 61
Maurer, A. 63, 126
Median Voter Theorem (1958) 73
Meirowitz, A. 47 n.20
member states (EU)
 as unitary actors 133, 134–8, 163
 domestic politics, effect of 134–5, 163, 164, 167, 206–7, 216
 governments' treaty variance 135–8, 197–201, 211–12
 political integration and 134, 162–3, 166, 168, 205–6, 211
 history of 169
 limits of 212–18
 national interest and 138–40
 partisan composition and 149–59, 163, 183, 209, 211. 212
 public opinion/median voters and 143–8, *156,* 162, 163, 184, 191–93, 211, 212
Meri, L. 128, 130
Merlo, A. 68 n.38
Michel, L. 127, 194–5
Miller, L. 195
Miller, V. 103
Milner, H. V. 37, 69
Milton, G. 116, 117, 127
Mitterrand, F. 130
Moberg, A. 110 n.32
Möller, P. S. 155
Monar, J. 37, 50, 57, 98
Monet, J. 130
Montenegro 218
Moravscik, A. 9, 11, 12, 13, 15, 30, 37, 40, 42, 46, 47, 48, 49, 51, 52, 55–6, 57, 63, 64, 67, 96, 100, 103, 106, 115, 131, 133, 134, 138–9, 166, 207, 209, 215
Moser, P. 39, 40 n.9, 63
Müller, W. C. 59, 60
Mundell, R. 44

Munger, M. C. 73, 171 n.8
Muthoo, A. 16, 65, 68

N

NATO 5, 99, 100, 107, 193
Nentwich, M. 102, 103 n.19
Netherlands, The
    EU policy preferences 20, 52, 79, 82, 191, 192
        political parties and 154, 155
    referenda 58 n.32, 206
        (2004) 11, 132, 213, 215, 216
Nice
    IGC 2000 6, 8, 10, 11, 15, 18, 20, 21, 30, 55, 96, 97, 207
        national positions 81, 82, *83*, 110, *114*, 136
        QMV and 110–11
        reform issues *31–7*, 43, 61, 69, 75
        voting threshold and 167 n.1
    Treaty of (ToN) 8, 9, 10, 11, 15, 47, *48*, 67, 80, 106–15, 131, 170, 183, 186, *190*, 195, 197, 198, 202, 210, 212
Nicolaïdis, K. 9, 46, 49, 57, 96, 100, 103, 134
Niemann, A. 99
non-separability, concept of 168, 169, 170, 172, 175
Norman, P. 68, 69, 126, 127, 130

O

Oates, W. E. 44, 45, 46
O'Halloran, S. 43, 44
Olson, M. 45
Opperman, T. 77 n.7
Ordeshook, P. C. 74
Ostrom, E. 24

P

Padoan, P. C. 56, 99
Page, T. 44 n.14
Pagoulatos, G. 127
Pahre, R. 64, 69, 217
PAP 201 n.55
Pappi, F. U. 18, 57
Peltomäki, A. 127

Pennings, P. 51
Persson, G. 192
Peters, B. 58, 217
Petersberg Tasks 100
Pijpers, A. 50, 97
Piris, J.-C. 9, 117, 118, 119, 121, 214
Plumper, T. 139
Poland 61, 64, 82, 191, 192–3, 194, 195, 217
    Constitutional Treaty 198, 200–1, 203, 210, 213 n.1
    EU referenda 58
Polish News Bulletin 201 n.55
Politiken 56, 195 n.38
Pollack, M. A. 40
Pollard, W. 74
Poole, K. T. 78
Portugal 58 n.32, 82, 154, 189, 194
    Constitutional Treaty and 199, 203
Pöter, M. 64
Pries, K. 194 n.31
principal agent theory 43–4
Prodi, R. 82, 84, 115, 127, 154
Proksch, S. O. 16, 68, 125, 127, 132, 210, 215
proportional representation 13, 61, 83, 101 n.13, 165, 205

Q

Qualified Majority Voting (QMV) 13, *14*, 27, 29, 38, 76, 116, 206, 210
    codecision and 101, 109, 111
    IGC reform *31–7*, 84, 86, *87, 88, 91, 93*, 102–3, 104, 108, 110–11, 112, 113, 115, 121, 123, 166, *177, 179*, 186, 194, 195, 197, 198, 200, 203, 207, 208
Quinn, K. M. 20, 78, 80, 171

R

Rabkin, J. A. 11
Radio Solvenia 198 n.41
Raffarin, J.-P. 154
Rasmussen, A. F. 154, 155, 192, 195, 200
Rasmussen, P. N. 154
Raunio, T. 42, 57, 59
Ray, L. 57, 59, 143
RDP Antena 1 radio 194 n.35, 199 n.47

Reflection Group 75
Riker, W. D. 73
Risse, T. 166, 211, 215
Rittberger, B. 42, 46, 49 n.24, 57, 109, 119
Rivers, D. 20, 80
Rokita, J. 190
Rome II 1, 67, 69, 80, 115–26, 167
    IGC 2003/4 6, 8, 15, 18, 20, 21, 30, 49, 67, 96, 97, 183, 185, 207, 208, 209
        codecision procedures 119
        conflict patterns at 52
        integration and 82
        national positions re integration 81, *82, 183*
        reform issues *31–7*, 39, 47, 61, 173
    see also Constitutional Treaty
Romer, T. 139
Rosenthal, H. 78, 139
Ruggie, J. 49
Rupel, D. 130
Russett, B. 78
Rynning, S. 107
Rzeczpospolita 201 n.55

S

Sampaio, J. 154
Sanchez-Cuenca, I. 214
Sandholtz, W. 49
Santer, J. 127
Sapir, A. 11
Schäuble, W. 97
Schelling, T. C. 57, 64
Schengen information system 205
Schimmelfennig, F. 19, 49 n.24
Schmitt, H. 56, 57, 58, 59, 143, 144, 145, 212
Schnauder, A. 198 n.43
Schneider, C. J. 139
Schneider, G. 38, 216
Schofield, N. 5, 73
Schröder, G. 82, 122, 186, 193, 194
Schulz, H. 30, 41
Schulz, T. 52, 57, 58, 122, 123, 145, 149, 162, 206
Schüssel, W. 191, 195
Scully, R. M. 39, 40 n.9
SDA-Service de base français 195 n.36

Selck, T. 51
Serbia 218
Serrano, R. 68
Services Juridiques 75, 76
Shapley, L. S. 38
Shaw, J. 23 n.1, 42
Shepsle, K. 59, 73
Shubik, M. 38
Single European Act (1986) 6, 8, 19, 133
Single European Market (SEM) 5, 8, 19, 55
    EU enlargement and 6, 138
Slapin, J. 15, 19, 68, 76, 106, 126, 209
Stoiber, M. 149
Slovakia 21, 76 n.6, 82, 217
Slovenia 76 n.6, 118, 173, 197, 217
Smith, J. 42
SonntagsZeitung 194 n.32
Spain 149
    EU policy and 60, 98, 189, 194, 200, 203
    integration and 82
    political parties and 154
spatial analysis and models 1, 15, 16, 20, *22*, 40 n.9, 63, 65, 70, 73–4, 96, 104
    development of 73
    unanimity core in 104, 106
Spring, D. 155
Steenbergen, M. 51, 56, 57, 60, *153*, 155, *156, 159*, 216
Stehn, J. 45 n.16
Steunenberg, B. 38, 63, 217
Stoiber, M. 21, 48, 52, 57, 59, 60, 98
Stokman, F. N. 74
Strom, K. 59, 60
Stubb, A. 98 n.3
subsidiarity, principle of *87, 92*, 101, 109, 119, 126, *177, 180*, 182, *188*
Sweden
    EU integration 6, 19, 82
    EU policy 60, 99 n.7
        preferences 52, 82, 191–2, 195, 200, 202, 210
    Social Democratic Party 82, 192

T

taxation policy 108, 111, 118, 121, *181, 187, 188*, 200, 206
    QMV and 210

Thatcher, M. 17
Thomassen, J. 57, 58, 59, 143, 144, 145, 212
Thomson, R. 31, 40, 51, 64
Thurner, P. W. 18, 37, 49, 57, 75, 76
Tiilikainen, T. 128, 130
Times, The 189 n.18, 191 n.23, n.24
Treaty Establishing a Constitution for Europe 97
treaty revisions (European) 29, 56, 63–7, 70, 133–4
    double-majority rule 167
    largest states preferences and 64–5, 67
    non-separable preferences, effect of on 167–70
    recurring stages of 54–5
    spatial analysis and 65–7, 70
    see also Intergovernmental Conferences (IGCs)
Treib, O. 55, 99, 169
Tsebelis, G. 15, 16, 40, 51, 63, 64, 65, 68, 106, 125, 126, 127, 132, 210, 215
Tucker, J. 143 n.6
Tullock, G. 12, 23, 24, 27, 30, 43, 44–5, 58
Tuomioja, E. 155
Turkey 218
Tusek, G. 130

U

Uebersax, J. 79
Ukraine 216
United Kingdom
    EU and 60, 61 n.37, 98 n.4, 209
        Common Foreign and Security Politics and 10, 99, 121
        Constitutional Treaty 200
        enlargement debate 15, 16, 82
        entry into 52
        party affiliation and 149, 154
        policy preferences 29, 49, 50, 64, 67, 98, 99, 121, 194
        QMV position 121
    Labour government 10, 49, 60, 82, 115, 131, 149, 154, 189, 194
    referenda 58
United Nations
    General Assembly 78
    Security Council 99

United States
    Congress 78
    Supreme Court 78, 80
University of Chapel Hill 155, *156*, *159*

V

Van Der Eijk, C. 42
Van Oosten, R. 74
Vanberg, G. 59, 60
Vaubel, R. 44
Veebel V. 122 n.54
Verhofstadt, G. 154
Voeten. E. 78
Volkens, A. 56, 134
von Aartsen, J. 155

W

Wacziarg, R. 11, 45, 170 n.7
Wallace, W. 42
Warntjen, A. 41
Weidenfeld, W. 37, 50, 107 n.23
Weiner, A. 23 n.1, 42
Weitsman, P. A. 216
Wessels, W. 37, 50, 98 n.3
West European Union (WEU) 5, *33*, 99, 100
    EU integration 107, 115, *177*
Westendorp, C. 75 n.4, 98
Westendorp Report 75, 98, 106
Widgren, M. 38, 169 n.5
Wilson, C. A. 68 n.38
Wlezien, C. 143 n.6
Wüst, A. 56

Y

Yang, J.-A. 68
Yataganas, X. A. 9 n.5, 37, 104, 106, 108, 110, 111, 112

Z

Zapatero, J. L. 154, 200
Zeitlin, J. 99 n.6
Zimmer, C. 11, 51
Zürn, M. 56, 134, 217

Lightning Source UK Ltd.
Milton Keynes UK
UKOW030043191011

180539UK00001B/8/P